This book describes in detail the ritual purity system of
the Hebrew Bible, and its development into the system of
the rabbis. Certain human conditions require purification
before contact is made with holy foods or areas. Recent
scholarly theories (Milgrom, Neusner, Douglas) are discussed, and new theories are proposed for the origin of the
Red Cow and the Scapegoat rites. It is argued that the
impurities concerned all derive from the human cycle of
generation, birth and death, from which the Sanctuary is
to be guarded; not because it needs protection from
demonic powers (as in other ancient purity systems), but
because of the reverence due to the divine presence.
While the priestly code of holiness displays traces of
earlier conceptions, its ritual has lost urgent salvific force,
and has become a protocol for the Temple and a dedicatory code for a priestly people; the sources distinguish it
from universal morality.

HYAM MACCOBY is an Emeritus Fellow of Leo Baeck
College London, where he taught until 1997. In 1998 he
was appointed Visiting Professor at the Centre for Jewish
Studies, University of Leeds. His many publications
include *Early Rabbinic Writings* (1998), *Judaism in the First
Century* (1989), *Paul and Hellenism* (1991), *Judas Iscariot and the
Myth of Jewish Evil* (1992, winner of the Wingate Prize), and
A Pariah People (1996). In addition, Dr Maccoby has
published articles in *New Testament Studies*, the *Journal for the
Study of Judaism*, the *Journal of Jewish Studies*, the *Journal for
the Study of the New Testament*, and the *Journal of Theological
Studies*.

RITUAL AND MORALITY

The Ritual Purity System and its Place in Judaism

HYAM MACCOBY

CAMBRIDGE
UNIVERSITY PRESS

CAMBRIDGE UNIVERSITY PRESS
Cambridge, New York, Melbourne, Madrid, Cape Town, Singapore, São Paulo, Delhi

Cambridge University Press
The Edinburgh Building, Cambridge CB2 8RU, UK

Published in the United States of America by Cambridge University Press, New York

www.cambridge.org
Information on this title: www.cambridge.org/9780521495400

First published 1999
This digitally printed version 2008

A catalogue record for this publication is available from the British Library

Library of Congress Cataloguing in Publication data
Maccoby, Hyam, 1924–
Ritual and morality: the ritual purity system and its place in
Judaism / Hyam Maccoby.
p.   cm.
Includes bibliographical references and index.
ISBN 0 521 49540 7 (hardback)
1. Purity, Ritual – Judaism – History of doctrines.
2. Purity, Ritual – Biblical teaching. 3. Bible. O.T. Leviticus – Criticism,
interpretation, etc. 4. Rabbinical literature – History and criticism.   I. Title.
BM702.M33   1999   98 35975
296.7 – dc21   CIP

ISBN 978-0-521-49540-0 hardback
ISBN 978-0-521-09365-1 paperback

Contents

Preface

In this book, I have given an account of the ritual purity system of the Hebrew Bible, and how it developed into the ritual purity system of the rabbis. I explore the motivations behind these systems, and the place they occupy in the total religious system and theology of Israelite religion and Judaism.

I am not concerned here (except peripherally) with dietary laws. These lay down what foods are permitted or forbidden to Israelites. They are often called 'purity laws', because the Bible does use in connection with them the language of 'pure' (*tahor*) and 'impure' (*tame'*). An Israelite who breaks these laws by eating a forbidden animal is guilty of a sin, for which a punishment is prescribed, and for which repentance is required. If the transgression is unwitting, there is no punishment, but there must be repentance for the negligence and a sin-offering brought to the Temple.

The laws of ritual purity, however, do not concern forbidden acts. They concern human conditions or states which occur despite human volition. Sometimes they are the consequence of actions which in themselves are meritorious. To be in a state of ritual impurity is never a sin; but the sufferer of ritual impurity has to be careful not to contact sacred areas or objects until he has rid himself of his impurity by the prescribed method of purification.

For example, an Israelite attends a family funeral. This in itself is a meritorious act, showing family feeling and respect for the dead. But proximity to a corpse causes a seven-day ritual impurity, which must be removed if the Israelite has occasion to enter the Temple, to offer, say, a thank-offering for the birth of a child, or to offer the Paschal lamb. Or a husband and wife have sexual intercourse. But this act, though meritorious, since it fulfils the commandment to be fruitful and multiply, and 'makes the loved companions greatly to rejoice', causes one-day ritual impurity to both husband and wife, which they must remove before their next visit to the Temple. Other impurities are incurred by natural processes: menstruation and childbirth; others by misfortunes: leprosy and abnormal genital discharges. Not one of these conditions is sinful. Many mistakes (especially in New Testament exegesis, see chapter 13) would be avoided if this were better understood.

What the dietary laws and the ritual purity laws have in common is that they form part of the priestly code laid down in the Torah for the Israelites as a priest-nation. It is significant that none of these laws is included in the Ten Commandments, or in any of the lists which were made from time to time (notably the rabbinic Seven Noachide Laws) to express basic human morality. Neither the dietary laws (*kashrut*) nor the purity laws were regarded as obligatory for non-Israelites. Nations or peoples castigated in the Bible for immorality (the generation of the Flood, the people of Sodom, the Canaanites) were never accused of breaches of purity, but only of basic morality.

There has been much scholarly interest in recent years in Israelite and rabbinic ritual systems, and this has done much to counter traditional polemical criticism of Jewish and Catholic 'ritualism'. Moreover, modern trends of structuralism and relativism have blunted the distinction between ritual and ethics to such an extent that a charge of 'ritualism' has come to seem meaningless.

Yet neither the Hebrew Bible nor the rabbinic literature supports the abandonment of the distinction between ritual and morality. The proliferation of ritual rules in Judaism, especially in the area of ritual purity, tends to obscure the fact that ritual in Judaism is ultimately subordinate to morality, or, more accurately, exists as the self-identifying code of a dedicated group whose main purpose is ethical.

Ritual in early Israelite religion took the place of magical apotropaic practices intended to counter demonic influences. Demons were abolished from the religious scheme, and all power given to the One God. Practices originally intended to propitiate or exorcise demons became devices for strengthening the morale and *esprit de corps* of a people dedicated to a revolutionary vision of a society based on love of neighbour. A question for the twenty-first century is whether the erosion of ritual leads to a more focussed morality or to the return of the demons.

But the ritual purity system cannot be completely explained as a monotheistic transformation of magical practices intended originally to combat demonic forces. Nor can all the various kinds of ritual impurity be explained as representing death, as Jacob Milgrom (and also Emanuel Feldman) have argued. There are certain aspects of both ritual impurity and its remedies that adumbrate an alternative mode of religious expression, in which both Eros and Thanatos are inextricably entwined. Monotheistic religion banished death and birth from the Godhead; yet it retained in some of its most dramatic rituals (those of the Red Cow, the Scapegoat, and the purification of the 'leper') vestiges of an ancient earth religion of generation, death and resurrection.

Acknowledgments

In writing this book, my chief scholarly debt has been to Jacob Milgrom, whose monumental work on Leviticus (the second volume of which is still awaited) must be the basis of all future work on the subject. While I have disagreed with him on some important topics (notably his theory of pollution of the sanctuary from afar), I have done so always with the greatest respect for his meticulous learning and lively theorising.

I wish to express also my appreciation of the work of Mary Douglas, who has brought both anthropological and literary insights to bear on Leviticus. As an anthropologist she has been able to display the developed culture and humanity of the priestly code; and she has also seen deeply into its sophisticated literary structure. I have valued greatly our exchange of ideas, and her personal kindness to me.

I am most grateful to Louis Jacobs for reading and commenting on articles which formed the basis of my chapter on ritual purity in the New Testament, and for his encouragement and support of my work. I thank Stefan Reif for his help and encouragement.

My chief support and unfailing source of keen constructive criticism of both style and subject-matter has been my wife and co-worker, Cynthia, whose contribution to my work is beyond assessment.

Chapter 2, 'The Corpse in the Tent' is substantially the same as an article of the same title published in the *Journal for the Study of Judaism*, 28, 2 (1997), while chapter 12, 'Corpse and Leper', was published in the *Journal of Jewish Studies*, Autumn 1998.

Abbreviations

4Q 394–399	See MMT
11QT	The Temple Scroll
Ant.	The Antiquities of the Jews
AV	Authorized Version
b.	Babylonian Talmud
BDB	F. Brown, S. R. Driver & C. A. Briggs, *A Hebrew and English Lexicon of the Old Testament* (Oxford, 1906)
B. Qam.	Baba Qamma
Chron.	Chronicles
Deut.	Deuteronomy
EJ	Encyclopedia Judaica
ET	Entziqlopedia Talmudit
Exod.	Exodus
Gen.	Genesis
Heb.	Hebrews
Jos. War	Josephus, *The Jewish War*
Lam.	Lamentations
Lev.	Leviticus
Lev. R.	Leviticus Rabbah
LSC	F. Sokolowski, *Lois sacrées des cités greques* (Paris 1969)
Manu	Code of Manu
Men.	Menahot
M.	Mishnah
MMT	Miqtzat Ma'asei Torah
MT	Mishneh Torah
NEB	New English Bible

Neg.	Neg'aim
Nid.	Niddah
NT	New Testament
Num.	Numbers
Pes.	Pesahim
R.	Rabbah
Sam.	Samuel
Sanh.	Sanhedrin
Shabb.	Shabbat
TM	Tum'at Met
Toh.	Toharot
t.	Tosefta
Vend.	Vendidad
y.	Palestinian Talmud (Yerushalmi)
Zab.	Zabim
Zech.	Zechariah

CHAPTER I

The sources of impurity: the human corpse

The various kinds of persons, animals and objects which cause impurity by touch or other means need to be listed and discussed. In particular, the question must be asked whether any pattern or basic theme can be discovered in all these varied causes of impurity.

In Judaism, the human corpse is by far the greatest source of impurity, in the sense that it causes the most severe level of impurity, and also contaminates in the greatest variety of modes. This very fact raises the possibility that death is the basic theme for which we are looking. Can it be that every source of impurity functions as a form of death? This has been argued by many scholars, and is supported by the fact that even animals in the Jewish system cause impurity only when they are dead. The theory, however, faces difficulties: in what way, for example, does the impurity caused by emission of semen, or by menstruation, or by childbirth, link with the concept of death?

In societal terms, the supreme impurity of the human corpse has some interesting consequences. It means, for example, that Judaism does not share with Christian societies the practice of interring the corpses of saints or other prominent people in shrines or other places of worship. For in death, all are equal: the corpses of saints are just as much sources of ritual impurity as those of other humans, and the essence of the Jewish system is that ritual impurity should be excluded from the Temple. In the holiest shrine in Christendom, the body of Saint Peter is allegedly buried. The medieval trade in relics, especially the bones, of saints is unimaginable in Judaism.[1]

After the destruction of the Temple, the focus of Jewish worship shifted to the synagogues, and in these the exclusion of impurity was no longer a requirement. On the contrary, it became imperative not to turn the synagogues into miniature Temples, since the sacramental function of the Temple was not transferred to the synagogue. Since by biblical fiat no sacrifices could be performed outside the Temple in Jerusalem, and the Temple no longer existed, any attempt to set up the synagogues as sacramental substitutes for the Temple was regarded as a transgression. From the standpoint of ritual purity, this meant that menstruating women, for example, were not excluded from the synagogue, a point misunderstood by many non-Jewish scholars and even by many ignorant Jews, who think that the reason why women are not called to the reading of the Law is that they may be menstruating.

Yet there is one form of impurity that is excluded even from the synagogue, and that is corpse-impurity, which makes it impossible for a synagogue to contain buried corpses as so many churches and cathedrals do (and as the temples of ancient Egypt did). The reason is that corpse-impurity is the one form of impurity to which an actual prohibition is attached: namely, it is forbidden for priests (Kohanim) to contract corpse-impurity wittingly. Priests are essential for certain aspects of the liturgy (the priests' blessing and being called up first to the reading of the Law), and therefore the synagogue must be conducted in such a way that priests can enter and take part. True, the purity of priests is only nominal, since the absence of the ashes of the Red Cow means that all priests are in a state of corpse-impurity anyway; yet the avoidance of corpse-impurity by priests is one of the 'remembrances of the Temple' that have become fixed practice among post-Destruction Jews.

---

[1] Nevertheless, the tombs (or alleged tombs) of prominent individuals have played some part in Judaism as holy places. Examples are the Cave of Machpelah in Hebron, tomb of the Patriarchs, and the tomb of Simeon bar Yohai in Meron. Veneration of such sites, however, began only in the Middle Ages, probably under Christian and Muslim influence.

The severity of corpse-impurity is shown in several ways. It lasts for seven days, like other severe impurities, but it requires a special method of purification, the sprinkling of the ashes of the Red Cow on the third and seventh day (Num. 19:12). Even more striking is 'tent' impurity, by which a corpse imparts impurity to all persons or vessels under the same roof, even without actual physical contact. This makes it unlike any other impurity (though the 'leper' has a milder version of it, see chapter 12). Further, corpse-impurity is not as easy to shake off as other impurities: it does not descend by such immediate stages. A man who touches a corpse incurs a seven-day uncleanness, and one might expect that if in turn someone touches this man, he would incur a lesser uncleanness, of one day, say, in accordance with the general pattern that uncleanness descends by degrees according to its remoteness from the source. But in fact, in the case of corpse-impurity, the pattern is rejected, or, rather, postponed. A person or vessel that touches a person (or vessel) that has touched a corpse incurs a seven-day uncleanness. It is only at the next remove that the pattern reasserts itself, and a one-day uncleanness is incurred. Further, corpse-impurity has ramifications not exhibited by other impurities. Not only a whole corpse, but even part of one, produces impurity. Not just a corpse, but the grave in which it is buried, is a source of impurity equal to the corpse itself. Most striking of all (in rabbinic theory at any rate) a corpse has a power of contamination in a vertical line both above and below it to an unlimited extent, so that anything hovering above it (even miles above) or below it (even as far as the 'deep') is contaminated by it. Only if it is lying in a 'tent', is this vertical force limited from above, though not from below (see chapter 2).

All this would seem to imply that corpse-impurity is an awesome force in Judaism that must dominate the consciousness of every Jew; that he must tread with the utmost care at all times in case he incur it. However, this is far from being the case. In non-Temple times, such as the present, corpse-impurity is a matter of no consequence at all, since all Jews are in a state of corpse-impurity (only Kohanim, as mentioned above, make a show of observing it). In Temple times, again, most Jews (i.e.

non-priests) were in a state of corpse-impurity most of the time
without concern. It was only when they had to enter the
Temple grounds, mainly at festival times, that they had to take
care to remove their corpse-impurity or other impurity by the
prescribed purifications. This is certainly true of the Second
Temple period; but opinions are divided about the First Temple
period, when, according to Milgrom (1991), Jews were indeed
very worried about corpse-impurity and other impurity. They
had to remove it by purification as soon as possible – otherwise,
it would pollute the Temple by flying horizontally through the
air towards it like a miasma, and fastening upon it. Reasons will
be given in chapter 14 and chapter 15 to reject this concept as
unwarranted by the biblical evidence and as postulating an
unacceptable discontinuity between First Temple and Second
Temple Judaism.

An unexpected feature of corpse-impurity, however, is a
strange leniency in respect of expulsion from holy areas. According to the Babylonian Talmud (Pesachim 67a–b), a corpse-
contaminated person, or even a corpse itself, is not excluded
from areas forbidden to other serious forms of impurity (menstruating or parturient woman, male/female suffering from
sexual flux, and 'leper'). This is a great exception to the rule
that corpse-impurity is more serious than any other. The reason
for this seems to be simply an awkward verse in the Torah that
the rabbis could not ignore. It is stated that Moses accompanied
the body of Joseph throughout the journeys of the Israelites in
the desert, and that the body's location at the resting-places in
the wilderness was 'with him' (Exod. 13:19), i.e. in the camp of
the Levites, since Moses was a Levite (b. Pes. 67a; Maimonides,
MT, Biy'at ha-Miqdash, 3:4). Now the camp of the Levites had
to be kept free of all other serious impurities, though only
'lepers' had to be excluded from all three camps. These were
defined as the Camp of God, i.e. the area of the Tabernacle, the
Camp of the Levites, i.e. the area surrounding the Tabernacle
area, and the Camp of Israel. When the Israelites entered the
Land, the three camps were redefined as the Temple grounds,
the Temple surrounds or Temple Mount, and the rest of
Jerusalem. Only lepers had to stay outside Jerusalem (and other

walled cities founded by Joshua), the 'pelvic dischargers' (Milgrom's term) were allowed in Jerusalem but not on the Temple Mount, while corpses and corpse-contaminated people were allowed on the Temple Mount but not in the Temple grounds. But how could this be reconciled with Numbers 31: 19, enjoining those who had killed in battle to remain outside the camp for seven days? The rabbinic answer is that this refers to exclusion from the Temple courtyard, i.e. from the camp of God, not to exclusion from the camp of Israel, or even the camp of the Levites.

This is not very convincing, and the simple explanation seems to be, as Milgrom argues, that biblically the corpse and corpse-impure were in fact excluded from the camp of the Levites, and even (in earlier legislation, see Milgrom, 1991, p. 316) from the camp of Israel too. This removes the anomaly by which corpse-impurity is treated more leniently than pelvic discharge. As for the corpse of Joseph, here again the simple answer is that this story dates from a time earlier than the priestly legislation about exclusion of impurities from various zones. Such an explanation was, of course, not available to the rabbis.

Another explanation, put forward by Maimonides (*MT*, Biy'at ha-Miqdash, 3:3), is that, in one respect, pelvic discharge is more polluting than corpse-impurity. For sufferers from pelvic discharge cause uncleanness to what they sit or lie upon, even if not in direct contact with them (see p. 32), and this is not the case with those affected by corpse-impurity. However, despite this one respect in which pelvic dischargers are more polluting than the corpse-contaminated, the general picture is the reverse, so it is hardly convincing that this one respect should be decisive for zoning. Moreover, Maimonides' explanation does not cover the case of the corpse itself, which does convey impurity to what is below it, not by 'sitting or lying', but by 'overshadowing' (see p. 17). So there is still no convincing rationale for the admittance of the bones of Joseph into the camp of the Levites while the pelvic dischargers are excluded.

A more detailed and analytical survey now follows of the polluting effects of a corpse.

1. *The corpse itself.* This includes portions of a corpse. It causes a seven-day uncleanness to persons or vessels by:
touching;
being in the same enclosed space ('tent');
overshadowing;
carrying (i.e. being carried, or moved, even if not touched).
2. *A person or vessel that has contracted uncleanness from a corpse.* These convey a seven-day uncleanness to other persons or vessels by:
touching.
3. *A grave.* Conveys a seven-day uncleanness by:
touching;
overshadowing.
4. *A person or vessel that has touched a person or vessel that has touched a corpse.* Conveys a one-day uncleanness to other persons or vessels by:
touching.
5. *A person or vessel suffering one-day uncleanness as in 4.* Does not convey uncleanness to other persons or vessels, but only to foodstuffs. This rule applies to any one-day uncleanness, not just to that derived from corpse-impurity.

I.e. if a person or vessel touches such a person or vessels, they remain clean. There are, however, some rabbinical enactments that modify this situation, especially as regards liquids, but such enactments are regarded as of human, not divine, authority, and, having been enacted in order to cope with some human difficulty, are, in theory, subject to cancellation in the light of changing circumstances.

COMMENTS

The communication of impurity by 'tent' and 'overshadowing' are peculiar to a corpse. 'Tent' has plain biblical authority (Num. 19), while 'overshadowing' has only tenuous textual support, yet is regarded as biblical by the rabbis (but see chapter 2 for the rationale of 'overshadowing', and its relationship to 'tent'). 'Tent' means any enclosed place with a ceiling or roof; if a person or vessel shares such a place with a corpse or portion of a corpse, that person or vessel becomes unclean even without actual contact. 'Overshadowing' occurs when the corpse is directly above or below a person or vessel either in the open air or within a solid block of material, no matter how far above or below the corpse the target is. These two methods of contamination are the most prominent examples of action at a distance in the field of ritual purity (unless one accepts Milgrom's theory, see chapter 14), though there is something similar to 'tent' in the case of the 'leper' (see chapter 12), and there are some shorter distance-mechanisms, viz. carrying or moving without direct contact, pressure through sitting or lying, and presence in the containing space of a contaminated earthenware vessel.

Contamination by 'carrying' is stated explicitly in the Torah only in the case of pelvic dischargers (Lev. 15:10). However, the rabbis extended it also to corpse-impurity by the use of an *a fortiori* argument.[2] They regarded this decision as of divine, not human authority, since it seemed a plain implication of the biblical code.

One must always be careful to distinguish in rabbinic law between those decisions that were regarded as having only human authority (*derabbanan*) and those regarded as having divine authority (*de'oraita*), even though sometimes arrived at by a process of human reasoning. The distinction is clear, even though the rabbis themselves sometimes had difficulty with it, wondering which modes of reasoning linked indissolubly with the biblical text, and which partook too much of human fallibility to be totally relied on in textual explication. Not taking the Karaite view (similar to that of early Protestantism) that the text was perspicuous, the rabbis had to struggle with the demarcation between the human and the divine, though they were quite clear that rabbinic legislation itself (by which new regulations and institutions were added to the biblical code) was entirely human and fallible. To give any greater authority to rabbinic legislation (in the form of a doctrine analogous to that of 'papal infallibility') would have been to

---

[2] Sifrei, Parah, on Numbers 19:16.

infringe against the biblical injunction, 'Thou shalt not add to it, nor shalt thou take away' (Deut. 12:32).[3]

'Carrying' is a kind of contamination from a distance, for it is effective even if the contaminating object is not touched by the carrier. Also, carrying need not be literal removal by the use of one's arms, or on one's head; it may be removal of the object in any way from its original location, for example by the use of a rod or beam. Many cases of carrying are also cases of over-shadowing, so one has to exercise one's imagination to conceive a corpse-impurity case where there is no overshadowing, yet the object is contaminated by being 'carried' or removed.

Corpse-impurity and Gentiles

The general rule (surprising as it may seem) is that non-Jews do not contract ritual impurity at all, and are therefore regarded as permanently clean, at least while alive. This applies to all sources of ritual impurity, not just corpse-impurity. 'Of all animated species there is no species which, while still alive, contracts or conveys uncleanness except man alone, provided that he is an Israelite' (Maimonides, *MT*, Corpse Uncleanness, 1:14). A Gentile cannot become unclean by touching a corpse, or carrying one, or overshadowing one, or being in the same room as one. A Gentile does not become unclean through parturition or menstruation or other discharges. A Gentile cannot even contract leprosy-impurity, which shows that the impurity of this condition is not a medical matter. A Jew who touches a Gentile thus never becomes unclean thereby.

This is not at all in accordance with the common view that Israelites or Jews by adopting a complicated system of purity condemn all non-Jews, who do not observe such rules, to a state of permanent impurity.

On the other hand, some people, on being informed that Gentiles cannot become unclean, are not too happy about this either. It seems to them a condescending state of affairs, that

---

[3] On this, see Maimonides, Introduction to *Mishneh Torah* (conclusion): see Isadore Twersky, *A Maimonides Reader*, New York, 1972, p. 41, for the correct placing of this passage (misplaced in some editions).

only Jews qualify for the rankings in the system of impurities, as if Gentiles are too unimportant even to be considered unclean. A Talmudic statement, likening Gentiles to animals in this respect (for live animals cannot become unclean either) is often quoted by antisemites to show that Gentiles are regarded as animals.

The real point is that Israelites are regarded as a priestly nation. Their purity code is that of a dedicated order, and therefore it does not apply to the rest of mankind, who, however, can opt to become Jews, whereby they become liable to observe the purity laws and also, from the moment of conversion, contract and convey uncleanness. Rabbinic Judaism considers that all humanity, whether Jews or not, are in covenant with God and are bound to keep the laws of morality as summarized in the Seven Noachian Laws, the first code of international law. To become converted to Judaism is not a matter of salvation, but of dedication. Those who are born Jews must function as Jews, but for other members of humanity, Judaism is a choice; just as it is a choice for a Catholic to become a priest or a member of a monastic order, by which he will become liable to obey rules not applicable to the majority of Catholics. This conception of the role of Jews as a priestly nation is not just rabbinic; it is also biblical.

The whole purity code found in the Torah and elaborated in the rabbinic literature is thus a protocol for a dedicated group living constantly in the presence of God, whose Tabernacle is in their midst. It is a kind of palace protocol or etiquette, observed in the court of a monarch, but not required outside the confines of the palace. Even for Jews, once the palace was destroyed, most of the rules became inoperative, though they continued to be studied. Studying the rules came to be a substitute for operating them, and, partly by this means, the Jewish self-perception as a priestly nation was preserved; though, of course, many of the laws of the priestly code, such as the dietary laws and the observance of the festivals, remained fully or partly valid even without the Temple.

The above picture, however, appears to be falsified by rabbinic rules that declare that live Gentiles do, after all, convey uncleanness (b. Niddah 34a; see Maimonides, *MT*, Tum. Met 1:14). The degree of uncleanness is that of a person with a 'running issue' or flux (*zab*), a seven-day uncleanness (see chapter 5). This is quite a serious degree of uncleanness, though less than corpse-uncleanness. This assignment of uncleanness, however, has no biblical authority, and is fully acknowledged in the rabbinic sources to be of human authority only. Consequently, a Jew who has touched a Gentile and then enters the Temple is not punished for sacrilege. This comes into the category of rabbinic enactments, which are, in theory, reversible. The reason for this enactment is given that it was intended to discourage social relations between Jews and non-Jews. The enactment was made, together with similar enactments, in 66 CE, just before the outbreak of war with Rome, at a time when relations between Jews and non-Jews were very strained. There is Talmudic evidence that later rabbis regretted these decrees (known as the Eighteen Decrees). The decision was after all a very illiberal one, because the rabbinically imposed uncleanness could not be remedied by purification procedures, unlike the biblically imposed impurities to which Jews were liable. In any case, the lapse of purity observance some time after the destruction of the Temple made the rabbinic law of Gentile impurity inoperative, since all Jews had become irremediably unclean, and contact with a non-Jew could not make them more unclean than they were already. This rabbinic law (of which much has been made by antisemites, as racist) was practically speaking of short duration.

A strong proof that the impurity of Gentiles is rabbinic is that it does not in fact disturb the rule that the established biblical sources of impurity do not affect Gentiles. Thus, even though a Gentile, by rabbinic decree, is unclean, in the degree of *zab*, he cannot contract further uncleanness by touching a corpse, or by becoming a 'leper'. A Gentile can have only the rabbinic uncleanness and no other. Even if he becomes a *zab* (i.e. contracts a sexual disease), which is the same uncleanness that he fictitiously contracts by rabbinic decree, a legal distinction is made between the two types of uncleanness, for the rabbinic status of *zab* allotted to a Gentile is not to be confused with the actual status of *zab*, which, being biblical, a Gentile cannot contract (see M. Zab. 2:3).

But what about dead Gentiles? One would expect that since a live Gentile is outside the whole system, a dead Gentile would be outside it too, and his corpse would have no power of contamination. But here we meet with an anomaly. The rabbis could not make the system entirely logical in this way, because a biblical text, about the Israelites' war with Midian (Num. 31:19), stands in the way. 'Whosoever hath touched any slain, purify both yourselves and your captives on the third day and on the seventh day.' The Midianites were not Israelites, yet their corpses conveyed a seven-day impurity. The rabbis concluded that the corpse of a non-Jew conveys impurity, but of course only to Jews. This was a decision of some consequence, because it meant that a Jew travelling in foreign countries was very likely to incur corpse-impurity by walking on ground in which human bones were lying, especially as non-Jews were thought to be not so scrupulous as Jews in carrying out burials. This became the basis of another rabbinic decree, that Gentile lands were to be regarded as conveying impurity to Jews, who therefore were required to undergo purification after a foreign visit, if they wished to enter the Temple precincts. Even though the impurity from a Gentile corpse was biblical (being based on the Midianite incident), the decree was regarded as merely rabbinic, since it was based on possibility, not proven fact. If a Jew was *known* to have contacted a Gentile corpse on a visit to, say, Rome, then his uncleanness was biblical; the decree, however, referred to putative impurity only.

Here again, antisemitic interpretations of the decree are not wanting. The fact is, however, that the matter is relatively trivial, being not part of the main purity system, but a temporary and limited offshoot. There can be no comparison with the Hindu purity law which forbids Brahmins to leave the holy land because of the impurity of foreign lands; this is an integral part of the Hindu purity system. In rabbinic Judaism, the decree, as in all purity matters, is tied to the Temple. Impurity is not evil in itself, but only in relation to the etiquette of entry to holy areas (and the consumption of holy foods). In the absence of the

Temple, the law is without application. In the basic system, that
of the Torah, foreign lands are not unclean.

One may ask, however, whether the rabbis' conception of the
difference between the Torah and themselves is a correct one.
From the standpoint of modern biblical study, is it correct to
say, as the rabbis said, that the Torah does not regard Gentiles
or Gentile lands as unclean?

Interesting work on this, as on many other ritual-purity
questions, has been done by Gedaliah Alon.[4] He criticizes some
of the rabbinic standpoints, arguing that the origin of the
decrees on Gentiles and Gentile lands is earlier than the date of
the Eighteen Decrees. But he confirms the rabbinic conviction
that these decrees are post-biblical. The Hebrew Bible knows
nothing of unclean Gentiles or unclean Gentile lands.

This is in spite of the fact that certain biblical texts can be
quoted to show that non-Jews and their lands were regarded as
unclean (e.g. Leviticus 18:24–25, Ezra 9:11). These texts,
however, can be shown to refer not to ritual impurity, as it is
conceived in a well-defined sense in relation to the Temple, and
for which purificatory rites are laid down. These texts, on the
contrary, use the term 'uncleanness' in a metaphorical non-
ritual sense, equivalent to 'abomination', in relation to immorality or idolatry (see chapter 16). True, in rabbinic times, a ritual
impurity, in addition to the metaphorical impurity, was attached
to idols and their appurtenances, but this again has no biblical
basis.

[4] Alon (1977), pp.146–86.

CHAPTER 2

The corpse in the tent: an excursus

One of the most difficult topics in the study of ritual purity is that of the corpse in the 'tent', and particularly the question of how the biblical law expressed so briefly in Numbers 19:14–16 proliferated into the complex system found in Mishnah Ohalot and elsewhere.

Numbers says simply: 'When a man dies in a tent, this is the law: everyone who goes into the tent and everyone who was inside the tent shall be ritually unclean for seven days, and every open vessel which has no covering tied over it shall also be unclean. In the open, anyone who touches a man killed with a weapon or one who had died naturally, or who touches a human bone or a grave, shall be unclean for seven days' (NEB).

These verses differentiate between a corpse that is enclosed in a 'tent' and a corpse that is in the open. When it is enclosed, it transmits impurity even to those people and vessels that have not touched it; simply to be under the same roof as the corpse is sufficient to incur impurity. In the open, however, a corpse (or even part of a corpse) transmits impurity by touch only. A grave, on the other hand, has its own individual impurity, by which it transmits impurity by touch in the open, even if the corpse itself is not touched.

Rabbinic law fills out this account in certain commonsense ways that are not problematic. The provision that corpse-impurity arises even from a small portion of a corpse is stated in Numbers only in relation to a corpse in the open (the 'bone'), but it is a natural extension to understand this as applicable also in the case of the enclosed corpse. It is also not problematic that rabbinic law seeks to define minimum quantities. How large does an enclosure have to be to count as a 'tent'? How small can a portion of a corpse be not to be dismissed as insignificant? This kind of quantity definition is characteristic of the rabbis and is to be expected. Even the idea that the biblical 'tent' does not mean an actual tent but any kind of enclosed space is hardly surprising, since the rabbis always regard the Written Torah as giving concrete instances which stand for more general concepts.

But certain other rabbinic concepts in relation to the 'tent' are surprising, even bizarre, since they do not seem to depend on any logical or generalising extension of the text. The chief concepts of this kind are the following:

1. that a person or vessel that 'overshadows' a corpse (i.e. is positioned vertically above a corpse, or part of a corpse) becomes ritually unclean;

2. that a person or vessel that is 'overshadowed' by a corpse, or part of a corpse (i.e. is positioned vertically below it), becomes ritually unclean;

3. that corpse-impurity can be conveyed from one enclosed space to another by means of an 'aperture' of a certain minimum size, and with the help of a certain kind of 'intention' on the part of the owner of the enclosed space.

These additional concepts seem so far from the biblical text that Jacob Neusner, in the course of his minute though unsatisfactory studies of the subject, has declared (his italics), 'If we started with Scripture and asked what it taught, we should never, *never* discover even the simplest datum of rabbinic law' (Neusner, 1975, p. 238). Neusner's treatment of the subject, then, proceeds in terms of a rabbinical concept of the Tent, which bears no logical relationship to the biblical tent.[1]

I shall argue, however, that the rabbinical concepts arise by natural and logical steps from the biblical data. Neusner admits that the rabbinical concepts did not begin with the rabbis of the second century, but show every sign of a long previous post-

---

[1] For criticism of Neusner's general tendency to see rabbinic literature as separated by a wide gulf from Scripture, see Maccoby (1990). For criticism of his thesis that the Mishnah actually sets itself up as a rival to Scripture, see Maccoby (1984).

biblical development, though some refinements do indeed belong to the second century (Neusner, 1975, pp. 243–44).

Neusner even finds discontinuity in the rabbinical concept of a minimum Tent of one cubic handbreadth. This, he argues, is alien to the biblical tent, which is simply an actual tent, large enough to contain a corpse. The biblical authors, he contends, never intended the law of the corpse-in-a-tent to go beyond this totally literal interpretation.

Even if the biblical authors were quite as simple-minded as this, there is no difficulty about seeing a legal continuity between Numbers and its rabbinic interpretation here. It is obvious that any reflection on Numbers is bound to come up with the question, 'What exactly is a tent, and how big does it have to be to exercise its special power of non-tangential impurity-transmission?' A corpse also needed definition, and the answer that even a small part of a corpse counted as a corpse had good scriptural authority in Numbers 19:15. There is thus no difficulty about a tent being small, since a corpse (or corpse-portion) can also be small. The progression from a large tent to a small enclosed space is thus quite understandable and need not give rise to any theory of an unbridgeable gap between biblical and rabbinic law.

The rabbinic theory of the 'aperture' (*halon*) connecting one space to another also arises very naturally out of the attempt to define a tent. This time we are concerned not with the minimum, but the maximum, tent. Can a whole house, consisting of a number of separate rooms, count as a single tent, or does this term refer to a single space only, so that a corpse lying in a house contaminates only the room in which it lies? The answer, a very natural one, is that several rooms can count as a single 'tent' if they are connected by an aperture; and then the minimum requirements of such an aperture are discussed. This, again, is a very logical and natural development of the biblical concept of a tent, and need not give rise to any claims of total discontinuity between the Bible and its rabbinic exegesis. It is the kind of discussion to which every legal text that is taken seriously is subjected. There are, however, some niceties of thought in the rabbinic discussion of the 'aperture' which will require further examination, since, at first sight, they seem remote from the biblical text.

The rabbinic concepts that do seem mysteriously remote from the Bible even in their most direct and uncomplicated formulation are those that concern 'overshadowing'. The rabbinic laws that prescribe impurity for persons or vessels situated either vertically above or vertically below a corpse or corpse-fragment are simple enough, but how do they derive from the biblical text about the tent? The expression 'overshadowing' (Hebrew *ma'ahil*) derives from the noun for 'tent' (*'ohel*) and the inference seems to be that 'overshadowing' is in some way an application of the law of the tent. But how does one logically proceed from the idea of a corpse lying in a tent to the idea of a corpse functioning as a tent or roof over a person or vessel, or the idea of a person or vessel functioning as a tent or roof over a corpse? There seems to be good reason, therefore, to think that these two kinds of 'overshadowing' are discrete additions to the biblical concept of the tent, not logical derivatives of it.

However, it is possible to explain the phenomena of 'overshadowing' in such a way as to show a logical and integral connection between the biblical tent and the rabbinic 'overshadowing'. This explanation will make it possible also to understand certain puzzling details of the law of 'overshadowing' which would otherwise remain mysterious.

The basic point to grasp about the rabbinic (or post-biblical) conception of the tent is that it is a device for *preventing impurity from travelling further upwards*. The concept of the tent, as outlined in Numbers, aroused wonder because it is the only explicit biblical example of *impurity that acts at a distance*. The question that presented itself, on the basis of the biblical data, was 'In what direction does the impurity travel?' And the answer given, with great plausibility (though it was not the only possible answer) was 'The distance-acting impurity of a corpse travels up and down from the corpse in a vertical direction.'

Instead of thinking of the tent as somehow collecting the distance-acting impurity of the corpse – a limited miasma which exhausts itself in reaching the roof and sides of the tent and can travel no further – the concept was that the impurity was of such strength that it could travel an unlimited distance vertically up and down.[2] It does indeed travel downwards through the floor of the tent until it reaches the 'deep' (*tehom*),[3] but on its upward passage it is checked by the ceiling of the tent and travels no further. This checking of an otherwise unlimited upward course was the fiat of the scriptural text, which in declaring that everything below the ceiling became unclean was also declaring that *everything above the ceiling was clean*.

Suppose, however, that there is no tent, and therefore the distance-acting impurity of the corpse is unchecked in its upward course. In this case, if the upward-travelling stream of impurity meets any object which is susceptible of impurity, i.e. a person or a vessel, that person or vessel will become unclean, being unprotected by any intervening tent-ceiling. This is the situation when a person or vessel 'overshadows' a corpse (a somewhat misleading expression, since, despite the etymological similarity between *'ohel* and *ma'ahil*, the tent and the 'overshadower' are two different things).

On the other hand, if a corpse 'overshadows' a person or a vessel, impurity is again transmitted to that person or vessel, since a downward flow of impurity will continue, causing impurity to any susceptible objects in its path. A downward flow, however, can be stopped by an *'ohel* construction; if a susceptible target is below the ceiling of the 'tent' and the corpse is above, the person or vessel is 'protected'. Unless stopped by a the ceiling or roof of a 'tent', the upward or downward flow of the impurity will cause impurity to all susceptible objects it meets on its vertical path.

Thus the impurity contracted through 'overshadowing' is not a gratuitous addition to the scriptural law of the tent, but a necessary consequence of a plausible interpretation of the tent as stopping the otherwise continuous flow of the distance-acting impurity of a corpse in an up and down vertical direction.

The matter has been obscured by the medieval Jewish commentators, whose codifying approach has led them to list

---

[2] For up-and-down motion of impurity, see Mishnah 'Ohalot 6:6, 7:1–2, 9:13,14,16, 10:6–7, 12:6–7, 15:1,3,7.

[3] Sifrei on Numbers 19:14–15.

all the phenomena of 'overshadowing' under the same technical term. Maimonides, for example, writes as follows:

'Uncleanness by overshadowing' applies to no uncleanness except that of a corpse; and it applies whether a person or vessel overshadows (*he'ehil*) the corpse ... or whether the corpse overshadows a person or a vessel, or whether a corpse and a person or a vessel are under one 'tent': in all these cases, the person or the vessel becomes unclean. 'Uncleanness by overshadowing' (*tum'at 'ohel*) wherever mentioned, means that such uncleanness of person or vessel was incurred by one of these aforesaid means. (*MT,* Tum'at Met, 1:10–11)

This listing of three kinds of 'overshadowing' is useful for rote learning, but is also misleading, because there is really only one kind of 'tent' contamination, which is the corpse lying in a tent with its target situated horizontally beside it, as described in Scripture, when the tent, in rabbinic theory, acts to pollute horizontally but protect vertically. The other two kinds of 'overshadowing' concern what happens when there is *no* tent to protect the target vertically, in which case the corpse contaminates vertically both upwards and downwards. (Note that it is the *ceiling* of the tent, together with its projected walls, that protects, not its floor – for the simple reason that a tent is defined by having a ceiling not by having a floor – so that the downward flow of contamination is only stopped when it encounters the roof of a tent situated below it.) The rabbinic sources are to some extent responsible for Maimonides' imprecision, because they too use the verb 'to overshadow' (*he'ehil*) for all three processes.

It may be useful at this point to give some further explanation of the relationship between horizontal contamination and vertical contamination. If a corpse is lying in the open, its contamination flows upwards and downwards from every part of the corpse, whether through the air or through solid rock. An analogy with rays rather than with a gas may be helpful to the modern reader. The corpse emits rays, but only in a vertical upward-and-downward direction. If, however, the corpse is in a tent, a horizontal component comes into play. The rays bounce off the ceiling of the tent and distribute themselves throughout the tent, so that any susceptible target becomes contaminated, whether on the same level as the corpse or above it, as long as it is below the ceiling. The ceiling need not be itself horizontal, but can be slanting or undulating, the only requirement being that it must leave the minimum space of one handbreadth clear above the floor. The tent is defined as anything below the ceiling. The walls of the tent may be fragmentary or non-existent; they do not matter because the ceiling itself defines its walls, i.e. anything under the same ceiling as the corpse becomes unclean, the walls being defined by the boundaries of the ceiling. Thus the horizontal action of the pollution arises because anything under the ceiling (however long or broad the ceiling may be) becomes polluted.

Of course, any physical analogy breaks down, because the rabbis had no physical conception of the pollution, but were simply trying to apply the biblical data. Sometimes (when dealing with the distribution of pollution within the tent) their solution seems to us to point to a conception of pollution as a gas. Sometimes (when dealing with the behaviour of non-tangential pollution in the absence of a tent) pollution seems to act like radiation. Scripture says that everything in the tent becomes unclean, so it is just a matter of defining the tent, not of picturing how the contamination works. Scripture says that everything *in* the tent becomes polluted, so that excludes everything above the tent. The tent does not protect objects below it from contamination, because it is the ceiling that defines the tent, not the floor. The earth is always there, but a tent comes into existence only when a ceiling is added above it, either intentionally or by chance. (Of course, if the floor is itself raised above the earth by the required minimum of a handbreadth, then it acts as the ceiling of a second tent.) The fact that the ceiling protects objects above it proves that without the ceiling, the contamination would proceed in an upward direction. This upward action of contamination must surely be complemented by a downward action, which itself can be halted by encountering the roof of a tent (here we arrive at a picture of a tent containing no pollution and resisting the pollution that hovers above it; this is a reversal of the biblical picture, yet an inevitable variation on it). Thus a whole theory of the distance-effects of corpse-contamination in and out of a tent arises simply from biblical exegesis.

It should be borne in mind, however, that such contemplation is stimulated by the extraordinary nature of the text, which posits a unique action-at-a-distance for tent-pollution, and invites theorising about what happens when this force is not restrained by a tent. The solution arrived at – that distance-acting pollution operates in a vertical up-and-down direction, but is stopped by the ceiling of a tent and then distributed throughout the tent – is imaginative, but is still strictly limited to the biblical data, adding nothing that is irrelevant to the solution demanded by those data.

Neusner has popularised the idea that corpse-pollution in a 'tent' is to be thought of in a rabbinic context as a kind of 'gas'. Biblical commentators have also interpreted the scriptural data as presupposing some physical miasma. Jacob Milgrom writes '... every person and object under the roof is contaminated, another example of the original notion that impurity was a dynamic, physical substance exuded by the contaminated body' (Milgrom, 1990, p. 161). Milgrom has emphasised to an unprecedented degree the idea of corpse-impurity as a physical miasma, even affecting the Temple from afar. Baruch A. Levine accepts this, writing (on Numbers 19:13), 'The impurity of the dead was so powerful that it affected the Sanctuary' (Levine, 1993, p. 466).

Whatever may be the case in the biblical context (and Milgrom's theory is far from proved, see chapter 14), Neusner's theory that corpse-pollution is to be regarded in a rabbinic context as a 'viscous (sic) gas' is far too simple-minded. He arrived at this physical explanation, which he attributed in a literal way to the rabbis as part of their thinking on pollution, by considering the way pollution behaves in a tent; but he failed to consider how distance-pollution behaves in the absence of a tent, regarding this as quite a separate issue, or hardly an issue at all. The reason why he thought that the gas was 'viscous' was that it needs an aperture of a square handbreadth to escape from one room to another. A thin kind of gas might escape through a smaller aperture; consequently, corpse-pollution must be a thick gas. This is entirely the wrong way to think about the matter. The whole point is 'When do we consider two adjacent tents to be connected, thus forming a single legal entity?' The answer was 'When they are connected by a non-negligible aperture.' The legal definition of non-negligible is in general a square handbreadth; anything smaller does not count as a viable connecting aperture, capable of turning two rooms into one. Yet this general measurement can change if an element of *intention* enters the matter. If the opening was put there intentionally as a means of connecting the two rooms (e.g. a small hole for conveying light from one room to the other), then the two rooms can be reckoned as one even if the aperture is *less* than a square handbreadth in size. The thickness or thinness of the 'gas' is not the point. It is a matter of the architecture of the two rooms.[4] Failing to understand this, Neusner is puzzled by the introduction of 'intention', which he calls 'an insoluble problem' (p. 250). He would like to regard 'intention' as one of the latest (Ushan) features of the law of tents, but is forced by the evidence to admit it as early (p. 251).[5]

When two rooms are connected in such a way as to make them legally one, then the corpse lying in one room is also lying in the other, and so the pollution that scripture ordains as affecting the room now affects both rooms. This case of connected rooms, in fact, shows that even in relation to tent-pollution, the rabbis did not think of pollution in terms of physical materiality. They thought merely in terms of applying and defining the scriptural terms involved. Pollution was not some substance that crept around rooms. It was a state or condition of people or vessels that were situated, together with a

[4] Neusner (1975, pp. 221, 223) strangely attributes to Philo the idea that the contaminating substance which fills the tent is the departing soul of the dead person who lies there. Philo's words are: 'For a man's soul is a precious thing, and when it departs to seek another home, all that will be left behind is defiled, deprived as it is of the divine image' (*Special Laws* 3:207). Philo is merely saying that the departure of the purifying influence of the soul leaves the corpse in a state of defilement.

[5] In M. 'Ohalot 13:1, the doctrine of intention is attributed to the Second Temple authorities, the Houses. Neusner writes, 'The attribution can be set aside, perhaps, with the claim that here Ushans assign as a datum of the Houses' conceptions what in fact is charateristically an Ushan concern. But what are we to make of Aqiva and Tarfon, who assume the same?' (p. 251).

corpse, in a certain kind of area, defined as fulfilling the requirements for the scriptural concept of a 'tent'. Having arrived at the conditions for impurity in this legal way, the rabbis might then indulge themselves, at times, in some physical metaphors, as when they refer to the up-and-down action of impurity (in the absence of a tent) as 'cleaving' (*boqe'a*), but such expressions are merely shorthand, and can be paralleled in other legal systems. Even up-and-down pollution is not caused by rays or any other physical mode of causation; it is simply the legal effect of the absence of an intervening tent, which would otherwise confine the corpse-impurity to a limited area, in accordance with scriptural law. There is certainly a physical aspect to all cases of corpse-pollution, namely that they occur in three-dimensional space. Unlike touching-pollutions or even carrying-pollutions, they mysteriously act across empty space, and our modern minds immediately jump to theories by which distant objects can be connected: gas, rays, perhaps even waves. Such explanations, however, are not the rabbis' province. They are content to know that action-at-a-distance has been decreed by the law.

There are, however, certain classes of objects which do not seem to behave in accordance with the above elucidation of the relationship between 'tent' pollution and up-and-down pollution. These anomalies will now have to be explained.

The Mishnah tells us (M. 'Ohalot 6:1) that when the ceiling of a 'tent' consists of a human being or a vessel – or even when these comprise not the ceiling of the tent but just the means by which it is propped up, i.e. the 'walls' – then the tent thus formed combines characteristics of tent-pollution and up-and-down pollution. Like a tent it 'brings' or conveys pollution; i.e. if it acts as a canopy over corpse-material, all people or vessels alongside the corpse and under any part of the same canopy become unclean. On the other hand, it does not 'protect'; i.e. the ceiling thus formed does not prevent the pollution escaping upwards to contaminate any person or vessel situated above it. Even more anomalous is the provision that objects above this kind of tent become unclean even if not in line with the polluting object lying below in the tent, as long as they lie above any part of the ceiling. This contradicts the rule that up-and-down pollution goes vertically from the polluting source, never spreading horizontally.

At this point, one might be forgiven for throwing up one's hands in despair, and concluding that the laws of tents have no rationale, since here we have cases that break every rule.

However, we need not despair, because there is a simple explanation. All these anomalous provisions are regarded as rabbinical enactments, not as part of the basic law of the 'tent'. This is proved by various leniencies which apply to the operation of these anomalous laws; i.e. breaking these laws does not bring the same penalties as breaking the basic laws (for example, someone who has become unclean under one of the anomalous laws, and then deliberately enters the Temple is not subject to penalty of extirpation). Maimonides puts the matter as follows:

We have already explained in Laws Concerning the Nazirite's Vow that if a Nazirite and an olive's bulk of flesh from a corpse are below a camel or below a bed or a similar object, although he incurs seven-day uncleanness he need not cut off his hair. From this we may infer that all the rules laid down concerning the uncleanness of 'tents' formed by persons or by beasts or by utensils rest on the authority of the Scribes; some of them are matters of tradition, some of them are preventive measures or precautions; therefore on account of them the Nazirite does not need to cut off his hair, nor, on account of them, is extirpation incurred by entering into the Temple or eating of its Hallowed Things. (*MT*, Tum'at Met 19:6, H. Danby's translation)

Thus, rightly considered, the anomalous laws only confirm the correctness of the relationship outlined above between tent-impurity and up-and-down impurity, for any laws that contradict this relationship turn out to be arbitrary decisions outside the basic categories, and therefore binding only to a limited degree. A plausible explanation offered in standard commentaries[6] for the enactment of these anomalous rules is that humans and vessels are too portable or unfixed to count scripturally as true 'ceilings' or 'walls' for tents. The rabbis,

---

[6] *Mirkebet Mishneh* on Maimonides, *Mishneh Torah*, Tum'at Met 19:6; *Tif'eret Yisrael*, on M. 'Ohalot 6:1; *ET*, ' 'Ohel ha-met', vol. 1, p. 109.

however, were afraid that if they were exempted, this might lead to the neglect of real 'tents'; so they made these 'materials' liable to act as 'ceilings', but were not able to release them from their scriptural liability to convey up-and-down contamination.[7] These 'materials' thus had the worst of both worlds. The reason why these 'ceilings' spread impurity along the whole area above them as well as below them (not just vertically from the corpse-material lying below them) is this: since rabbinically the area below has been turned into a 'tent' which is full of pollution, yet since, also rabbinically, the ceiling formed does not 'protect' from rising pollution, the whole of the rabbinically enacted 'tent' pollution rises through up-and-down action (nevertheless this result was so anomalous that a distinction was introduced between the *degree* of contamination immediately over the corpse and that over the other areas of the 'tent').

It may be useful now to consider a passage from the Mishnah that illustrates graphically the relationship between 'tent' pollution and up-and-down pollution.

There were courtyards in Jerusalem built over rock, and beneath them the rock was hollowed for fear of any grave down in the depths; and they used to bring women while they were pregnant and there they bore their children and reared them. And they brought oxen with doors laid upon their backs, and on these the children sat bearing in their hands cups of stone. When they reached Siloam, they alighted and filled the cups with water and got up again and sat upon the boards. R. Jose says: The child used to let down his cup and fill it without alighting. When they came to the Temple Mount they alighted.

Beneath both the Temple Mount and the courts of the Temple was a hollowed space for fear of any grave down in the depths. At the entrance of the Temple Court was set a jar of [the ashes of the] Sin-offering. They brought a male from among the sheep, tied a rope between its horns, and tied a stick and wound it about with the [other] end of the rope, and threw it into the jar. The sheep was smitten so that it started backward [and spilled the ashes], and the child took of the ashes and mixed enough to be visible on the water. R. Jose says: Give not the Sadducees occasion to cavil! But, rather,

---

[7] Live animals, however, such as the camel mentioned above by Maimonides, were given full (though rabbinical) status as 'tents' (able both to pollute and protect), for reasons that need not be investigated here.

one [of the children] took [the ashes directly] from the jar and mixed them. (m. Parah 3:2–3, H. Danby's translation)

This passage shows how the construction of a 'tent' could be a means of protection from vertical distance-pollution. The mixing of the ashes of the Red Cow with water had to be done in a state of the utmost purity; otherwise the resultant mixture would not be efficacious as a purification (by sprinkling) from corpse-pollution. Extraordinary steps are described (perhaps in partly legendary fashion) to ensure that the purity of this operation would not be affected by underground sources of corpse-pollution. Empty underground 'tents' were constructed to stop upward-flowing pollution from graves deeper underground.

In case some above-ground pollution should be encountered, a separate 'tent' was constructed above ground. This consisted of the 'doors' laid upon the backs of the oxen bearing the children. This was a protection not from 'graves' but from possible corpse-mould lying on the road traversed, which would cause pollution if 'overshadowed' by the children.

It should be noted that the underground pollution feared was not from corpses themselves, but from 'graves'.[8] That a grave is a source of impurity on its own, is derived from the biblical text that lists 'grave' as a separate source (Num. 19:16). The rabbinic doctrine of the polluting action of a grave is that its behaviour is similar to that of a corpse in the open, i.e. it transmits pollution either by being touched on any part of it, or by vertical over-shadowing. What if a corpse lies in a tomb, with space of more than a handbreadth between corpse and ceiling of tomb? This would act as a tent, if the tomb has a doorway, for a tent must have a doorway (*MT*, TM 7:1) – even a room with no doorway counts as a grave. What if a corpse lies in a coffin with one handbreadth space above it? The coffin does protect like a tent (scripturally, but not rabbinically) because the coffin lid is counted as a doorway. If there is no space in the coffin, it acts like a corpse or a grave (*MT*, TM 12:6).

---

[8] The Temple Mount contained many underground passages, and it may be that these were used at times for the construction of catacombs.

The introduction of the Sadducees as possibly mocking at the extraordinary purity measures is puzzling, because recent research has shown that the Sadducees were actually not more lenient but stricter in purity matters than the Pharisees or (later) the rabbis.[9] The explanation here may be that the Pharisees were famously lenient in the *preparation* of the ashes, allowing this to be performed in a state of minor impurity, and even deliberately performing it in impurity in order to flout the more stringent Sadducee doctrine (M. Parah 3:7). Yet the Pharisees were very stringent, as this Mishnah shows, in the purity of the rite of mixing the ashes with the water. The Sadducees might mock, not because of this stringency, but because of the apparent inconsistency between the leniency in preparing and the stringency in mixing the ashes. Therefore, Rabbi Yose sought to lessen the inconsistency. More probably, however, Rabbi Yose, speaking in the second century CE, did not have the historical Sadducees in mind, and was not connecting the matter to any first-century Pharisee-Sadducee controversy. By his time (the Sadducees having become defunct) the word 'Sadducee' may have been already used loosely to signify merely 'heretic' or 'sceptic', as we know to be the case in later times. Rabbi Yose may simply have felt that excessive anxiety in avoiding impurity (even in anecdotal form about Temple times) might lead to ridicule from sceptics.[10]

The passage shows that great anxiety was indeed felt about the possibility of corpse-impurity or grave-impurity when certain Temple rites were performed. This does not mean that the average Jew, even in Temple times, went around in constant fear of incurring corpse-impurity. On the contrary, attending a funeral, and even more so laying out corpses for burial, were regarded as highly meritorious, despite the corpse-impurity involved. Only priests, not ordinary Israelites, were actually

---

[9] See Baumgarten, J.M. (1980) and Maccoby, H. (1994).

[10] What would have been the purpose of spilling the ashes through the agency of a sheep? The answer may be that if, despite all the precautions, the children had incurred impurity, they would impart it only to the small amount of ashes used for mixing with the water, not to the main body of ashes reserved for future use.

forbidden to incur corpse-impurity.[11] Yet even a High Priest
was obliged to do so if he came across an unburied corpse by
the wayside, since the duty of burying such a corpse (*met mitzvah*)
took precedence over all ritual purity laws (M. Nazir 7:1). Only
before entering the Temple was it imperative for the average
person to perform the sprinklings which purified from corpse-
impurity.[12]

After the destruction of the Temple, these sprinklings could
not be performed, in the absence of the means of purification,
the ashes of the Red Cow. Consequently, all Jews, whether
priests or non-priests, were in a state of corpse-impurity (though
the priests, as a memento of Temple times, continued to avoid
funerals or graveyards, in a pious pretence of avoiding impurity). All the laws of tents elaborated in Mishnah 'Ohalot and
elsewhere were therefore academic, and were studied with such
care only as a religious or intellectual exercise, or as a preparation for the eventual rebuilding of the Temple.

Nevertheless, there can be little doubt that the principal laws
and concepts had been handed down by tradition, and were not
invented in the second century by ingenious rabbis to employ
their leisure hours.[13] There may be some legendary exaggera-
tions in the above account of the Temple precautions taken
against corpse-impurity, but there is no reason to dismiss the
whole story as unhistorical. It seems that in Temple times, long
before Usha, the 'tent', conceived in abstract terms as a covered

---

[11] This does not mean that corpse-impurity was of no importance to non-priests, who
did have to enter the Temple at times, especially during festivals. On such occasions
they would need purification. But they could certainly remain in impurity for much
longer periods than priests, who constantly handled sacred food (*terumah*), and were
positively forbidden to incur corpse-impurity, except in emergencies. This is what
Maimonides means when he says, ' ... Scripture warns none but the sons of Aaron
and the Nazirite against incurring uncleanness from a corpse, thereby implying that
for all other people it is permissible, and that it is permissible even for priests and
Nazirites to incur uncleanness from other unclean things, except only corpse
uncleanness' (*MT*, VI, 16:9), a passage which Hannah K. Harrington seems to
misunderstand as meaning that Maimonides exempted non-priests of all concern for
corpse-impurity ('Maimonides ... states that corpse impurity applies only to the
priests', Harrington, 1993, p. 70).

[12] See Maccoby (1988), pp. 94–100, 104–5.

[13] 'We can hardly be surprised by the evidences of the relatively greater antiquity, the
longer pre-history, of Ohalot, as compared to the pre-history of Kelim' (Neusner,
1975, p. 243).

cubic measure of space, was regarded as a protection against pollution, not just as a cause of it. Known in conjunction with this was the concept of the unlimited up-and-down motion of corpse-pollution, cleaving through air or solid rock.

The question may be put: 'To what extent did the rabbis understand the logical links between the various laws of the Tent?' Did they understand that the protective function of the Tent and the laws of vertical 'overshadowing' were related to each other, and were both derived directly from the text of Numbers 19:14–16, as argued above? The answer seems to be 'No', since they derived the laws of overshadowing by strained exegesis from side-texts, not from logical extrapolation from the main text about the tent.[14] Thus the codifying method of Maimonides was anticipated by the Tannaitic literature, and overshadowing was regarded as chiefly validated by the Oral Law, with some support from texts that, in themselves, would not have given rise to such halakhic results. This is why it is stated about the laws of 'tents' that they have 'little Scripture and many laws' (b. Hagigah 11a), despite the exegeses which were adduced.

But this is by no means the only instance of rabbinic loss of earlier rationale – the degeneration of logic into codification. A good example is the law prohibiting the wearing of a garment woven from a mixture of wool and linen (*sha'atnez*). The rationale of this was fully understood by Josephus, who says that this mixture was 'appointed to be for the priests alone' (*Ant.*iv. 208).[15] This cogent reason for forbidding the mixture for profane use had been forgotten by the rabbis, who regarded the law of *sha'atnez* as inscrutable and mystical. They simply codified and defined the law among other biblical precepts, without attempting to explain it. Similarly, the rationale of 'overshadowing' as a logical consequence of the biblical law of the 'tent' was lost. This need not prevent us from restoring the

---

[14] Overshadowing of corpse over person or vessel is derived from 'shall be unclean seven days', Numbers 19:16. Overshadowing of person or vessel over corpse is derived from 'over the face of the field', Numbers 19:16. See Sifrei Zutta ad loc.

[15] The garments of the priests were indeed made of this mixture, see Exod. 28:3–6, 39:29. The hangings of the Tabernacle itself were of the same mixture, see Exod. 26:1, etc.

rationale, and thus vindicating the logical continuity between scriptural and rabbinic law.

The laws of the 'tent' proliferated into many side-issues which have been omitted here. Nevertheless, the appearance of a chaotic mass of laws is deceptive. Once the clue of the relationship between the 'tent' and 'overshadowing' has been grasped, a consistent system is revealed, based not on rabbinic inventiveness, but on the exegesis of Scripture.

CHAPTER 3

The sources of impurity: menstruation

The bodily discharges that cause serious impurity are menstruation, childbirth, and 'running issues' from either male or female (i.e., abnormal discharge of semen, in the case of the male, and abnormal uterine bleeding, in the case of the female). Another discharge that causes less serious impurity is normal discharge of semen, whether by involuntary nocturnal emission, or by voluntary sexual activity.

How do these discharges relate to the greatest source of impurity, the human corpse? Is there a common theme here? Jacob Milgrom argues that there is.

Moreover, in the Israelite mind, blood was the archsymbol of life ... Its oozing from the body was no longer the work of demons, but it was certainly the sign of death. In particular, the loss of seed in vaginal blood ... was associated with the loss of life. Thus it was that Israel – alone among the peoples – restricted impurity solely to those physical conditions involving the loss of vaginal blood and semen, the forces of life, and to scale disease, which visually manifested the approach of death ... All other bodily issues and excrescences were not tabooed, despite their impure status among israel's contemporaries, such as cut hair or nails in Persia and India and the newborn child as well as its mother in Greece and Egypt. Human feces were also not declared impure (despite Deut. 23:12; Ezek. 4:12). Why, wonders Dillman, does not the Bible label human feces impure, as do the Indians (Manu 5.138ff), Persians (Vend. 17.11ff) and Essenes (Jos. *War* 2.8,9; cf 11QT46:15)? The answer is clear. The elimination of waste has nothing to do with death; on the contrary, it is essential to life ... The association of blood with life and its loss with death is fully comprehended in the rabbinic law that a quarter of a log (about two-thirds of a pint) of human blood can cause defilement (b. B. Qam. 101b; cf. b. Sanh. 4a). Thus the rabbis go beyond Leviticus in ruling that not only does vaginal blood defile but if blood issues in large enough quantities from any part of the body it also defiles. The equation of sperm and life is, of course, self-evident ... This view is echoed by Shadal (on 12:2): 'the discharge of blood or seed (involuntary) is the beginning of death' (Shadal's parenthetical insertion is in error, for voluntary emissions, such as during intercourse, are equally defiling). (*Leviticus 1–16*, p. 767)

These remarks contain much of interest and value, yet they also contain some uncharacteristic errors. There is no rabbinic law that says that an effusion of blood from a live person is a source of impurity. The passages cited by Milgrom (b. Qam. 101b; and b. Sanh. 4a) refer to blood that has oozed from a corpse (see Maimonides *MT*, TM, 2:13, based on M. 'Ohalot, 2:2). Only a whole limb cut off a live person counts as dead and defiles (M. 'Ohalot 2:1).

This tells against Milgrom's theory that the impurity of discharges derives from their depletion of the body, tending towards death (and that only substances representing death must be excluded from the Sacred, which is synonymous with Life). For no discharge is more dangerous to the body than loss of blood, yet the blood shed by a wounded person is not a source of impurity. Some of the discharges that produce impurity are indeed life-diminishing (abnormal discharges of semen or menstrual blood), but they are not enough to substantiate a theory that requires that all life-diminishing discharges defile.

Moreover, normal loss of semen hardly comes into the category of life-diminishing discharges. As Milgrom himself points out (in his above-quoted comment on Shadal, i.e. Samuel David Luzzatto) it is not just involuntary discharge of semen that defiles, but also the voluntary discharge of intercourse. Involuntary loss of semen might be regarded as life-diminishing, but a discharge that produces new life cannot be so regarded. In some varieties of religion, notably Yoga, loss of vital fluid is a more important spiritual consideration than the production of new life, but Judaism, whether biblical or rabbinic, is certainly not such a religion.[1] The problem remains that normal inter-

---

[1] Milgrom (p. 934) quotes with approval the suggestion of Nachmanides that death is

course is nevertheless defiling, and the reason for this needs to be discovered.

It seems that the sources of impurity in Judaism are too various to be subsumed under one concept, even death. Some of the defiling processes are pathological, and some normal. Some, as we shall see, arise out of the classification of animals as permitted or forbidden for eating. If an overall concept is to be found, it will have to be of a more complex, perhaps dialectical or binary, nature.

Further discussion of this matter must be postponed, however, while we accumulate a more detailed conspectus of the sources of pollution.

Menstruation

The defilement of menstruation is firmly based on a biblical text (Lev. 15:19–24). This lays down that the menstruant woman suffers a seven-day uncleanness, but that someone who touches her suffers only a one-day uncleanness ('until the evening'). This source of impurity is thus far less serious than the corpse, which imposes a seven-day impurity on anyone who touches it.

Nevertheless, the menstruant has certain modes of defilement that are not found in the corpse. These are the defilements through couch and chair. If she lies on a couch or sits on a chair, and then someone touches the couch or chair, the toucher incurs a one-day uncleanness. It does not matter if the menstruant does not actually touch the couch or chair; mere pressure on them, even through several cushions, is enough. This mode of defilement is thus somewhat similar to defilement through 'carrying', which we have encountered in the case of the corpse, where we noted that carrying, or even moving, need not involve direct contact. Defilement by couch or chair is a kind of contamination through space, though not as striking as the forms of distance-contamination noted in the case of the corpse ('tent' and 'overshadowing') in which the defilement

---

involved in ordinary intercourse because we cannot be sure that it will result in new life. Consequently, there is a waste of semen on many occasions. This seems a rather far-fetched argument.

66

actually travels through *empty* space. We do not find in the Jewish system, however, the forms of distance contamination found in Hinduism, such as defilement through casting one's shadow over the polluting source ('overshadowing' does not mean this).

What does the defilement by couch or chair imply about the status of the couch or chair itself? Does it incur a seven-day uncleanness, or a one-day uncleanness? The general rule is that an object with one-day uncleanness does not cause any uncleanness to another person or object, only to foodstuffs. The logical conclusion, then, is that the couch itself suffers a seven-day uncleanness, and this is the conclusion drawn in the rabbinic literature. In practice, this means that a menstruating woman has her own couch and seat, which undergo purification at the same time that she does.

This does not mean, however, that menstruants have to be isolated from the community. Such isolation is prescribed in the Torah only for lepers (and even this was not practised in rabbinic times, see p. 146). In many cultures it has been indeed the practice to isolate menstruants, who lived in special huts during their period of menstruation some distance away from the community. Among Jews, this practice was found among the Falashas, the Ethiopian Jews who were detached from the main body of Jews at an unknown period. There is disagreement among scholars as to the origin of the Falashas, but if they are indeed derived from a pre-rabbinic era, their practice may point to an ancient pre-rabbinic and even pre-biblical observance.

Even in rabbinic circles, there is evidence of a minority opinion that menstruants should be treated as a kind of social outcast. This evidence is in a curious work, discovered only in 1890, called *Baraita di-masseket Niddah* (Horowitz, 1890), the date of composition of which is far from certain, but it is quoted by medieval authorities, so probably dates from the late Geonic period, i.e. ninth or tenth century. Its material, however, probably has an even earlier history, and the work as a whole represents a dissident, or even heretical view about the menstruant (*niddah*). The work is severe in the extreme, forbidding the menstruant to perform her usual household tasks, to enter the synagogue, or even to light the Sabbath lights. Even this work does not demand that the menstruant should be isolated in a special dwelling during her period, but it does demand that her husband also should be debarred from the synagogue, and, if he is a priest, debarred from giving the priestly blessing.

This work appears to stem from a minority group among the rabbis of the second century, who were perhaps connected with the first-century group known as the House of Shammai. A Shammaitic connection can be inferred from its version of a well-known rabbinic legend favourable to the House of Hillel. Instead of a voice from Heaven commending the House of Hillel, the voice is made to commend the House of Shammai. It is well known that the Shammaites had more severe and illiberal attitudes than the House of Hillel, but this work is so hysterically anti-menstruant that it could belong only to a minority even among the Shammaites. It seems possible, however, that the *Baraita di-masseket Niddah* was of Karaite origin, drawing on traditions deriving from the Sadducees. The hinted-at Shammaite connection, in this case, may have been merely an attempt to gain Rabbanite authority.

Unfortunately, once this illiberal tract began to circulate in rabbinic circles from the tenth century onward, it began to have an influence. The more liberal party won, having the better case in terms of Jewish tradition, and consequently the support of the great rabbinic authorities, notably Maimonides, who rejected the practice of isolation of the menstruant (when put forward as having Talmudic authority) as heretical and contrary to Talmudic teaching (Blau, 1957–61, II, p. 588). Ashkenazi Jews eventually ceased to isolate the menstruant,[2] but certain customs of isolation lingered among Sefardi Jews until the present day.

In an important article, Yedidiah Dinari analyses the reasons why the practice of isolating the menstruant persisted in many communities despite the contrary pronouncements of both

---

[2] Ashkenazi authorities who denounced menstruant-isolation practices include Joel Sirkes (Bach), David Halevi (Taz), Isaiah Horowitz (Shelah). See Dinari (1979–80), p. 323.

Tannaitic and Amoraic authorities (Dinari 1979–80). He adduces much evidence to show that the practice of isolation stemmed not from the *halakhah* but from popular belief that the menstruant was physically dangerous to those in her proximity. This belief led to a practice that had no basis in either purity law or the laws designed to separate husband and wife from temptation to intercourse: this was the practice of making a distinction between the time a woman was actually menstruating and the time when she had finished menstruating and was awaiting immersion (*yemei libbun*). Popular belief made this distinction because once a woman had finished menstruating, she was obviously no physical threat. Competent legal authorities, however, constantly complained that the distinction was invalid halakhically.

Halakhically, there were only two considerations: purity and temptation. As to purity, competent authorities continually stressed that this was not a valid consideration after the destruction of the Temple. As to temptation (a consideration still valid after the destruction of the Temple), there was concern that the wife should avoid arousing her husband, but continuance of household duties was not regarded as arousing, and Rabbi Aqiba even ruled leniently that a wife might continue to use cosmetics during her menstruation, in order not to impair too drastically her attractiveness to her husband (b. Shabbat 64b).

Yet there was also pressure to find some halakhic support for the popular fear of the menstruant. This pressure did not begin in the late Geonic period (as some scholars have argued), but existed even in the first and second centuries. According to a Tannaitic source, a menstruant was forbidden to attend to household duties (Abot R. Natan 1, 1–4). However, even this prohibition shows that she was not banished from the home. The Mishnah (M. Niddah 7:4), on the other hand, does refer to 'a house for impurities' (*bet ha-tum'ot*), i.e. a place set aside for menstruants, but it is a vexed question whether this means an isolated dwelling-place for menstruants, or a place for self-examination and disposal. The reading found in some manuscripts and in the Talmudic Mishnah is *bet-ha-teme'ot* ('house of the impure'), but even this is not a decisive argument for a 'place that segregates impure persons' (*contra* Harrington, 1993, p. 271), any more than a place labelled 'Gentlemen' means a place that segregates gentlemen. The Dead Sea Scrolls sect, far more severe in ritual purity matters than the rabbis, 'quarantined her (the menstruant) within their community' (Milgrom, 1991, p. 949). Even they, however, did not banish her from the community. The puzzling statement of Josephus (*Ant.*, 3.261) that menstruants were removed from the city refers to the time of Moses, not his own time.[3]

The tendency to fall back into more primitive legal attitudes towards the menstruant is connected to the concomitant tendency to relapse into primitive attitudes of fear and superstition. Some superstitions are found in the folklore of the Talmud itself: that the breath of a menstruant is dangerous, and that if she walks between two men, one of them will die (b. Pesahim 111a). Remarkably, no such superstitions are found in the Torah itself, which considers the menstruant merely as one source of impurity. Fear of menstruation is found in all societies, ancient and modern, and such fears (arising from men's awe of the female processes of reproduction) tended to swamp the Torah's attempt to reduce the matter to procedure, protocol and purification. The fear of menstruation as harmful and contaminating is one side of the coin: the other is a great awe and reverence for a holy process from which men are excluded: this aspect finds expression in the rite of the Red Cow (see chapters 8–9), as well as in the Talmudic view (common in the ancient world) that menstrual blood is actually the material out of which the embryo is formed in the womb (j. Kilayim 8:3).

The story of menstruation in Jewish observance is thus one of sporadic relapse from the comparatively rationalistic stance of the Torah, which stands out from that of other ancient systems in its lack of hysteria and superstition. In the Torah, menstruation is merely one of the conditions which produce impurity, and impurity itself is not condemned as sinful, but regarded as a natural state, which, however, has to be corrected by purification before contact with holy areas or foods. Milgrom, too,

---

[3] So Albeck (1958), Additional Comments on M. Niddah 7:4, though Dinari disagrees.

would agree with this formulation. He lays stress on the sinfulness (in the biblical but not in the rabbinic system) of *remaining* in a state of impurity instead of taking the first opportunity to correct it. But he is clear that it is not sinful to contract impurity in the first place, since this is an inevitable concomitant of ordinary living. Mary Douglas also points out another unique feature of the biblical system of impurity: that it does not serve to mark out different castes or privileged groups within the community (Douglas, 1993–94, p. 113). The conditions which produce impurity are in no way class-orientated. Menstruation, for example, cuts across all classes: a priest's wife who is menstruating causes just as much impurity to all who touch her as the wife of the poorest peasant, or (more to the point) of a slave or *mamzer*. Noone causes impurity just because he or she is a member of a certain class. While certain classes, or semi-castes, do exist in the biblical and even rabbinic systems (see p. 198), ritual purity has nothing to do with the demarcation of these classes.

We may now tabulate the impurity effects of menstruation (see Lev. 15: 19–24):

1. *The menstruant herself.* Suffers a seven-day uncleanness. Causes a seven-day uncleanness to whatever she sits or lies upon (the rabbis add, to what she rides upon, by analogy with the *zabah*). Causes a one-day uncleanness ('until evening') to any person or vessel that touches her. Causes a seven-day uncleanness to someone who has sexual intercourse with her.

2. *The person who has intercourse with her.* Causes a one-day uncleanness to what he sits or lies upon. These in turn do not cause impurity to persons or vessels, but cause impurity to foodstuffs (see p. 39).

3. *Her bed or couch.* Cause a one-day uncleanness to all persons or vessels that touch them.

4. *Method of purification.* The Torah specifies a seven-day period of impurity, followed by immersion. The rabbis imposed a more complicated system (see below, p. 44). No sacrifice is prescribed for the menstruant's purification, since her condition is normal (see p. 48).

THE PROHIBITION AGAINST INTERCOURSE
WITH A MENSTRUANT

Quite apart from the ritual purity laws applying to a menstruant, there is a prohibition attaching to her: it is forbidden for anyone to have intercourse with her (Lev. 18:19). This prohibition applies also to those who are similar to the menstruant in their mode of impurity: the woman with an irregular flow (*zabah*), and the parturient in days of her primary impurity (see p. 48). If through inadvertence, such intercourse nevertheless happens, the person having intercourse with her suffers uncleanness (no. 1 above), but, as in all cases of inadvertence, he is not reckoned a sinner. (He must nevertheless bring a 'sin-offering', in Temple times, since these offerings are allotted especially for reconciliation or atonement after committing a sin inadvertently.)

The prohibition against intercourse with a menstruant has put this form of impurity into a special category: menstruation (with its analogues) is the only form of impurity that has survived the destruction of the Temple and has remained as a subject of practical observance to the present day. It is only because of menstruation and its associated conditions that the *miqveh*, or purity pool, has remained as a Jewish institution in post-Destruction times.

Intercourse with a menstruant is the only way of incurring impurity that is also a forbidden act. Every other way of incurring impurity is free from sin, since impurity in itself is not sinful. To touch a corpse is not forbidden (except to a priest); it may even be a virtuous and praiseworthy act (for example, if one is engaged in the duty of preparing a corpse for burial). For a man to emit semen is not forbidden; it is in fact a duty for a married man. Yet these acts cause impurity. Even to remain in a state of impurity is not a sin (certainly not in rabbinic law, and, in biblical law, only if one subscribes to Milgrom's theory). The only time that sin enters the picture is when a person, knowing himself to be in a state of impurity, enters sacred areas or comes into contact with sacred foods such as the sacrifices, or the priestly food (*terumah*). Even in Milgrom's theory, the only reason why a person must not remain in a state of impurity is that this state affects the Sanctuary from afar – not because impurity is sinful in itself. Also, even according to Milgrom, the definition of 'from afar' has definite limits, and outside these limits it is not sinful to remain in a state of impurity.

But in intercourse with a menstruant, both the man and the woman are committing a sin (even this is sinful only for Jews, not for non-Jews). Consequently, the prohibition remained in force even after the destruction of the Temple. This prohibition has nothing to do with the Temple, but only with sexual relations. That is why the prohibition against intercourse with a menstruant is included in the list of sexual offences (Lev. 18:19), not in the passage about the ritual impurity of a menstruant (Lev. 15:19–24).

However, the situation remains that here, for once, is a condition of ritual impurity that is also associated with a prohibition (other than the prohibition attaching to all impurities against contact with sacred areas and objects). As long as the menstruant remains in a state of impurity, her husband must not have sexual relations with her; and this prohibition is in force outside holy areas and even outside the time during which the Temple was functioning. This explains the survival of the need for purification of the menstruant even to the present time, and also the survival of the means of purification, the *miqveh*. It is necessary to reckon the days of impurity and purity of the menstruant just as in Temple times, because it is only during her days of purity that she is permitted to have intercourse with her husband. The other laws relating to a menstruant – that she must not enter the Temple, or touch holy food, and that these prohibitions also apply to those who touch her or her couch or chair – are in abeyance because of the absence of the Temple. There never was any prohibition against touching the menstruant or her couch or chair; only against coming into contact with sanctities afterwards, without purification. Even a priest is not forbidden, even in Temple times, to touch a menstruant or her couch or seat; the only form of impurity that a priest is forbidden to incur intentionally is corpse-impurity, except in special circumstances (the death of a close relative, or the need to bury an abandoned corpse).

We have here a somewhat paradoxical situation, for the prohibition against intercourse with a menstruant (forbidden) is bound up with the ritual impurity of the menstruant (not a sinful condition, but one that needs to be carefully reckoned). We have two realms of *halakhah* that are distinct, with different criteria, yet which, in this case, intersect. This may lead to complications, for sometimes the criteria for impurity, when adjudged in cases of doubt, are not quite the same as the criteria for forbiddenness. But this is a matter of detail which need not concern us here.[4]

Here it is necessary to counter some common misunderstandings. The commonest relates to the fact that the husband, even in the post-Temple period, is forbidden to touch his wife or sleep in the same bed while she is menstruating. This is misinterpreted as a matter of ritual purity, but it is in fact entirely a matter of avoiding temptation to sexual relations. The prohibition is, of course, not biblical, but rabbinic, coming into the category of rabbinic precautionary legislation, intended to act as a 'fence to the Law'. It is not forbidden for someone other than the husband to touch the wife, say by shaking hands, for it is a matter of indifference whether impurity is communicated in this way.

Another common misapprehension is that the reason why women are not called up to the reading of the Law (in Orthodox synagogues) is that their touch, if they are menstruating, would bring impurity to the Torah scroll from which the reading is made. There is no prohibition whatever against the touching of a Torah scroll by a menstruating woman. The synagogue and its appurtenances do not come into the same category as the Temple; on the contrary, it is regarded as reprehensible to treat a synagogue as similar to the Temple. Menstruating women were excluded from the Temple in ancient times during their

[4] See Tosafot on b. Baba Qamma 11a, s.v. *de-eyn miqtzat shilya*, which suggests that certain situations of doubt (in a private, as opposed to a public domain) may be judged more severely in relation to impurity (where possible defilement of sacred food is in question), but more leniently, in relation to prohibition of intercourse.

period of impurity, but they are not excluded from the synagogue. The reason why women are not called up to the reading of the Torah is rather surprising: it is 'for the honour of the public' (*kebod tzibbur*) (b. Megillah 23a). This means that there is no halakhic reason why women should *not* be called up, but that this was eschewed in order not to hurt the feelings of men who might resent the implication that they lacked the knowledge to read from the Hebrew scroll. (At that time, being called up to the reading of the Torah meant actual reading of the passage in unpointed Hebrew, not, as is usual nowadays, simply reciting the blessings for a reading by an expert.) This is a ruling that clearly depends on a particular social situation (the confinement of education, mostly, to men). Even Orthodox authorities (such as Rabbi Eliezer Berkovits) have seen a need to reverse this outdated ruling in the light of the spread of Hebrew education to women in modern times, and the consequent disappearance of any threat to public order in a display of women's learning – especially as the present procedure requires no virtuoso knowledge from the person called up to the reading.

The fact that the impurity of menstruation involves a prohibition of sexual relations has meant that the whole rabbinic discussion of the biblical laws of menstrual impurity has remained of practical importance in Jewish religious life even when other ritual purity matters have become academic. This explains why the Babylonian Talmudic commentary (Gemara) on the Mishnah tractate Niddah (Menstruation) has survived, while no Gemara on the other tractates of the Order of Purities exists in either the Babylonian Talmud or the Palestinian Talmud, either because they were lost or because they were never written. Nevertheless, many comments on ritual purity matters other than menstruation are to be found in the Gemara of tractates outside the Order of Purities (Toharot).

In their discussions, the rabbis take into account matters not covered by the biblical treatment. The rabbis were aware that while some women have regular periods of menstruation, others have irregular periods. Others again experience a change in the pattern of their periods, moving from one regular pattern to another. Rules had to be developed to govern women's behaviour in such varying circumstances. On the whole, the matter was left in the hands of women themselves, who were trusted to apply the rules correctly, and report accordingly to their husbands. However, in cases of doubt, which were not infrequent, women had to consult rabbis, to whom they brought the special cloths used to collect exudations. Some of the rabbis became specialists in the assessment of bloodstains or other stains of various colours, in order to pronounce whether they were menstruous or not. A positive side to this kind of practice is that in Jewish society, menstruation was not a furtive affair which men pretended not to notice, or regarded with disgust, but a matter of communal and religious concern, in which men and women co-operated to produce mutually satisfactory behaviour. Men and women were equally concerned not to transgress a biblical commandment. They were not to be over-concerned, however, as the following ruling shows: although it is generally praiseworthy for a woman to check herself for any possibility of a flow, she should not do this while in bed with her husband, as this might cause him anxiety and affect his performance. A saying of Rabbi Meir (second century) illustrates the rabbis' attitude towards the psychological effects of the laws of menstruation: 'The Torah has said, Let her be unclean for seven days so that she will be as beloved to her husband as in the hour when she entered the bridal canopy' (b. Niddah 31b).

One aspect was again left to the rabbis to administer, in the absence of biblical guidance. This was the question of the blood shed by a virgin bride on the occasion of the consummation of her marriage. Was this to be regarded as menstrual blood, in which case the consummation would have to be interrupted in order to avoid transgression of the law against intercourse with a menstruant? The answer was that blood deriving from a vaginal wound was not menstrual, and that therefore the consummation could proceed to its natural conclusion. On the other hand, there were some doubts and unease about this decision (since it was thought that the trauma of defloration might bring on menstruation), so it was decreed that a period of seven days should elapse between the first act of intercourse and the second. This period of seven days, however, was not to be observed with the same strictness (regarding separation of the couple) as a period of genuine impurity.

The use of the miqveh by men

In view of the fact that the *miqveh* survived as an institution in post-Temple times only for the sake of menstruants, it may be asked why, at certain periods and in certain areas, it was customary for men too to practise immersion. There is no special sexual prohibition attached to men's impurity arising from emission of semen, as in the case of menstruation. As for all the other forms of impurity that may affect men (corpse-impurity, or gonorrhea for example), there is no need for ritual purification in the absence of the Temple and its sanctities.

Yet in various pietistic sects that have arisen in Judaism, it has been the practice for men to visit the *miqveh*, especially after emission of semen.

Here it is necessary to introduce an important concept: the voluntary practice of ritual purity as a pietistic exercise. This has taken various forms in Jewish history, from the biblical institution of the Nazirite onwards (see Appendix A). Some ritual purity practices have even spread from the pietistic groups to the general Jewish community. This was certainly true of the practice of purification after sexual intercourse, which became widespread in the first two centuries: so much so that the rabbis introduced a new form of purification (pouring drawn water over the head and body) for this purpose. This unbiblical form of purification emphasized the voluntary non-obligatory nature of the practice, of which, however, the rabbis thoroughly approved as a matter of human decency rather than purification from biblically defined defilement. Their saying was: this practice ensures that 'the learned should not frequent their wives like cocks frequenting hens' (b. Berakhot 22b). To avoid farmyard behaviour was not the original purpose of purification, but an adaptation to ordinary life of an originally Temple-oriented practice. To a considerable extent purification procedures were adapted to the needs of ordinary decent, cleanly living (alongside already existent hygienic, non-ritual practices) (see pp. 60–61).

The rabbinic system of menstruation

Milgrom writes (p. 935):

The rabbis contend that 'seven days' means pure days, in other words, that the counting begins after the discharge has stopped, in effect equating the menstruant with the *zabah* (v. 28; cf. b. Nid. 57b, 69a). Strikingly, so do the Falashas (Ethiopian Jews), who never had contact with rabbinic traditions (Eskoli 1936), in contrast to the Karaites, who contend that the impurity does not extend beyond the seven-day period.

This is not quite correct. The rabbis never denied that, biblically, the impurity of the menstruant lasts only seven days from the onset of menstruation. In this respect, the menstruant differed from the *zabah*, who had to count seven clean days after the cessation of her flow. But the Talmud eventually found this system unworkable for the menstruant, in view of the need for each woman to work out her own pattern of menstruation by establishing her individual cycle (*veset*), which might subsequently change. Rules were laid down for all this, but were so complicated that they became unmanageable. Consequently, the Talmud deliberately shifted to the more workable, though severer system of regarding the menstruant as equivalent to the *zabah*, counting seven clear days after the cessation of her flow. This system was acknowledged to be rabbinic, and the reason for the shift was humbly given as inadequacy on the part of the rabbis themselves, combined with the willingness of 'the daughters of Israel' to accept a severer regime than the Torah, or even the rabbis, demanded. Maimonides, after carefully outlining the complexities of the how to establish a cycle, expresses the matter as follows:

All that we have said about the menstruant and the *zabah* and the parturient is Torah law, and they practised according to these judgments when the Great Bet Din was in existence and there were great Sages who could discern the various types of blood; and if a doubt arose for them about appearances (of blood) or the days of *niddah*, or the days of *zibah*, they (the people) would go to the Bet Din and ask, as the Torah had assured them, as it is said, 'If anything should be too hard for you to judge, between blood and blood, between decision and decision,' (meaning) between the blood of *niddah* and the blood of *zibah*. And in those days the daughters of Israel took great care of this matter, and watched their periods, and continually counted the days of *niddah* and the days of *zibah*.[5] And there would be great trouble in the counting of the days, and often they would come into doubt ...

And in the days of the Sages of the Gemara, the matter fell into very great doubt as to the appearance of various kinds of blood, and the calculations of periods became corrupted, because there was not the power in all the women to count the days of *niddah* and the days of *zibah*. Therefore, the Sages took severe measures in this matter, and decreed that all the days of a woman should be like the days of her *zibah*, and that any blood that she saw would be regarded as doubtful blood of *zibah*.

And further, the daughters of Israel took an even more severe measure upon themselves. They adopted the custom, all of them in every place where Israel was, that every daughter of Israel who saw blood, even if only a drop as small as a grain of mustard, and the blood stopped, would count seven clean days, even if she saw it in the days of her *niddah*. Whether she saw it one day, or two days, or all seven days or more, when the blood stopped, she would count seven clean days like the Great *Zabah*, and immerse herself on the eighth night (or on the eighth day, in case of emergency, as we have said), and after that she would be permitted to her husband.' (*MT*, Issurei Biah, 11:1–4)

Whether this is an accurate historical account may be doubted. The unanimous acceptance by the 'daughters of Israel' of the system instituted by the rabbis, in an even severer form, has a mythical air. Nevertheless, it is clear that the rabbis were well aware of the unbiblical nature of their final system, and they felt the need to say that it had the backing of the

[5] 'The days of *zibah*' (i.e. days when an appearance of blood would be counted as assigning the woman to the category of *zabah*) were the eleven days following the seven days of menstruation (*niddah*). One appearance of blood during this period counted as a Small *zibah*, requiring only a one-day uncleanness, but three appearances counted as a Great *zibah*, making the woman a full *zabah*, requiring seven clean days and a sacrifice. If there was an appearance of blood only after the eleven days of *zibah*, this counted as an early onset of menstruation. The period of eleven days, during which blood-appearances counted as belonging to the category of *zabah*, not *niddah*, was derived from tradition (*halakhah le-Mosheh mi-Sinai*). The average cycle of menstruation was regarded as thirty days.

people most concerned – the women. They still retained the awareness that, as far as Scripture is concerned, menstruation is a natural and normal experience of women that must be distinguished from the abnormal, and more polluting, flow of the *zabah*.

CHAPTER 4

The sources of impurity: childbirth: the 'zabah' and 'zab'

While menstrual flow is regarded as normal, yet polluting, the flow of uterine blood at an abnormal time is regarded as even more polluting. Is this because such a flow is regarded as a form of illness? But illness in itself is not polluting, for many serious forms of illness (e.g. bubonic plague) carry no charge of impurity at all. Certainly some of the sources of impurity are illnesses, notably 'leprosy', but most are not. Many people, contemplating the phenomena of ritual impurity, are irresistibly drawn to the view that the whole system is hygienic in inspiration, being designed to prevent the spread of disease by infection. The conveyance of impurity through touching or proximity in an enclosed area recalls modern ideas of germ-infection by contact or through the air. Certainly the idea of infectious disease was known in ancient times, especially in the form of plague. Yet this analogy breaks down at many points. The most we can say is that there is probably a hygienic component in the origins of the purity system. The system as we find it in operation in the Bible and rabbinic literature has no aim of preventing the spread of harmful infection, but merely of protecting holy areas and foods from desecration. No reasons are offered why these particular conditions or objects convey pollution to the holy, though we may speculate whether there is any basic concept uniting the various pollutions, or whether they are in fact a miscellaneous collection deriving from various historical milieux.

Childbirth is certainly a normal enough condition, even a highly prized one, yet it gives rise to an impurity that is greater than that of menstruation. Is this because of a patriarchal prejudice against women? Are women's reproductive processes regarded with disgust? This can hardly be the answer, since disgust does not necessarily produce pollution. In the Judaic system, faeces and urine are not polluting in the ritual purity sense (see p. 64), even though they are in other ritual purity systems. It may prove more helpful to explore the possibility that ritual impurity has a relationship to the emotion of awe, rather than disgust. Some things may be polluting in proportion to their awesomeness. There may also be an inner relationship between holiness and impurity, so that one is the shadow of the other: perhaps what is now impure was once holy.

Childbirth. When a woman gives birth, she becomes unclean for seven days, if the child is male, and for fourteen days, if the child is female (Lev. 12). During this period of uncleanness, she must not have sexual relations with her husband, as in the seven days of menstruation, and of course must not contact holy areas or foods. But there now follows a period of thirty-three days, in the case of a male, or sixty-six days, in the case of a female, in which she retains a modified form of uncleanness. During this supplementary period, she may have sexual relations with her husband, but must not touch holy things or enter the Temple. To effect purification at the end of this period, she must offer a sacrifice of a lamb and a dove, or (if she cannot afford a lamb) two doves, one for a burnt-offering and one for a sin-offering (Lev. 12:1–5). Thus her uncleanness is more severe than that of a menstruant, both in the addition of the supplementary period and in the requirement of a sacrifice (a menstruant requires only ablution) for purification. According to the majority of the rabbis, the parturient actually requires ablution after the end of her seven-day impurity, like a menstruant, as well as being required to bring the sacrifice after the supplementary period. This seems a natural deduction from the expression, 'According to the days of menstruation shall she be unclean' (Lev. 12:2). Just as a menstruant undergoes ablution to make her available to her husband,[1] so the parturient requires ablution, even though she remains unclean for other purposes. The rabbis remark

[1] Actually, even this is not stated explicitly in Scripture, but it is easily derived by *a fortiori* argument from the ablution of one who discharges semen.

(b. Niddah 29b) that just as the menstruant must wait after morning ablution 'until the evening' before touching holy things (but may have intercourse at once), so the parturient must wait after ablution for 'a long day' of thirty-three or sixty-six days (but may have intercourse at once).

Why is the period of impurity twice as long for the birth of a female child as for the birth of a male child? This appears to be a clear case of discrimination against the female. Among the Hittites (who may have had cultural influence on the Israelites), there was also a longer period of impurity after the birth of a girl than after that of a boy (four months as opposed to three months),[2] and similar differentiation has been observed in the non-related culture of North India (though in South India, strangely enough, the period of impurity is longer for a boy than for a girl).

Must we then agree with the judgment of Martin Noth, 'The cultic inferiority of the female sex is expressed in giving the female birth a double uncleanness effect'? Not necessarily, for impurity is not always a sign of disrespect, sometimes the reverse. 'The bones of an ass are pure, and the bones of Yohanan the High Priest are impure' (M. Yadaim 4:6).

For the purification of the island of Delos, it was decreed that 'neither births nor deaths were permitted to occur there' (Thucydides, 3.104). This Greek example of purity law may throw light on the Hebrew purity laws which also exclude both death and birth from the holy place. Impurity, it may be, is an expression of the birth-death cycle that comprises mortality. The temple, whether in Israel or Greece, was the abode of the immortal; even more so in Israel where God is neither born nor dies, than in Greece, where a god escapes death but not birth. Thus it is not adequate to say (as Milgrom and Feldman do) that the temple excludes death (the dangers attendant on childbirth being merely an example of the threat of death). It is not just

---

[2] Milgrom (1991), p. 744. Milgrom here attributes to Rabbi Simeon ben Yohai (b. Niddah 31b) the theory that 'originally the mother of a male was impure for fourteen days, just as in the case of the female, but the term was reduced to seven to allow the circumcision ... to take place in a state of purity'. More likely is Rashi's interpretation that Rabbi Simeon is asking why the circumcision does not take place on the seventh day.

death that the temple excludes, but the whole cycle of mortality, which actually provides the basis for an alternative spirituality, and therefore has a power and awesome quality of its own (see chapter 9 for further discussion). The female, more than the male, is involved in the birth-death cycle, and is therefore a greater focus of impurity, just because she represents a potentiality for a different religious orientation.[3]

Like the menstruant, the parturient, according to the rabbis, conveys impurity (during her initial period of uncleanness) to what she sits, lies or rides upon. This is not stated explicitly in the Torah, but can be reasonably derived through an *a fortiori* argument. This kind of argument, known as *qal va-homer*, is regarded by the rabbis as the main tool of human logic. If the menstruant, who is unclean for seven days, causes impurity to what she sits or lies upon, all the more so the parturient, who is unclean in some sense for forty or eighty days.

The laws pertaining to the parturient may thus be summarized as follows:

1. *The parturient herself* is unclean for 7+33 or 14+66 days; she causes uncleanness to persons or vessels by:
   touching (one-day);
   sitting, lying or riding on (seven-day);
   being carried (or shifted) by (one-day);
   maddaf (see below) (one-day).
2. *A couch or seat that has contacted uncleanness from a parturient* causes a one-day uncleanness to persons or vessels by:
   touching or carrying.

MADDAF

A strange feature not only of the parturient but of the menstruant and the flux-sufferers (*zab* and *zabah*) is that they convey impurity by *maddaf*, which means that utensils carried in the air above them (i.e. situated above and in the vicinity of their bodies)[4] become unclean (for one day). *Maddaf* is a rabbinic

---

[3] For an interesting medical theory of the longer impurity caused by the birth of a female child, see Magonet (1996).
[4] This is called 'the space above a *zab*' ('*elyono shel zab*), see b. Niddah 32b, bot.

institution, according to b. Niddah 4b, but elsewhere (b. Niddah 32b), it is treated as Toranic. If rabbinic, several questions present themselves. What induced the rabbis to make this post-scriptural innovation? At what period was this innovation made? What relationship, if any, exists between *maddaf* and the 'overshadowing' (as distinct from the 'tent') that features in the law of corpse-impurity? (see pp. 16–17).

In Hindu purification law, there are circumstances in which impurity can be transferred by the falling of the shadow of the impure person. Judaism, whether biblical or rabbinic, makes no use of shadow as a means of transfer, but does regard situation in space above as tending to contamination. In the case of the corpse, even situation below the corpse can incur contamination (see p. 17). Hindu law is thus in a sense more material, for it requires some impact, or mediating entity, even if only that of a shadow.

In the case of the leper, the rabbis definitely rejected the concept of 'overshadowing' (see p. 145). Even here, however, the concept exerted some influence, for we find that one rabbi, Simeon b. Yohai, wished to apply a kind of overshadowing even here (see Tosefta, Neg. 7:3). He was overrruled, but the exist-ence of a minority opinion in the second century can often point to a previous history of the overruled opinion. It seems likely that the concept of 'overshadowing' had a long history and was practised among some groups in relation to leprosy until finally a majority decision of the rabbis abolished it.

Similarly, *maddaf* probably had an early origin, perhaps even earlier than the redaction of the Torah. It seems hard to believe that the rabbis introduced it in the second century, at a time when its operation was purely academic, since any person or object affected by it had no Temple to pollute. It was probably a demotic extra-biblical tradition, which the rabbis retained, but were reluctant to accord any authority higher than rabbinic. It should be remembered that the status 'rabbinic' was allotted even to laws mentioned in the Bible (e.g. the institution of Purim), if they were non-Mosaic (i.e. not contained in the Torah, or Pentateuch); even a biblical institution, such as the law against buying and selling on the Sabbath, attributed to

Nehemiah on the basis of Nehemiah 10:31, had the status of 'rabbinic'. The rabbis' own definition of 'rabbinic' thus differed greatly from that of modern scholarship. The law of *maddaf*, even though unmentioned anywhere in the Bible, might be ancient and yet 'rabbinic'. Indeed, some of the institutions found in rabbinic law are older than than the Bible. Some of them, such as the 'water-libation' ceremony of Sukkot, were given biblical status, either by forced exegesis, or by being included in the Oral Torah as 'Mosaic-Sinaitic laws' (i.e. laws given orally by God to Moses, *halakhah le-Mosheh mi-Sinai*). Others, with which the rabbis were perhaps not fully in sympathy, were demoted to 'rabbinic' status. Others were voted out of existence, even though they had the authority of the past.

The idea that a parturient caused impurity even to those in her surroundings is by no means peculiar to Judaism. An interesting Greek purity law was that of Cyrene (LSC 115A 16–20, Milgrom, 1991, 763), which decreed that for three days the new mother pollutes all who enter under her roof. This particular kind of pollution is found in Jewish purity law only in relation to the corpse and the leper, who pollute respectively in a 'tent' and a 'habitation' (see p. 143). A corpse, being the severest contaminant, pollutes both by 'tent' and in the open air by 'overshadowing'. The other two less severe sources of pollution share these modes: the leper shares with the corpse a kind of enclosed-space pollution but not the 'overshadowing', while the parturient, menstruant and flux-sufferers, share a kind of 'overshadowing' (i.e. the *maddaf*), but not the enclosed space mode. Even what is shared is not fully shared: the leper's 'habitation' is less contaminating than the corpse's 'tent'; the parturient's *maddaf* is less contaminating than the corpse's 'overshadowing' (it does not pollute downwards as well as upwards, and even upwards is much more limited).[5] It seems that the

---

[5] It may seem puzzling, however, that it is stated, 'Greater stringency may apply to a *zab* than to a corpse [correct reading] ... since he conveys *maddaf*-uncleanness to what lies above him ... which a corpse does not convey' (M. Zabim 4:6). A corpse does convey uncleanness to what is above him, even though it is not called *maddaf* but *tum'ah boqa'at ve-'olah* ('overshadowing' or 'impurity cleaving upwards'), so where is the lesser stringency? The answer to this conundrum is that there are circumstances in which *maddaf* would operate but not the 'overshadowing' effect of the corpse. Suppose

'overshadowing' which R. Simeon wished to attach to the leper was more like *maddaf* than like the corpse's 'overshadowing' – a limited upward, but not downward influence.[6]

THE ZABAH AND ZAB

The menstruant and the parturient are not suffering any unusual or pathological condition, yet are polluting. The *zabah*, on the other hand, is suffering a definite disorder, though not necessarily a severe one. Scripture does not define her condition precisely (only saying that she has a flux of 'many days, outside the time of her menstruation', Lev. 15:25). By rabbinic definition, she experiences a flow during the eleven days (known as *yemei zibah*) following the first seven days of her menstrual cycle (see p. 45n for the distinction between the Small *zabah* and the Great *zabah*). But because of difficulties in calculating menstrual cycles, in the end the distinction between menstruant and *zabah* became eroded (see above) and finally vanished. This is undoubtedly a case of discontinuity between scriptural and rabbinic codes of purity, but not in the sense that the rabbis changed or reformed biblical law. They continued to study it, hoping that it would be re-instituted at some time in the future (perhaps Messianic days) when more skilful and knowledgeable rabbis would be able to administer it in the form originally intended.

Like the menstruant and the parturient (and her male equivalent, the *zab*), the *zabah* has the peculiarity, in ritual purity law, of causing a special kind of impurity to what she sits or lies or rides upon. Unlike the menstruant, but like the parturient, her purification requires not merely ritual immersion, but the bringing of a sacrifice. Unlike the graduated

---

a corpse were situated immediately below the ceiling of a 'tent', and the vessel immediately above it, no uncleanness would be conveyed because of the 'protection' of the ceiling. In similar circumstance, a *zab* would convey *maddaf* uncleanness to the vessel above, since the 'protecting' effect of the 'tent' (*'ohel*) does not exist for him.

[6] There remains some doubt, however, about the definition of *maddaf*. While Maimonides plumps for the definition 'utensils carried above a discharger', and declares the category rabbinic, Rabad, criticising him, is of the opinion that there are two distinct meanings of the term, one of which is biblical and the other rabbinic.

sacrifice of the parturient (who, if wealthy brings a lamb and a bird, but if poor, two birds), the sacrifice of the *zabah* consists of two birds for rich and poor, which suggests that the *zabah* is somewhat less polluting than the parturient, though more than the menstruant, who does not bring a sacrifice at all.

The details of the *zabah* may thus be outlined as follows (see Lev. 15:25–29):

The zabah herself is unclean for the duration of her flow plus seven days.

Her couch, seat and saddle are unclean for seven days.

Anyone who touches her is unclean for one day.

Anyone who touches her couch, seat or saddle is unclean for one day.

Any man who has intercourse with her is unclean for seven days.

Her purification consists of immersion followed by the bringing of a sacrifice of two birds.

The zab. The male equivalent to the *zabah* is the *zab*, who is also suffering from a genital 'running issue'. Medically, there is no real equivalence, because the *zab* is suffering not from a mere irregularity, but from a venereal disease, which nowadays we would call gonorrhoea. This causes a flow of semen, which, if repeated three times, even in one day, renders the man unclean with a seven-day uncleanness (see Lev. 15:1–15).

Like the other genital dischargers, the *zab* causes impurity to what he lies, sits or rides upon. Anyone touching these suffers a one-day uncleanness, and must wash the clothes he was wearing at the time of contact, but conveys no uncleanness to utensils which he touches when separated from the source of impurity. The *zab*'s seven-day impurity (i.e. seven days from the end of his affliction) requires a purification not only of bathing, but of bringing a sacrifice on the eighth day, like the *zabah*.

A strange verse that caused trouble to the rabbinical exegetes is Lev. 15:11: 'And every person whom the *zab* touches, while he has not rinsed his hands with water, shall wash his clothes and bathe in water and be unclean until the evening.'

What is meant by saying ' . . . while he (the *zab*) has not rinsed his hands with water'? If the person who touches the *zab* must bathe in water (the ritual pool) how can mere hand-rinsing remove uncleanness from the *zab* himself? The rabbinic answer

(Sifra) is that this so-called 'hand-rinsing' is actually an expression for the bathing of the whole body, which is indeed necessary for the removal of the *zab*'s uncleanness (together with his sacrifice). The reason why the Torah refers here to 'hand-rinsing' instead of the expected 'bathing' is to convey a special lesson: that bathing need only be external. Just as the hands are external, visible organs of the body, so only external, visible body-parts need be bathed. No-one is obliged to swallow the waters of the ritual pool in order to cleanse his or her internal organs. So the hand-rinsing prescribed for the *zab* means 'external organ rinsing', and this is a lesson that is valid not only for the *zab* but for all who require ritual bathing. This is a not untypical form of rabbinic exegesis, in which an unexpected expression is interpreted as conveying a teaching that reaches beyond the immediate context. (See p. 158 for the relevance of the external nature of purification to Jesus' saying about the washing of hands.)

For the modern scholar, however, this interpretation is forced, and we must conclude that the Torah does indeed prescribe a hand-washing for the *zab*. The rabbis could not accept this because it did not fit into their schematization of the ritual purity laws, which, while in general based on a close reading of Scripture, did not allow for certain exceptions or anomalies included by the Scriptural authors.

Why, then, did Scripture provide an exceptional method of purification for the *zab*, by which a mere hand-washing made his touch non-polluting to people and objects? Jacob Milgrom suggests (1991, p. 920) that this exception was made in order to permit the *zab* to remain within the community, instead of being banished like the leper. There is evidence that such banishment was indeed prescribed at some period, for it survives in one scriptural text, Num. 5:2. Moreover, there is evidence in Josephus that it was still practised in his day (*Wars* 5.227, *Ant*.3.261). Even the rabbinic literature attests the pressure of the old tradition, for the *zab* is excluded in rabbinic law from the Temple Mount. By prescribing hand-washing for the *zab*, Milgrom argues, his presence in his home was made possible.

The difficulty with this explanation, however, is that, if correct, it ought to apply to the menstruant and the parturient as well, whom Scripture does not banish from the community even though no hand-washing purification is prescribed for them. Nor is even the *zabah* provided with a hand-washing purification. It seems likely, then, that the hand-washing purification has nothing to do with the question of banishment, but is a survival of an older form of purification by which the hands alone could be temporarily purified while the rest of the body remained unclean. Whether Scripture intends this leniency to apply to all the other genital dischargers too, is doubtful; probably not. The expression just happened to survive in the case of the *zab*, and should be regarded as an inadvertence; a failure to excise, in one case, a reference to a practice that had been abolished.

It is interesting that the Sifra records, at this point, a remark of Rabbi Eleazar ben Arakh: 'From this passage the Sages drew support for the view that the purity of hands is derived from the Torah.' The whole question of the washing of hands is important not only for rabbinic but for New Testament studies, since Jesus is reported to have come into conflict with the Pharisees on this issue (Matthew 15, see pp. 155–60). The date of the introduction of the rabbinic hand-washing prescription has been much discussed, and the rabbis themselves debated whether it was ancient or recent (R. Eleazar's remark forms part of this debate). We have to bear in mind, also, that an ancient practice may be continued or reintroduced at a later date with a different significance. The pressure of ancient tradition makes for the preservation of the practice, but new conditions and thinking mould it into a different form.

While full discussion of the hand-washing issue is reserved for a later page, it should be mentioned here that R. Eleazar's remark is not intended to suggest that the *zab*, in fact, may purify his hands by washing even while the rest of his body remains unclean. R. Eleazar is saying that though the prescription for hand-washing occurs in a passage about the *zab*, it does not refer to the *zab* at all, but is merely an incidental remark with the purport: 'Just as the *zab* has his own mode of purification (immersion), so unclean hands have a mode of purification (rinsing).' This incidental remark, in R. Eleazar's view, is sufficient to give the institution of hand-washing scriptural status. R. Eleazar's view is discussed in these terms in the Babylonian Talmud (Hullin 106a), where two Amoraim, Abaye and Rava, differ about whether hand-washing is a rabbinical or scriptural institution.[7]

The details of the *zab* may thus be summarized as follows:

The zab himself is unclean for the duration of his flow plus seven days.

Vessels or persons who touch the zab suffer a one-day uncleanness.

The zab's couch, seat or saddle suffer a seven-day uncleanness.

Persons or vessels that touch or carry the couch, seat or saddle suffer a one-day uncleanness, and must wash clothes, in the case of couch or seat. In the case of saddle, clothes-washing is required on carrying, but not on touching.

Purification is by immersion of himself and clothes, and bringing of a sacrifice of two birds.

---

[7] Milgrom (1991, p. 921) misunderstands this passage, thinking that it refers to some hand-washing that formed part of the final purification of the *zab*.

CHAPTER 5

Normal emission of semen

While the *zab*'s emissions are abnormal and pathological, even normal emission of semen causes uncleanness, but of a lesser kind (Lev. 15:16–18). Whether this emission is involuntary (known in rabbinic literature as *qeri*, i.e. accidental), or voluntary (in sexual intercourse), it causes the man a one-day uncleanness. He must immerse himself in the ritual pool, and await evening for full purification. In this case, Scripture does not prescribe a washing of clothes, and the rabbis take this to be the norm in cases of one-day uncleanness, the more serious genital dischargers being an exception. Further, any person or vessel that touches the man who has had an emission of semen remains pure. Food, whether solid or liquid, holy or profane, does become unclean if touched by him. While he is awaiting final purification (between his immersion and the evening) he can pollute only holy food, and causes no impurity to ordinary food by his touch. In this condition (known as *tebul yom*), he must avoid touching holy food, but may touch or eat ordinary food even if he is a member of a purity society (*haber*), sworn to eat even ordinary food 'in purity' (see Appendix A).

On the other hand, semen itself is a more serious source of impurity, being what the rabbis call a Father of Uncleanness (see Appendix B). Any person or vessel that comes in contact with semen incurs a one-day uncleanness. This is true also of all the products of genital discharges. In the case of the more serious genital dischargers, even their normal liquid discharges (spit and urine) are polluting (see below), but not in the case of the *ba'al qeri*.

In the case of sexual intercourse, not only the man, but also the woman, becomes unclean. The rabbis are puzzled about this. Is it because she comes in contact with semen? The answer is No; because only external contact produces uncleanness, just as purification is applied only externally.[1] The rabbis concluded, therefore, that this was 'a decree of the King', for which no human rationale could be found. The rabbis also considered the argument that, since semen was not the cause of the woman's uncleanness, she ought to be made unclean even by intercourse when no semen was emitted (Sifra). They admitted that this would indeed be a logical conclusion, but it was ruled out by the wording of the text, 'And a woman with whom a man lies with emission of seed (*shikhbat zer'a*) – they shall bathe in water and be unclean until the evening' (Lev. 15:18). Thus the presence of semen is necessary, even though it is not the semen that causes her uncleanness. Her uncleanness is caused by the sexual act, not by the semen, but the sexual act must be a complete one. This is a typical rabbinic argument, in which an apparently redundant phrase is given legal significance, and shown to be necessary in order to counter a logical train of reasoning that would otherwise have been unanswerable. One scholar (Neusner, 1990) has argued that this shows that the Sifra (in particular) is engaged in an anti-logic campaign, since so often (as here) a train of logical reasoning is refuted by citing an

---

[1] The only exception to the rule that impurity is external only is the case of the 'bird in the gullet' (see M. Parah 8:4, M. Toharot 1:1, M. Zabim 5:9). If a person eats the flesh of a clean bird that died naturally (i.e. not by the prescribed procedure of slaughter), 'at the moment when an olive's bulk is in contact with his gullet he becomes a 'Father of Uncleanness' so that (at that moment) he conveys first-grade uncleanness to garments or vessels which he touches or carries. After the olive's bulk is swallowed he suffers only first-grade uncleanness' (Danby, 1933, p. 714). Maimonides writes (*MT*), 'From tradition it is learned that the verse, *And every soul that eateth that which dieth of itself or that which is torn of beasts* ... *shall wash his clothes and bathe himself in water* (Lev. 17:15), refers only to one who eats carrion of a bird that is permitted for food ... And how does it convey its uncleanness? It does not convey uncleanness by contact or carriage or when it is in his mouth, but only when it is in his gullet, for it is said, *And every soul (nefesh) that eateth* – that is, it conveys uncleanness only when it is the place of the *nefesh*' (*MT* 'Other Fathers of Uncleanness' 3.1). This strange rule seems to have arisen out of contemplation of the word *nefesh*, 'soul', the gullet being regarded as the seat of the soul or life. A possible alternative explanation is that rabbinic tradition preserved an archaic meaning of *nefesh* as 'neck'. This meaning of the word is found frequently in Ugaritic, and was used by Michel Dahood to explain difficult phrases in the Psalms. See Dahood (1965), p. 41, and his comments on Ps. 7:3, 22:21 and 105:18.

apparently irrational text. It would seem, however, that this tactic of the Sifra is at root a logical procedure, defending the Torah as a system of axioms, none of which can be deduced from each other. A chain of reasoning is produced which ought to lead to a certain conclusion; but it transpires that God, the wholly logical author of the Torah, has foreseen this precise line of reasoning and forestalled it by the insertion of the necessary qualifying phrase. Our attempts to deduce one law from another are often frustrated by the text itself, but this is only the beginning of a true understanding. This does not mean that human reason is *always* frustrated in its attempts to draw conclusions from God's word. Many rabbinic laws are derived from the text by the hermeneutical methods called the *middot*. But quite often, as here, these same methods lead to a conclusion that is denied by the text; and this denial actually reinforces the rabbis' faith in their own methods of logic, which are so strong that they have compelled God to insert special phrases in his Scripture to pre-empt their expected logical activity.

But can we seek some positive reason why a woman is rendered unclean by a sexual act involving an emission of semen? This question, I suggest, should be approached on a more philosophical or discursive level, since no explanation is offered either in Scripture or in rabbinic literature. It seems that the woman becomes unclean through a sexual act not because she is contaminated by semen, nor because of the mere act itself, but because of the combination of the two in a process of creation. The human cycle of procreation and death must be excluded from the realm of the eternal God, who creates life without suffering death. A sexual act without emission of semen is too uncreative to count as defiling; whereas mere external contact with semen would indeed defile the woman, but not in this particular way, and not in this actual case.

Bathing after sexual intercourse has an interesting history even when no element of Temple-pollution is present. This is certainly true in rabbinic practice, in which bathing after intercourse survived long after Temple times, but more as a matter of decency than of pollution (see p. 43). The fact that considerations other than purification were present is shown by

the mitigation of the mode of washing: instead of the requirement of full immersion in the ritual pool, it was declared
sufficient to rinse 'the head and most of the body' with 'drawn
water' (i.e. water which would not qualify for the contents of a
ritual pool). This mode of washing made it clear that no
scriptural support for the practice was claimed; this was
merely a rabbinic institution. Yet it was widely practised for a
period, and was even extended to function as a purification
before prayer or study, a form of purification unknown to
Scripture.

Yet there is evidence even in Scripture that bathing after
emission of semen was required even if there was no intention
of entering the Temple. It has been inferred that a war party
was required to observe conditions of sexual purity (I Samuel
21:5), and that even celebration of the New Moon required such
purity (I Samuel 20:26).

In the first case, David pleads with the high priest to allow his
men to eat the holy bread, and the priest replies that they may
do so 'if the young men have kept themselves at least from
women'. David assures him, 'Of a truth women have been kept
from us about these three days, since I came out, and the vessels
of the young men are holy, and the bread is in a manner
common, yea though it were sanctified this day in the vessel.'
Upon this, the priest allows them to eat the shewbread.

The rabbinic explanation of this passage (b. Menachot 96a) is
that David and his men were allowed to eat the shewbread
because they were in danger of dying from starvation. Jesus'
citation of this passage in the corn-plucking incident is thus of
halakhic interest (see Maccoby 1986, pp. 40–42). But in that
case why was David at such pains to assert that his men were in
a state of ritual purity? On rabbinic principles, even people not
in a state of ritual purity were entitled to eat holy food if their
life depended on it. The rabbis would probably answer that the
priest, if he was reluctant to accept the seriousness of the
emergency, might acquiesce if assured that profanation was not
also involved. David used both arguments in the hope that they
would reinforce each other, and result in the feeding of the
starving troop.

But of course the authors of 1 Samuel were not rabbis, and the rabbinic doctrine of the cancellation of all ritual duties by emergency threatening to life (*piqquach nefesh*) had not yet been formulated. The scriptural text tells us that it was forbidden to eat sacred Temple food (even after its removal from the Table) unless in a condition of purity. But does the incident tell us something else, that a war-troop was required to be in a state of ritual purity? Otherwise, there is some difficulty in explaining why David and his men were in fact ritually clean, having abstained from sex, and presumably having avoided contact with other impurities too. The text does not mention such a requirement directly, and indeed David's company is not represented as a war-troop but as a group of fugitives, but many scholars have seen the incident as reflecting the purity practice of a war-troop, especially in the light of the practice of other cultures.

The scriptural passage that speaks explicitly of purity in a war-camp is Deut. 23:9–13 (Heb. 10–15). This states:

9. When the host goeth forth against thine enemies, then keep thee from every wicked thing.
10. If there be among you any man that is not clean by reason of uncleanness that chanceth him by night, then shall he go abroad out of the camp, he shall not come within the camp.
11. But it shall be, when evening cometh on, he shall wash himself with water; and when the sun is down, he come into the camp again.
12. Thou shalt have a place also without the camp, whither thou shalt go forth abroad:
13. And thou shalt have a paddle upon thy weapon: and it shall be when thou wilt ease thyself abroad, thou shalt dig therewith, and shalt turn back and cover that which cometh from thee:
14. For the Lord thy God walketh in the midst of thy camp, to deliver thee, and to give up thine enemies before thee; therefore shall thy camp be holy: that he see no unclean thing in thee, and turn away from thee.

For the rabbis, this passage could not be taken at face value as referring to a war-camp. For in the rabbinic system, there was only one area from which impurities (other than leprosy) were excluded, and that was the Temple. Wherever the Torah mentions 'camp' as an area from which impurity was to be excluded, the rabbis take this to mean the Temple area, which indeed comprised two 'camps', that of the Divine Presence (*machaneh Shekhinah*) and that of the Levites) (*machaneh leviyah*). These designations referred in the first instance to the concentric camps in the wilderness at the time of the journey to the Promised Land, but by transfer they referred to the Temple in Jerusalem, the 'camp of the Divine Presence' being the Temple itself, including its courtyards, and the 'camp of the Levites', the Temple Mount. Genital dischargers were all excluded from the Temple Mount (unlike the corpse-impure, see p. 4–5).

So when Deuteronomy says that the emitter of semen must withdraw from the camp, the rabbis (Sifre) take this to mean from the Temple Mount, i.e. he must not enter even the outer Temple area until he is purified. As for the reference to the war-camp in verse 9, this is taken to be a topic completed in that verse alone: one should avoid sinning in a war-camp particularly, since in a situation of danger, 'Satan accuses' – the verse thus does not refer to ritual purity at all.

This, of course, is far from the intention of the authors of Deuteronomy. It seems likely that the passage derives from a time when, although the centralization of Temple worship had already taken place (a constant theme of Deuteronomy), sanctity had not yet been withdrawn from the war-camp. This kind of sanctity is evidently unknown to the rabbis, for not even a minority opinion refers to it. The obliteration of the war-camp as a locus of sanctity and ritual purity had taken place long before the rabbis discussed this passage. Yet it is still known to the sectarians of the Dead Sea Scrolls, though it should be remembered that their war-camp is messianic. As for the 1 Samuel passage, while no explicit mention is made of war-camp purity, we may surmise that in some earlier version the matter was made plainer.

The other non-legal passage referring to impurity through seminal emission (1 Sam. 20:26) is also somewhat puzzling. David absents himself from King Saul's table at the time of the New Moon. 'Nevertheless Saul spake not any thing that day: for he thought, Something has befallen him, he is not clean; surely he is not clean [Septuagint: he has not been purified].' The expression 'something has befallen him' (*miqreh*) is typical for an involuntary emission of semen. But why should David require purity to attend the king's table, even if it is the New Moon? The rabbis could only suppose anachronistically that Saul and his entourage observed the purity rules of the *haberim*, who dedicated themselves to 'eating ordinary food in purity' (see Appendix A).[2] But a simpler answer is available, in historical terms. The Jerusalem Temple had not yet been built, and the country was dotted with shrines at each of which purity observances were required. The king's palace perhaps functioned also as a shrine at which sacrifices were performed, and if so it is natural that ritual purity would be demanded at the king's festival table. The passage should not be understood to mean, as some scholars have asserted, that ritual purity was required at all times and not only in relation to sanctities.

The details of the semen-emitter may thus be summarized as follows:

The semen-emitter himself suffers a one-day uncleanness. He conveys uncleanness to foodstuffs, but not to persons or vessels.

Semen itself is a Father of Uncleanness and conveys one-day uncleanness to persons and vessels.

A woman who engages in sexual intercourse involving emission of semen has a one-day uncleanness, conveying impurity to food, but not to persons or vessels.

NON-GENITAL BODILY EMISSIONS

In the Deuteronomy passage quoted above, there is also mention of the need for dealing with excretion in a manner that would not defile the 'camp' (Deut. 23:12–13). It is clear that excretion, unlike emission of semen, is not defiling in the ritual purity sense, for no ritual washing, or waiting until the evening, is prescribed for it. Nor is it said anywhere in the Torah that either excrement or urine themselves cause ritual impurity by

---

[2] Even this does not quite cover the case, for after bathing the semen-emitter does not have to wait until evening before eating non-holy food. Rashi therefore adds that Saul conjectures that David has not yet bathed (this actually fits in well with the reading of the Septuagint).

contact or any other means. Nevertheless, excretion must take place outside the 'camp', and this appears to be a matter of seemliness, rather than ritual purity. Here we find in the Torah an important distinction between ritual purity and ordinary cleanliness – a distinction also important in rabbinic thought, yet often overlooked or minimised in scholarly discussion (see pp. 154–55).

Since the rabbis define the 'camp' not as a war-camp but as the Temple Mount, does this mean that in rabbinic law excretion within the Temple area is forbidden? This would make things very difficult for the priests whenever they had to engage in protracted duties in the Temple. Consequently, the rabbis concluded that 'camp' in the text about defecation does not include the whole Temple Mount, but only the Temple itself (i.e. the 'camp of the Divine Presence', sometimes called the 'camp of the Cloud', since the divine cloud rested upon the Tabernacle in the Wilderness). Indeed, the Mishnah refers to a lavatory within the Temple area, situated next to the ritual pool and reached by a tunnel (M. Tamid:1:1).

The sectarians of the Dead Sea Scrolls, however, took the matter more literally and forbade defecation not only in the Temple Mount but in the whole of Jerusalem.[3] This, however, was a messianic ideal, and perhaps assumed some miraculous modification of the human bodily system. Milgrom suggests (1991, p. 536) that the Dead Sea Scrolls sectarians were influenced by Ezekiel, who appears to regard excrement as ritually defiling (Ezek. 4:10–15), when he protests against God's command to eat excrement as a symbol of coming doom. This, however, is not certain. Perhaps, as Rashi thinks, Ezekiel was referring here to the prohibition against eating anything disgusting (*miy'us*), even if not ritually defiling or included in the lists of forbidden foods. This prohibition was derived from Lev. 20:25, 'Ye shall not make your souls abominable.'

The attitude of the rabbis is shown by their statement that urine would be a useful ingredient in the Temple incense, 'but one may not bring urine into the Courtyard because of respect'

---

[3] Whether they in fact regarded excrement as defiling in the ritual purity sense is not quite clear from 11QT 46:13–15, or from Josephus *War*, 2:8.148.

(b. Keritot 6a). Urine is thus regarded not as a defiling substance which it would be sacrilege to bring into the Temple, but as too low on the scale of being to be suitable for Temple dignity. Here again we see a distinction between defiling substances, which carry a charge of transgression and awe, and merely unsuitable substances which offend good manners. Urine is actually regarded as a useful substance in some contexts; for testing the nature of menstrual stains, for example (M. Niddah 9:6).

One rabbi roundly protested against the idea that excrement was defiling: 'Rabbi Yose said: Is excrement impurity [*tum'ah*]? Why, it is nothing but cleanliness [*neqiyut*]' (y. Pesah. 7:12). By this he meant that an evacuation of excrement leaves the body clean (in contrast with an evacuation of semen, which leaves it ritually unclean). Here Rabbi Yose moves from one conception of purity to another: from ritual purity to hygienic cleanliness – the two states are distinguished by a difference of terminology. In the same spirit as Rabbi Yose's saying is the rabbinic belief that saintly persons have complete evacuation of their bowels shortly before death, so that they can come into the Divine Presence (on resurrection) in a seemly state (b. Shabb. 118b, and comment of Tosafot; also Bereshit R., 82).

It is of some ideological and psychological significance that excrement is not regarded as ritually defiling, either in Scripture or in rabbinic literature, in contrast with its status in the purity systems of other cultures.[4] In Judaism, it appears, preoccupation and guilt about bodily functions has progressed beyond the infantile, and is firmly located in the sexual realm. Excrement is merely soiling and unmysterious, while sexual substances, in some much more serious way, impinge upon the holy.

[4] Human faeces are impure in Hinduism (Manu 5.138ff.), and Iranian religion (Vend. 17.11ff.).

CHAPTER 6

Animals and purity

One of the confusing aspects of purity in Judaism is that the same word, 'unclean' (*tame*) is used in two (at least) very different contexts. One is the context of animals forbidden for food, and the other of ritual impurity, which requires purification but is not in itself a forbidden state. Though quite distinct, these two areas sometimes impinge on one another.

In ritual purity, the first important principle is that live animals (with one exception, the Scapegoat) are never a source of impurity. Only animal carcases can be a source of impurity, whether the animal is permitted for food or not. A live pig, for example, is totally 'clean' in the ritual purity sense. To touch one does not produce impurity.

In the case of dead animals, however, the two senses of 'unclean' already impinge on one another: for the carcase of an 'unclean' animal (in the sense of 'forbidden for food') produces 'uncleanness' (in the sense of 'ritual impurity') more readily than the carcase of a 'clean' (permitted for food) animal, the latter causing impurity only if it dies of natural causes.

The main text is Lev. 11:8: 'Of their flesh shall ye not eat, and their carcase shall ye not touch; they are unclean to you.' Other important texts are Lev. 11: 24–28 (unclean animals); Lev. 11:29–38 ('creeping things'); Lev. 11:39–40 (clean animals that die).

An important preliminary question emerges: 'How literally must Lev. 11:8 be taken when it says,

' ... Their carcase shall ye not touch'?' Here we find what seems to be a total conflict between Scripture and the rabbis. For the rabbis say unequivocally that it is *not* forbidden to touch the carcase of an unclean animal (or to incur any other impurity, except that priests must not incur corpse-impurity); only that, having incurred impurity by touching such a carcase, a person must undergo purification before contacting holy areas or foods. This understanding is crucial to the whole rabbinic system of purity, in which impurity is not a sin, but a condition incurring no blame, and indeed very often even meriting praise, since it is linked inevitably with meritorious actions such as burying the dead or engaging in marital intercourse. Must we see here an unbridgeable discontinuity between Scripture and the rabbis?

Even Milgrom (who thinks that Scripture does regard impurity as a sin if prolonged unnecessarily) does not think that Scripture is here literally forbidding persons to touch the carcase of an unclean animal. Milgrom does see a discontinuity between Scripture and the rabbis (in the matter of prolonged impurity), but not such a total discontinuity. He points out that no punishment is prescribed for touching a carcase, and that other texts exist which imply that there is no such prohibition. For example, it is forbidden to a priest to touch a human corpse (Lev. 21:1), but not to a non-priest. It is incredible that a non-priest, permitted to touch a human corpse, should be forbidden to touch an animal corpse. It is possible that priests were forbidden scripturally to touch animal carcases (Lev. 22:8 and Ezek. 44:31), but this is not an incontrovertible interpretation, since these texts refer to eating, not touching. The rabbis, certainly, did not forbid priests to touch animal carcases.

Why than does 11:8 state so plainly that it is forbidden, even to a non-priest, to touch an animal carcase? Milgrom suggests that it is a kind of recommendation, rather than a law, having the status of a 'fence' to the law. The rabbis, however, suggest that we must insert a parenthesis 'if one needs to be in a state of purity', as at festival times, when even non-priests attending the Jerusalem rites required purification. This seems a reasonable suggestion, which, however, Milgrom cannot accept, because other texts which the rabbis interpret parenthetically are interpreted by him literally to mean that the Temple is affected from afar by impurity. Indeed, this text (11:8) threatens Milgrom's whole theory of the contamination of the Temple from afar. For if Milgrom accepts that this text is not to be read literally, why does he have such difficulty in accepting that other texts should be read non-literally? For example, when the Torah says that impurity must be removed by purification so that the Temple will not be polluted, why should this not be read parenthetically, meaning 'if you intend to enter it'? (For further discussion, see p. 173.)

Many scholars, however, unlike Milgrom, have accepted uncritically that Lev. 11:8 forbids the incurring of impurity. This has led to misinterpretations of the New Testament: for example, that Jesus' association with sinners and tax collectors showed that he flouted the laws of ritual purity (see p. 149). Since there was nō law forbidding people to incur impurity, Jesus was not flouting any impurity law. What may have aroused criticism was his association with people who were real sinners, in the sense of being extortionate gangsters co-operating with Roman tax farmers. But Jesus, like many messianic claimants both before and since, hoped to induce repentance even in the most desperate sinners. The argument between Jesus and his critics thus had nothing to do with ritual impurity (see chapter 13).

UNCLEAN ANIMALS

Chapter 11 of Leviticus deals with animals forbidden for food and also animals whose carcases convey impurity. These categories are by no means co-extensive, for some types of creatures are forbidden for food without causing impurity. Only the carcases of land animals cause impurity. Creatures of the sea and the air even when forbidden for food do not cause impurity. Even among land creatures, there are some categories of forbidden food that do not cause impurity, notably insects.[1] It may be asked why there is this disparity. Why are certain

---

[1] It is an error in E.P. Sanders' generally excellent survey of ritual purity (Sanders, 1990) that he interprets the 'swarming things' of Lev. 11:33–6 as 'principally insects'(p. 138). In context, the impurity applies only to the eight categories of rodents and reptiles mentioned in 11:30, as all rabbinic literature interprets. Sanders admitted the error in a later book (Sanders 1992, p. 520).

creatures forbidden for food as 'unclean', yet are not conveyors of impurity?

First, however, let us establish that this is the case. One of the main clues lies in the terminology, as Milgrom convincingly shows. Wherever the word *sheqetz* ('abomination') or the associated verb *shaqetz* is used, this is a sign that the creature referred to is forbidden for food, but does not cause impurity, for wherever this word is used, there are no directions for purification. Where there are such directions, a different terminology is used based on the verb *tame'*.

The first category dealt with is that of land quadrupeds or 'cattle' (*behemah*), of whom the requirement to make them eligible for food is that they should both chew the cud and have cloven hooves. Some have neither requirement, and some, such as the camel, the rabbit and the pig, are excluded as having only one characteristic, not both. All these animals that are ineligible for food cause impurity when dead. The person who touches the carcase has a one-day impurity, but if he carries the carcase, he communicates impurity to his clothes too (11:25).

The second category is that of sea creatures, of which only those with scales and fins may be eaten. Those excluded are forbidden for food, but nothing is said about their carcases communicating impurity, and the language used is that of 'abomination' not impurity.

The third category is that of birds, and again those excluded, not by criteria, but by individual mention, are declared to be 'abomination' and nothing is said about impurity.

The fourth category is that of flying insects. These are banned for food, with certain named exceptions (various kinds of locust), but no mention is made of impurity. Again, the language of 'abomination' is used.

The fifth category is that of 'creeping things' (*sheretz*). Here we change to the language of 'impurity', and we are told that he who touches their dead body has a one-day impurity. But these are a strictly limited number of species, mentioned by name, and hard to assign to any particular category. They are 'the weasel, and the mouse and the tortoise, after his kind; and the ferret, and the chameleon, and the lizard, and the snail, and the mole' (AV). These and these only among creeping things convey impurity when dead. He who touches their dead body incurs a one-day impurity. Also details are given of the impurity which they impart to vessels and foodstuffs.

The sixth category is that of the animal which is permitted for food, but dies a natural death, instead of being slaughtered in the prescribed manner. This carcase conveys a one-day impurity to one who touches it. This passage seems out of sequence, so that Milgrom argues that it is a later interpolation, and in earlier practice, permitted animals never conveyed any impurity at all.

The seventh and final category is that of 'creeping things' generally (other than those detailed under category five). These are treated in the language of 'abomination', and no procedure for purification is included, so it is clear that they do not cause impurity. Nevertheless, the term *tame'* is also used of them (11:43–44), and this is something of a difficulty. The rabbinic literature has no doubt about the matter: insects do not cause impurity. Milgrom concludes (also on stylistic and structural grounds) that these two anomalous verses come from a different source, in which the distinction between animals forbidden as food and animals transmitting impurity was expressed differently. There is no need to suppose that Scripture and the rabbis differ on this matter.

In the New Testament we read of the Pharisees, who 'strain at a gnat' (Matt. 23:24, AV). This means that when a Pharisee finds a gnat in liquid that he is drinking, he puts the liquid through a fine sieve to extract the gnat.[2] This is not a matter of ritual purity, as some commentators have thought. It is entirely a matter of forbidden food, for an insect, such as a gnat, conveys no impurity but is forbidden for ingestion as *sheqetz*. Similarly, in the Mishnah, where the question of the invalidation of the Red Cow water by dead insects is discussed (M. Parah 9:2), the discussion concerns only the discoloration of the sacred water by the exudations of the insects, not any fear of ritual contamination.

---

[2] The idea that the word 'strains' means 'becomes anxious' is a modern misconception.

In the rabbinic literature, the term *sheretz*, in ritual purity contexts, always means the eight species of category five, never creeping things generally, for which the term used is *remes*. This is a change of terminology from that of Scripture, in which *sheretz* is used to designate all creeping things, including the eight species. The rabbinic usage aims merely to avoid confusion, not to alter scriptural doctrine.

It is a question of some interest why certain categories of dead forbidden animals cause impurity and others do not. Why are sea creatures, birds and insects exempt from impurity, while the larger land animals are contaminating? The Mishnah provides a schema, if not exactly an explanation, for these distinctions (M. Kelim 17:14):[3]

> Uncleanness can arise in what was created on the First Day; no uncleanness can arise in what was created on the Second Day; uncleanness can arise in what was created on the Third Day; no uncleanness can arise in what was created on the Fourth Day and on the Fifth Day, excepting what was made from the wing of the vulture and plated egg of the ostrich.[4] (R. Johanan b. Nuri said: How does the wing of the vulture differ from other wings?); and everything that was created on the Sixth Day is susceptible to uncleanness.

Milgrom (1991, p. 658) sees this schema as providing, or implying, an explanation in deeper terms. He sees the main distinction as between creatures derived from land, and those derived from water. Since water is the means of purification, and can never be impure (unless detached from its source), all creatures whose derivation is from water are insusceptible to impurity.

This explains the immunity of both fish and birds (since both, according to the Creation account, came out of the waters, Gen. 1:20). But it hardly explains the immunity of land insects. Milgrom refers to Gen. 1:20 again, which mentions 'swarms of living creatures', but this refers to sea insects, and perhaps flying insects, reckoned among the birds. It does not refer to

---

[3] The Mishnah actually is dealing not with the defiling quality of the dead animals, but with the related question of susceptibility to impurity of vessels made out of the corpses of such animals.
[4] These two exceptions were rabbinical rulings, made because the items in question were hard to distinguish from ordinary vessels.

crawling land insects (*remes ha-'adamah*) which are separately mentioned in Gen. 1:24–25, as having been created on the sixth day.

This however is an objection to the Mishnah too. But it seems likely that the Mishnah classification is intended merely as a mnemonic (though a somewhat imperfect one, since it fails to accommodate the land insects). The explanation of the immunity of certain categories remains mysterious.

A clue may perhaps be found in the very disgust with which the crawling land insects (as distinct from winged insects, some of which are permitted) are forbidden as food. More than any other creatures, they are banned as 'abomination'. It seems that only those forbidden land creatures that are regarded with some respect as possible food are burdened with susceptibility to impurity, as an extra discouragement. Similarly among the birds, those that are forbidden for food are predators or scavengers which arouse disgust. As for sea creatures, their insusceptibility to impurity may have another explanation. The sea is regarded as another world, whose workings are not covered by the Torah.[5] Sea creatures do not require a special mode of slaughter, like land creatures. They are divided into permitted and forbidden, but they remain alien. Unlike land creatures, they contribute nothing to the sacrifices of the Temple.

Why were the eight species of 'creeping things' singled out from all other varieties of 'creeping things' to be conveyors of impurity? The AV translation of the list is given above. That of the NEB is : 'the mole-rat (note: or weasel), the jerboa, and every kind of thorn-tailed lizard; the gecko, the sand-gecko, the wall-gecko, the great lizard, and the chameleon.' Milgrom translates: 'The rat, the mouse and large lizards of every variety; the gecko, the spotted lizard, the lizard, the skink, and the chameleon'. The list has no biological unity, for it comprises

---

[5] See Hullin, 127a, 'Everything that is on dry land is also in the sea, except the weasel.' This view of the sea as an alternative world may derive from biblical passages depicting the sea as the antagonist of God, who subdues it (Job 38:8, Pr. 8:29, Nah. 1:4). This in turn derives from Babylonian myths of the combat between Marduk and Tiamat.

both rodents and reptiles which, on a modern taxonomy, would not be listed together. What they have in common is their size. They are small, scuttling creatures, too small to be included in the larger mammals, but standing out as larger than most 'swarming' creatures. Thus (to continue the line of explanation offered above) they do not excite the disgust (as food) appertaining to the tiny insects, and share in the more respectful treatment accorded to the larger animals. They are considered worthy to be regarded as contaminating in their death (note that the most contaminating species of all, when dead, is the human).

The 'creeping things' are animals that were often found in houses, and their dead bodies were not infrequently found inside vessels. Impurity was incurred by humans and vessels more often from 'creeping things' than from any other source. This accounts for the fact that in the rabbinic literature the 'creeping thing' or *sheretz* is regarded as the paradigm case or archetype of impurity. Where we might speak of an ingenious arguer as 'one who can prove that black is white', the rabbinic phrase is 'one who can prove that a *sheretz* is pure (*metaher sheretz*)'. Curiously enough, according to the Talmud, one of the qualifications for membership of the supreme judicial body the Sanhedrin was this ability to prove that a *sheretz* was clean (b. Sanhedrin 17a). One of the duties of a member of the Sanhedrin was to explore every possibility of innocence of the accused; he therefore had to have the kind of intellect that could prove that black was white.

Because vessels or utensils (including furniture) and foodstuffs were more likely to incur impurity from 'creeping things' than from any other source, we find the law of impurity of vessels and foodstuffs expounded in Scripture in the context of 'creeping things' (Lev. 11:32–38), though in fact all other primary sources of impurity have the same effect on vessels and foodstuffs:

32. And upon whatsoever any of them, when they are dead, doth fall, it shall be unclean; whether it be any vessel of wood, or raiment, or skin, or sack, whatsoever vessel it be, wherein any work is done, it must be put into water, and it shall be unclean until the even; so shall it be cleansed.

33. And every earthen vessel, whereinto any of them falleth, whatsoever is in it shall be unclean; and ye shall break it. 34. Of all meat that may be eaten, that on which such water cometh shall be unclean; and all drink that may be drunk in every such vessel shall be unclean. 35. And every thing whereupon any part of their carcase falleth shall be unclean; whether it be oven, or ranges for pots, they shall be broken down: for they are unclean, and shall be unclean unto you. 36. Nevertheless a fountain or pit, wherein there is plenty of water, shall be clean: but that which toucheth their carcase shall be unclean. 37. And if any part of their carcase fall upon any sowing seed which is to be sown, it shall be clean. 38. But if any water be put upon the seed, and any part of their carcase fall thereon, it shall be unclean unto you.

Other relevant texts are:

Lev. 15:12: And the vessel of earth, that he toucheth that hath the issue, shall be broken: and every vessel of wood shall be rinsed in water.
Num. 31:23: Every thing that may abide the fire, ye shall make it go through the fire, and it shall be clean: nevertheless it shall be purified with the water of separation: and all that abideth not the fire ye shall make go through the water.

(Note also: Lev. 6:28: 'But the earthen vessel wherein it [the sin-offering] is sodden [NEB: boiled] shall be broken: and if it be sodden in a brasen pot, it shall be both scoured, and rinsed in water.' (For the 'washing away of holiness', see p. 116).

These verses (together with various scattered texts referring to the washing of clothes by polluted persons) are the basis of the extensive rabbinic writings on the impurity of utensils, the chief of which are the tractates Kelim and Makhshirin in Mishnah and Tosephta and the relevant chapters of the Sifra.[6] Every scriptural phrase is subjected to intense scrutiny, and a comprehensive and consistent theory is developed, which, however, is remarkably faithful to the intentions of the priestly text.

VESSELS

The chief distinction is between earthenware vessels and others. Earthenware vessels cannot be purified, and thus must be

---

[6] The couch, chair and saddle of the genital dischargers are treated separately in the tractate Zabim.

broken, to prevent their coming into contact with holy foods (it would not matter if they came into contact with ordinary foods, which it is permitted to render unclean).

Another distinctive thing about earthenware vessels is that they cannot be made unclean by contact with a source of impurity on their outside, only by contact on their inside. This important rule is derived from v. 33 (above), which says that a dead 'creeping thing' contaminates an earthenware vessel only if it falls inside it. The rabbis extended this rule to include every source of impurity including even a human corpse: none of them could render an earthenware vessel impure by contact with its outside. There is actually some scriptural justification for this extension of the rule, for we learn in Num. 19 that in the tent in which a corpse lies, an earthenware vessel protects its contents from pollution if it is tightly stopped. The corpse pollutes all the air within the tent, but an airtight earthenware vessel keeps out the polluting air, and the vessel is impervious to the polluting air beating on its outside. The rabbinic extension thus has the status of a Toranic, not a rabbinic law.

The biblical distinction between the inside and outside of an earthenware vessel was adapted by the rabbis to formulate a distinction of their own (never claimed to have scriptural authority) between the inside and outside of ordinary washable vessels. It has been suggested that this rabbinic distinction is the basis of Jesus' saying about hypocrites, whom he compares to those who clean the outside of a vessel but leave the inside unwashed (Neusner, Milgrom). See, however, pp. 151–54 for a refutation of this derivation of Jesus' saying.

Why are earthenware vessels treated as a special category? These are vessels that have been fired, but not glazed; if not even fired, they count as dried mud, not as earthenware, and, like the earth itself, are not susceptible to impurity at all. It seems clear that this is because of the porousness of earthenware vessels, which makes them liable to absorb unclean substances in a way that cannot be remedied by mere washing. But why are their outsides exempted from contamination? Milgrom suggests plausibly that the reason is economic: these very common vessels would represent a serious loss to householders if they had to be broken every time they brushed against a source of impurity such as a dead mouse. On the other hand, they were the cheapest of vessels; to calculate the loss one would have to weigh their cheapness against their preponderance. There are some interesting parallels in Hittite and Hindu purity law in respect to earthenware vessels (Milgrom, 1991, pp. 675–77). But these other codes, while making a distinction between earthenware and other vessels, do not reproduce the Hebrew exemption of the outside from contamination. Perhaps the reason is that Hebrew earthenware vessels were glazed on the outside but not on the inside.

Another important principle about vessels is expressed in this passage: that receptacles dug into the earth, or existing naturally in the earth, are not susceptible to impurity (v. 36). Only receptacles standing above the earth count as vessels for ritual purity purposes.

FOODSTUFFS

Also in the passage about 'creeping things', we find a treatment of the topic of transmission of impurity to foodstuffs. Again, this is really a topic to which every source of ritual impurity is relevant, but it is treated in relation to 'creeping things' because they are the most prevalent source of impurity in the home.

The principle enunciated in v. 34 and again in v. 38 is that foodstuffs cannot be rendered ritually impure when they are in a dry state. Only after they have been dampened with some liquid can the impurity be transferred to them from a dead 'creeping thing' or other source (the rabbinic gloss, however, is that one dampening is enough; if they then become dry again, they remain susceptible). Drinkable substances, of course, are already susceptible by their liquid nature, and therefore need no 'preparation' (*hekhsher*, the rabbinic term) to receive impurity.

According to Scripture, the only liquid that functions as a 'preparer' for impurity is water. The rabbis, however, add other liquids as 'preparers' (*makhshirin*): wine, blood, oil, milk, dew, bees' honey (M. Makhshirin 6:4). The Sifra explains that this interpretation derives from a reading of v. 34, by which the expression 'any liquid' is transferred from its natural meaning in context (as referring to a liquid in the contaminated earthenware vessel), and regarded as an expansion of the word 'water', earlier in the verse, producing 'water or any liquid'.[7] It is strange, however, that fruit juices are excluded from the list of liquids. The reason given for this is that the names of fruit juices always include a qualifier (*levai*), e.g. 'apple-juice', 'pomegranate-juice', and only unqualified liquids are included in the list (to the objection that 'bees' honey' contains a qualifier, the answer is given that if the unqualified word 'honey' is used, it is understood to mean 'bees' honey'). This linguistic reason for the exclusion of fruit juices from the list of 'preparers' seems artificial.

I suggest that the actual reason for the exclusion of fruit juices was economic, though not openly so. If all fruit juices were regarded as 'preparers' for impurity, this would have required much extra care and expense in the gathering of the fruits, which would be 'prepared' for impurity by their own juices exuded during the harvesting, and would therefore have to be harvested by workers in a state of purity (to prevent impurity befalling the part of the harvest due to the priests, the *terumah*). This requirement of purity of the harvesters was unavoidable at wine-pressing and olive-pressing times (M. Hagigah 3:4), because oil and wine were well established in the list of 'preparers'; the evidence is that this requirement was widely observed. But extension of the requirement to all fruit harvests was thought to be expecting too much of small farmers.

I suggest further that the criterion for inclusion in the list of 'preparing' liquids was originally not linguistic but substantive. The criterion was that all eligible liquids had to be drinkable. The scriptural phrase from which liquids other than water were deduced was not just 'liquid' but 'liquid that may be drunk' (*mashqeh 'asher yishaqeh*), and this would naturally be taken to mean that any potable liquid should be included. Further, strong traces of this original criterion remain in the halakhic

---

[7] The interpretation of 'water' as meaning 'any drinkable liquid' is then transferred from v. 34 to v. 38 by the principle known as 'likeness of expression' (*gezerah shavah*).

details: e.g. blood that is given for food (to animals) is included, but not blood that is let for healing (M. Makhshirin 6:5–6).

The criterion of potability proved unworkable because of its economic effects on the fruit harvest, so the linguistic criterion was substituted; thereby it was possible to exclude fruit juices from the list. Following this, further modifications ensued, incompatible with potability: e.g. under the definition of water were now included urine and rheum (M. Makhshirin 6:5), which would have been excluded by a consistently applied criterion of potability.

This is a good example of rabbinic development of scriptural law, though extension of 'preparers' from water to other liquids (probably derived from traditional exegesis rather than initiated in the second century CE) hardly ranks as serious discontinuity. The modification by which fruit juices were excluded, however, may have been a second-century innovation, as we know of other legislation during that period with the purpose of bringing relief to the hard-pressed small farmers.[8]

Another aspect of the rabbinic doctrine of 'preparation' has been claimed by Neusner as a prime example of rabbinic discontinuity with Scripture. This is the rabbinic rule that the dampening of food or grain does not count as 'preparation' for impurity unless it is done intentionally by a human agency and for a human purpose. Thus dampening by accident or by rainfall does not count. Neusner claims that the idea of intentionality is typical of second century rabbinic thinking, and has no support in Scripture.[9]

Yet the language of Scripture does in fact lend support to the rabbinic doctrine of intentionality, for verse 38 reads: 'If water should be put on seed ...' This contrasts with the expression in v. 34: '... on which water may come', which expresses any kind of dampening, whether intentional or not. The rabbis responded to the expression of v. 38 sensitively, and concluded

[8] For example, Judah I dispensed certain areas from the payment of tithes (y. Demai 2:22c, b. Hullin 6b). He also attempted (unsuccessfully) to abrogate the sabbatical year in agriculture (y. Demai 1:20a). Judah I (or Judah II) abolished the ban on the use of Gentile oil (M. Abodah Zarah 2:6). See Alon (1984), pp. 730–37.

[9] See, for example, Neusner (1988), p. 88, 'when Scripture refers ... to grain's being made wet, it makes no provision for the attitude of the owner of the grain ...'

that it referred to human intentionality rather than chance dampening. Again, this is unlikely to be a second century exegesis and more likely to have been traditional, but even if second century, it is not an arbitrary invention, but a response to a real feature of the scriptural text. In general, as Milgrom has argued cogently (1991, pp. 485–86), Neusner's denial of intentionality in Scripture does not bear scrutiny, for many scriptural texts show a strong awareness of the importance of intention in human behaviour and law.

CHAPTER 7

Impurity and sacrifices

One of the most intriguing areas involving the impurity of animals is that of sacrifices. It is understandable that dead animals in general should be a source of impurity, but it is, at first sight, bewildering that the performance of holy sacrifices of animals in or just outside the Temple area should produce impurity, in some cases, in those performing them. An examination of these cases may throw light on the inner nature of impurity itself.

SIN-OFFERINGS

One of the commonest kinds of sacrifice in the Temple was the sin-offering (*hatta't*), which was brought by individuals in expiation of unwitting infringements of the prohibitions of the Torah. But sin-offerings are also prescribed on a less individual basis: for the High Priest for derelictions in his performance on behalf of the community, and for the community itself, when it has been guilty of some communal offence, or for a ruler (Lev. 4), or for everyone indiscriminately (whether guilty of specified offences or not) on the expiatory occasion of the Day of Atonement (Lev. 16). According to Lev. 16:28, the sin-offerings brought to atone for the sins of the whole community on the Atonement Day have the effect of causing impurity not to the officiating priest, but to the priest who carries out the carcase of the sacrificed animal for burning. But in rabbinic doctrine (M. Parah, 8:3), this is also true of all the sin-offerings whose remains are burnt outside (Lev.4:12, 21,26) i.e. sin-offerings of a public nature: the priest who burns the remains of the animal becomes impure, even though he is required to burn them in 'a clean place' outside the camp (Lev.4:12). Ordinary individual sin-offerings, however, do not require burning of their remains outside; these belong to the officiating priest, who must eat them in the sanctuary (Lev. 6:26; Heb. 6:19).

Many theories have been put forward to explain this ritual impurity derived from sacrificial animals. Milgrom's view (1991, pp. 262–63) is that the impurity derives from the transfer of human guilt to the animal, which in its turn transfers impurity to those handling it in the process of sacrifice. This impurity, he argues, would actually affect even the sacrificing priest, were it not for the sanctity of the Temple which neutralizes the impurity. But when the remains of the sacrificed animal are carried by an ordinary priest or non-priest outside the Temple for the performance of the final rites (the burning of the remains and the deposit of the ashes), the counteracting influence of the Temple sanctity is no longer present, and the sins which the animal bears cause impurity to the bearer. This interpretation receives reinforcement from the rabbinic doctrine that the impurity of the bearer does not commence until he reaches the area outside the Temple grounds.

Neusner has a different theory, according to which the element of outsideness is even more important. According to this view, all areas outside the Temple are impure (Neusner 1988, p. 46). Consequently, the bearer of the remains of the sacrificed animal becomes impure simply by virtue of performing rites on the outside. All rites performed outside the Temple (including the Scapegoat rite and the Red Cow rite) automatically confer impurity upon their participants. The sins borne by the animals concerned thus have no relevance to the impurity of the human participants.[1]

Objections can be urged, however, against both these views. Both appear to undervalue the element of purity in the situation. Thus Scripture emphasises that the place to which the remains of the animal must be borne (even though it is outside the Temple) must be a pure one, and also that the human

---

[1] This theory was previously put forward by Y. Kaufmann (1937–56), I, pp. 542–43.

participants must be in a state of purity at the time when they undertake the rite. The whole paradox of the rite is that it must be performed in conditions of purity, yet it causes impurity to those who perform it. No explanation can be satisfactory unless it takes this paradox into account.

In Greek religion, there is a distinction between sacrifices performed inside the temple, and those performed outside. The distinction turns on the contrast between the Olympian sky-gods, and the more primitive earth-gods, whose worship persists but in a less prestigious form. In Judaism, despite the centralization of Temple worship and the abolition of the 'high places', certain rites are performed outside the Temple: the Scapegoat on the Day of Atonement, the Red Cow rite for the provision of the water of purification for remedying of corpse-pollution, the calf-sacrifice for the discovery of a murdered body (this, however, is a special case, see p. 91), and the burning of the remains of sin-offerings. These rites have an anomalous, primitive air about them. We have to consider whether they are remnants of more primitive religious practice, and that is why they exhibit a mixture of the holy and the unclean. They are banished from the Temple, yet to a 'clean place' where they are performed in a 'clean' state. Yet they cause uncleanness to their participants, and this uncleanness perhaps arises from the ambivalent air surrounding them, as survivals of pagan practice. Can it be that the Israelite distinction between inside and outside rites somehow parallels the Greek distinction between inside and outside rites?

In the case of the sin-offerings, it should be noted that the parts that are burned to ashes and thrown on a dump, and thus rejected for Temple worship, are parts specially prized in other religions of the ancient world. The entrails and heart were the centre-pieces of Greek sacrificial practice, being devoured with the greatest honour and relish by the participants;[2] yet these are

---

[2] 'The animal is skinned and butchered; the inner organs, especially the heart and the liver (*splanchna*), are roasted on the fire on the altar first of all. Occasionally the heart is torn still beating from the body before all else. To taste the entrails immediately is the privilege and duty of the innermost circle of participants' (Burkert, *Greek Religion*, p. 57–7).

rejected and burned in the Jewish practice of the sin-offering, which includes them with the dung (Lev. 4:11) in a disposal operation (the entrails, however, after washing, are included in the wholly-burnt offering, Lev. 1:9). Only the fat around the entrails, the kidneys and the fat around them and part of the liver, are included in the sin-offering itself, and burnt into smoke for God's consumption.[3] There is no mention in the Torah of the inspection of entrails for favourable omens, as found in Greek, Assyrian, Ugaritic and Etrurian sacrificial practice. Could it be that the impurity suffered by the priest who disposed of the entrails and remaining parts of the body is the last element of awe in a procedure that has been transformed from a solemn rite into a chore?

It may be objected to the above theory that there are certain sacrifices of which the ashes are taken outside without causing impurity to the carrier. These are the burnt-offerings (Lev. 6:4), which take place every day in the Temple. But it is clear that the actual burning of these sacrifices takes place *inside* the Temple, on the altar. The removal of the ashes to the dump is thus a mere disposal operation, and has no aspects of being a rite itself. The sin-offering, on the other hand, does have such aspects, because the burning of the remains of the animal takes place outside (including the burning of parts of the animal which in other cults are regarded as especially sacred).

Further, it is significant that the remains themselves are not a source of impurity. Anyone who touches them while they are being transported to the place of burning remains pure. This shows that it is not the animal that causes impurity but the rite of burning itself. This is acknowledged by Milgrom, but his theory still seems to depend on some sort of transfer of human sins to the animal. Such a causation of impurity would be different from every other mechanism of pollution in the Hebrew system. No human being becomes a source of impurity through sinning, but only through contracting certain bodily states (leprosy, gonorrhea, etc.). So why should an animal to

---

[3] In Greek practice, all the succulent parts were eaten by the human participants, a practice that gave rise to much jesting in the Athenian comedy tradition, where the gods are shown complaining about this shabby treatment.

which human sins have been transferred become a source of impurity?

Milgrom's strongest point, however, is that there are parallels in other Middle Eastern cults for the impurity of the priest after performing a cleansing or purifying sacrifice. In Babylonian religion, even the officiating priest in the temple suffers impurity after such a sacrifice. Milgrom's argument is that Hebrew purifying sacrifice retains this idea, but relegates it to the outside part of the procedure. This argument deserves respect, but I would suggest that its plausibility depends on taking the sin-offerings in isolation from the general pattern of outside procedures. When the phenomena of the Scapegoat and the Red Cow are taken into the reckoning (see below), there are grounds for the conception that outside procedures can have a validity of their own, other than being merely the dénouement of inside procedures. In this overall pattern, the impurity of the burning of the sin-offering assumes a different dimension.

THE SCAPEGOAT

Redolent of primitive thought and practice is the rite of the Scapegoat. Here we have a rite that is openly revealed as stemming from pagan belief in demons, a belief that has been banished from the rest of the Priestly document, and from the Torah generally. The person who performs the last stage of the Scapegoat ritual becomes unclean and must wash his clothes. This is usually interpreted as the effect of his participation in the transfer of sins. But it is certainly worth considering that his uncleanness may be the effect of his transaction with the demon Azazel. If so, then all the outside rites which cause uncleanness may retain vestiges of pre-Hebraic thinking, and for that reason show a combination of cleanness (denoting holiness) and uncleanness (denoting the uneasiness of regression and also a kind of negative holiness). Only in these outside rites do we find this ambivalence of the clean and the unclean, and their outsideness denotes that they belong, even if subliminally, to powers other than the God whose presence rests on the Temple – powers of the earth rather than of the Heavens.

The ritual of the Scapegoat is the most dramatic of the Israelite religious year. It is also the most alien to the spirit of rabbinic Judaism, which bowdlerized it, and removed the pagan elements from it. This process of taming of paganism is characteristic of the rabbis, but by no means a new development, for the same process is found within the Hebrew Bible itself, where, nevertheless, outcrops of primitive rock remain, indications of violent disturbances which the authors of the Hebrew Bible are struggling to surmount. In the rabbinic writings, the struggle is over, and a highly civilized plateau has been reached. The fascination of the biblical writings is that in them the struggle is still going on.

At the apex of the Day of Atonement ritual in the Temple, two goats stand before the High Priest in the adytum of the Temple, its holiest part except for the Holy of Holies. One of the goats must die, and the other must be escorted to the wilderness, carrying a great burden of sin, to join the demon of the wilderness, Azazel. Which will die and which will live in exile is to be decided by lot; that is to say, by the decision of God, or (in earlier thinking) of Fate.

In the Priestly account as we have it, each of the two goats expiates a different category of sins. One goat dies to expiate sins committed against the sanctity of the Temple; while the other is driven out to expiate, or carry away, the sins of the whole community, whether in the moral or the religious sphere. There is a certain overlapping here, and it is not clear why the mode of expiation in the one case is death, and in the other expulsion. It seems likely that the distribution of the roles of the two goats is a later rationalization. The basic narrative of the two goats, one of which dies while the other is expelled, is earlier than the explanation evolved to account for their duality.

The earliest narrative, indeed (as I have argued elsewhere), concerns not two goats but two human figures. One of them dies, and the other is banished into the wilderness. We see the outlines of such a story in many myths and legends: Cain and Abel, Osiris and Set, Baal and Mot, Romulus and Remus, Balder and Loki, even Laius and Oedipus. This is an ancient pattern of human sacrifice, in which the necessary salvific death is procured for the tribe by the agency of a dark figure of mingled evil and sanctity, whom I have called the Sacred Executioner. The tribe is protected from the guilt of murder by a ritualized shifting of guilt to a prepared figure, who carries away the burden into the wilderness outside the community, where he bears an accursed but charmed life, protected even by the god of the tribe, but in other versions by the evil god of the wilderness who shares his guilt.

When animal sacrifice replaced human sacrifice, the old pattern remained, but the human participants in the rite were replaced by animals. The secret that was lost was the nature of the guilt for which the live goat was banished: the sacrificed goat died for the tribe, but the live goat (or rather his earlier human counterpart) made an even more important contribution to the welfare of the tribe – he killed the sacrifice for them. This is the forgotten guilt which the live goat carried away into the wilderness, not the neatly distributed portion of community sins that the Priestly authors allotted to him (see also pp. 135–40).

The dialectic of the sacrificed goat and the living goat is further blurred in the rabbinic modification by which both goats meet with death. Whereas the biblical text clearly posits that the non-sacrificed goat is left to live in the wilderness, the rabbinic account of the rite describes how the goat is led to a precipice and pushed over it to its death.

Bible

And the goat shall bear upon him all their iniquities unto a land not inhabited: and he shall let go the goat in the wilderness. (Lev. 16:22).

Rabbinic

Certain of the eminent folk of Jerusalem used to go with him to the first booth. There were ten booths from Jerusalem to the ravine which was at a distance of ninety *ris* [which measure seven and a half to the mile]. At every booth they used to say to him, 'Here is food, here is water', and they went with him from that booth to the next booth, but not from the last booth; for none used to go with him to the ravine; but they stood at a distance and beheld what he did. What did he do? He divided the thread of crimson wool and tied one half to the rock and the other half between its horns, and he pushed it from behind; and it went rolling down, and before it had reached half the way down the hill it was broken in pieces. He returned and sat down beneath the last booth until nightfall. And from what time does it render his garments unclean? After he has gone outside the wall of Jerusalem. R. Simeon says: From the moment that he pushes it into the ravine. (M. Yoma 6:5–6).

Josephus

And besides these, they bring two kids of the goats; the one of which is sent alive out of the limits of the camp into the wilderness for the scapegoat, and to be an expiation for the sins of the whole multitude; but the other is brought into a place of great cleanness within the limits of the camp, and is there burnt, with its skin, without any sort of cleansing. (*Ant.* III. 240)

Josephus does not mention the killing of the scapegoat at the ravine. This may simply be because he is following the expression of the Hebrew Bible in his account of Jewish religious practices. It is hardly likely that the killing of the scapegoat is a post-Temple fiction; much more likely that it was the practice of the Second Temple, motivated not by a sacrificial purpose (for the method of killing is non-sacrificial) but by a fear that the goat, laden with sins, might return into inhabited regions. The basic idea of the ceremony remains that the goat is set free to wander in uninhabited territory. Support for this may be found in the ceremony of the cleansing of the leper (see Chapter 11), in which two birds feature, one of which is sacrificed and the other is allowed to fly away into freedom (Lev. 14:4–7).

The term 'scapegoat' arises from an interpretation of the term 'Azazel', found in Greek and Latin sources, and from there adopted in European translations. It is taken to be derived from Hebrew *'ez azal*, meaning 'the goat who escapes'. This interpretation, however, is forced, and intertestamental literature (1 Enoch, Dead Sea Scrolls) shows that Azazel was the name of a demon or fallen angel. The way in which the two goats are labelled, one 'for the Lord' and the other 'for Azazel' (Lev. 16:8) also shows that Azazel is some supernatural power.

The later history of the term 'scapegoat' is curious, for it has become a term for a person who suffers for the sins of others and does not escape. Thus in the Christian story, Jesus is sometimes called a scapegoat for the sins of humanity, though in fact his function is much more like that of the other goat, the one that was sacrificed. More akin to the role of the scapegoat is Judas Iscariot, who (in some versions) wanders the world in expiation of his sin; but this is to see the Christian story as reviving the original pre-biblical meaning of the ceremony of the two goats. In the Hebrew Bible as we have it, this original meaning has been suppressed, and the two goats are equally expiating figures, though the reason why one lives and one dies has become opaque.

The Scapegoat is the focus of genuine disagreement or discontinuity between Scripture and its rabbinical exegesis. In Scripture, there can be no doubt that the Scapegoat is the subject of a transfer of sins. It bears the sins of the community away, and thus clears the community of sin, enabling it to make a new start once every year. In rabbinic thought, however, there is no transfer of sins to the Scapegoat, since sins can be expiated only by repentance and reparation. Even partial repentance makes the Day of Atonement, together with its Scapegoat rite, inefficacious. If a person repents of a past sin, but retains an intention to continue that sin in the future, the Day of Atonement does not expiate even his past sin. This turns the rite of the Scapegoat into a mere symbol. When the sins of the community are loaded on to the back of the Scapegoat and sent into the desert, this merely symbolizes the repentance of the community and its desire to maintain the values of the settled community against the chaos of the desert.

Yet the discontinuity is not quite as great as it appears. On the rabbinic side, there is enough disagreement among the rabbis to show that the final decision about the insignificance of the Scapegoat was not reached without difficulty. For one very important and influential rabbi, no less a person than Rabbi Judah the Prince, the redactor of the Mishnah, attempted, though unsuccessfully, to stem the tide of reformist exegesis. He stated, 'The Scapegoat atones for all sins in the Torah, whether repented or unrepented' (b. Yoma 85b, b. Shebuot 13a, b. Keritot 7a).[4] This view, though it was overruled by Rabbi Judah's colleagues, testifies to the survival of an unsophisticated belief in the transfer of sins to the Scapegoat.

At the same time, Scripture itself testifies to a reluctance to accept the Scapegoat at face value as a magical atonement for unrepented deliberate sins. The Prophets inveigh against such an interpretation, when they declare the inefficacy of all sacrifices without repentance. The authors of the Priestly document also express their belief in the power of repentance (Lev. 26:41–42), a belief that is hard to reconcile with the atoning efficacy of the Scapegoat. It seems likely that the Priestly authors regarded the Scapegoat as a last resort, when all other methods of atonement had failed (and this is likely to have been the attitude of Rabbi Judah the Prince too.) The prevailing view among the rabbis, that the Scapegoat had no atoning power at all without repentance, had a long struggle for victory, and yet was present as a contending view all along. Similarly, the other primitive aspect of the Scapegoat, the name Azazel, has a chequered exegetical history. There is a reluctance, shown in the earliest translation, the Septuagint, to admit that this is the name of a supernatural power or demon. The rabbis never admitted this, and yet retained memories of a fallen angel called Azael or Azazel. That the Scapegoat is sent into the domain of a demon or minor deity called Azazel, carrying the sins of the community, is too much of a scandal to be admitted into monotheistic consciousness. That the Scapegoat is actually dedicated in a Temple ceremony to this demon, alongside the goat that is dedicated to God, expresses a dualism that was banished from Judaism and could not be admitted into biblical

---

[4] It is a problem that Maimonides rules that the Scapegoat atones for minor transgressions (but not for major ones) even without repentance (*MT*, Teshubah 1:2, see also his Commentary on the Mishnah, on M. Shevuot 1:6). Karo objects in the *Kesef Mishneh* that this is not in accord with either the minority opinion of Rabbi Judah the Prince that the Scapegoat atones for all unrepented sins or with the majority opinion that it atones for none. For a full discussion of the many solutions offered to this problem, see Kapah (1984), pp. 575ff.

exegesis. Yet the residue of remembrance of the demon Azazel may be found in the ceremony of the accompaniment of the Scapegoat into the wilderness by elders of the community, and above all in the lingering of its aura in the form of the impurity suffered by the Scapegoat's chief companion. Here we see impurity as the mirror-image of sanctity, an effusion that signifies the supernatural in its despised, rejected and yet lingering form; banished to a region outside the influence of the Temple, and yet attached somehow to the Temple ceremonies by an indissoluble link.

THE CALF WHOSE NECK IS BROKEN

An outside ceremony that has no links with the demonic, however, is that of 'the calf whose neck is broken'. This is the ceremony laid down in Deuteronomy (but not in Leviticus) to be performed when a murdered body is discovered and the murderer is unknown (Deut. 21:1–9):

1. If one be found slain in the land which the Lord thy God giveth thee to possess it, lying in the field, and it be not known who hath slain him:
2. Then thy elders and thy judges shall come forth, and they shall measure unto the cities which are round about him that is slain:
3. And it shall be, that the city which is next unto the slain man, even the elders of that city shall take an heifer, which hath not been wrought with, and which hath not drawn the yoke;
4. And the elders of that city shall bring down the heifer unto a rough valley, which is neither eared nor sown, and shall strike off the heifer's neck there in the valley:
5. And the priests the sons of Levi shall come near; for them the Lord thy God hath chosen to minister unto him, and to bless in the name of the Lord; and by their word shall every controversy and every stroke be tried:
6. And all the elders of that city, that are next unto the slain man, shall wash their hands over the heifer that is beheaded in the valley:
7. And they shall answer and say, Our hands have not shed this blood, neither have our eyes seen it.
8. Be merciful, O Lord, unto thy people Israel, whom thou has redeemed, and lay not innocent blood unto thy people Israel's charge. And the blood shall be forgiven them.

9. So shalt thou put away the guilt of innocent blood from among you, which thou shalt do that which is right in the sight of the Lord.

Considered as a sacrifice, this ceremony is a curious one. It is performed outside the Temple, like the Scapegoat rite and the Red Cow rite, but, unlike them, it has no Temple aspect linking it to the Temple cult. In some respects it is like the Red Cow – the sacrifice is a female animal which must be unworked – but its purity aspects are exiguous. The washing of hands by the elders is a symbolic act, not a washing away of cultic impurity. What they wash away is their moral responsibility for the death of the murdered person. Like the Scapegoat, the heifer dies by a non-cultic mode of death (if we accept the rabbinic version of the Scapegoat's death), but there is no residual impurity attaching to the performers of the sacrifice as in the case of the Scapegoat.

The reason for this is that there are no demons or sublimated spirits involved. The ceremony is a local one, but shows no sign of derivation from local cultism. The Temple is left out of the matter (except for the involvement of the priests) as irrelevant to a matter of local concern. The object is to clear the locality of guilt, not impurity. Nothing is said about cleansing the land of blood-impurity, contrary to the interpretation of some commentators.

Jacob Milgrom, for example (Milgrom, 1971) sees the rite as transferring the land polluted by the corpse to an uncultivated plot. The killing of the heifer re-enacts the murder; the blood of the heifer, identified with the blood of the slain, is transferred to the wilderness where it will not bring a curse to the land (see Num. 35:33, 'The land cannot be cleansed of the blood that is shed therein, but by the blood of him that shed it'). He sees the rite, therefore, as very ancient.

The land where the sacrifice is performed, however, is not wilderness but land that happens not to have been cultivated: it corresponds to the requirement that the heifer should not have been worked with. It fits in with the concept of making a new start; or of using materials for the ceremony that have not been corrupted by human use. There is no hint in the passage of a concern for the defilement of the land; instead the concern is that the murder might be laid to the charge of the people or its leaders. The death of the heifer, rather than re-enacting the murder, enacts the execution of the murderer who could not be found. Its mode of death is thus more like an execution than a sacrifice. Moreover, there is little persuasiveness in the idea that murder-defilement can be transferred to an uncultivated plot. Although Num. 35:33 does say that murder defiles the land, this cannot be taken to imply that murder is acceptable outside the Land or in uncultivated parts of the Land. The sinfulness of murder does not consist in its effects on the fertility of the Land.

The rabbinic sources add that the ceremony is to be performed only if full enquiry has failed to discover the identity of the murderer. Moreover, if the identity of the murderer is discovered after the ceremony has been performed, the murderer must go on trial just as if no ceremony had been performed. The ceremony thus does not atone for the murder. There is a rationalistic motivation – a desire to clear up a tragic and inexplicable incident with dignity and without blame to the local authorities. The ceremony has taken features from the Red Cow rite, but in the way of imitation or even pastiche. The Red Cow rite itself is no such civilized, carefully plotted public display, but a genuine survival of primitive thought.

CHAPTER 8

The Red Cow: the paradoxes

Among the animal sacrifices that cause impurity to their participants, the most mysterious and paradoxical is that of the Red Cow, the animal whose ashes, mixed with water, provide the means of purification from the most severe impurity of all, corpse-impurity.[1]

The Red Cow is the sacrifice that breaks all the rules, and reduced the rabbis to such mystification that they declared that even Solomon, in all his wisdom, did not understand it. Their puzzlement derived from the mixture of purity and impurity in the rite of the Red Cow. Its overall purpose was purification; yet in both the preparation and performance of the rite, participants became unclean. There is an ambiguity about the whole procedure that reflects an ambiguity in the concept of impurity itself.

Numbers 19:2 tells us that the Red Cow must be 'without spot, wherein is no blemish, and upon which never came yoke'. The priest must bring the Red Cow outside the camp, where she is to be killed, 'before his face'. The priest must take some of the blood of the cow on his finger, and sprinkle it seven times in the direction of the Temple. Then the cow is to be burnt before

---

[1] On the question of nomenclature: should we speak of the Red Cow, or, as many commentators have it, the Red Heifer? A 'heifer' is defined by OUP as 'a young cow that has not had a calf'. In the Hebrew Bible, the term is *parah 'adumah*, which means 'red cow', and the use of the adult term *parah* is probably what motivates the Mishnah to rule that the animal must be from two to five years old in order to be sacrificed. The Hebrew term for a female calf, on the other hand, is *'eglah*, the term used for the animal whose neck is broken for an unsolved murder (Deut. 21:1–9). I think it best to speak of the Red Cow, and reserve the word 'heifer' for the female calf. This, in fact, is the nomenclature of NEB, which translates 'cow' in Num. 19 and 'heifer' in Deut. 21. It was AV that introduced confusion by translating both as 'heifer'.

the priest, 'in his sight': 'her skin, and her flesh, and her blood, with her dung, shall he burn.' The priest then takes cedar wood, hyssop and scarlet wool, and throws them into the burning cow.

: At this point, impurity appears. The officiating priest is now unclean, and must wash his clothes and body in the ritual pool. He remains unclean until the evening. Also the person (not necessarily a priest) who assisted the priest by burning the cow becomes similarly unclean. He must wash his clothes and body and be unclean until the evening.

Now a third person enters the scene. He must be clean, and he gathers the ashes of the cow and takes them to a clean place outside the camp, where they are preserved, so that when required they may be mixed with water and used to purify from corpse-impurity. This mixture of water and ashes is called 'water of separation' (*mei niddah*).

But this third person, who gathers and deposits the ashes, has become unclean in turn, and must wash his clothes and body and be unclean until the evening.

Now the process of purification is described (from v. 17). Again we need a clean person to officiate (v. 18). He takes some of the ashes of the Red Cow and puts them into a vessel with running water (literally 'living water', i.e. water from a stream). He uses hyssop as a sprinkler, and sprinkles on the corpse-impure person on the third and seventh day of his impurity. This completes the work of the Red Cow for the corpse-impure, who now, on the seventh day of his impurity, washes his clothes and body, is unclean until the evening, and then finally becomes clean.

But the priest who performed the sprinkling also becomes similarly unclean (v. 21, but differently interpreted by the rabbis, see below).

Also, most surprising of all the 'water of separation' becomes itself a source of impurity (v. 22). Anyone who touches it or carries it (when it is not being used for purification purposes) becomes unclean. Moreover, anyone who touches or carries the ashes alone becomes unclean (Num. 19:10).

Yet, although the 'water of separation' (or 'sin-offering water' as it is called in the rabbinic literature, from the expression 'it is a sin-offering' in Num. 19:9) causes impurity to those who touch or carry it, it is regarded (in the rabbinic literature) as the purest of the pure, and extraordinary measures are taken to safeguard its purity by preventing it from coming into contact with even the slightest suspicion of impurity which might impair its efficacy as an agent of purification from corpse-impurity (see M. Parah 3:2–3). In fact, the 'sin-offering water' is the apex of the purity system, the only substance so holy that it can be contaminated even by a fourth degree of impurity; an impurity so refined that it leaves unaffected even the sacrifices themselves (M. Hag. 2:5, 7).

This dialectic of purity and impurity is characteristic of the Red Cow in all its phases of preparation and use for purification. One writer, however, has attempted to demystify the matter. Jacob Neusner argues that the paradoxes can be dissolved by applying the historical method. He contends that the purity aspects of the Red Cow preparation are all rabbinic; biblically the Red Cow was prepared entirely in impurity. This was because the Red Cow was slaughtered and burnt outside the Temple. Any rites that took place outside the Temple were scripturally devoid of purity. The rabbis of the second century, however, having to cope with the absence of the Temple, wished to transfer the purity regulations of Temple times to ordinary life, and in part pursuance of this aim, imported elements of purity into their version of the (now unperformed) ritual of the preparation of the Red Cow. In this aim of transferring purity to everyday life, the rabbis had been preceded by the Pharisees of Temple times, who (Neusner contends) are to be identified with the 'fellowships' (*haberim*) who practised a priest-like ritual purity in the home.

Neusner repeated this view (despite criticism from Joseph M. Baumgarten[2]) in his *A Religion of Pots and Pans?* as follows:

The priestly author stresses, first of all, that the rite takes place outside the camp, which is to say, in an unclean place. He repeatedly tells us that anyone involved in the rite is made unclean by his participation in the rite, thus, 19,7, the priest shall wash his clothes; Num. 19,8, the one who burns the heifer shall wash his clothes; Num. 19,10, and he

---

[2] Baumgarten, 1980, pp. 169–70.

who gathers the ashes of the heifer shall wash his clothes and be unclean until the evening. The priestly legislator therefore takes for granted that the rules of purity which govern rites in the Temple simply do not apply to the rite of burning the cow. Not only are the participants *not* in a state of cleanness, but they are in a state of uncleanness, being required to wash their clothes, remaining unclean until the evening only then allowed back into the camp which is the Temple. Accordingly, the world outside the Temple is by definition not subject to the Temple's rules and is not going to be clean. (p. 29)

These assertions are contradicted by the biblical assertions that at each stage of the preparation of the Red Cow and its use for purification the participants must be in a state of cleanness (Num. 19:9 and 18–19). Neusner, however, assumes that because the participants are unclean at the end of the rite, they must also be unclean at its beginning. The biblical account, however, is at pains to stress that the participants are made unclean by the rite itself, and this not only does not imply that they are unclean at the start, but actually implies that they are clean at the start. It is plainly stated that the man who gathers and stores the ashes is clean at the start (v. 9) and unclean at the end (v. 10) of his activity. The rabbis said that the Red Cow rite was performed in cleanness, even though it took place outside the Temple, not because they had a new philosophy of extra-Temple cleanness, but because this appeared to them to be the most natural way to read the meaning of Scripture, even though, as they fully acknowledged, the phenomenon of being made unclean by a rite for which cleanness was required was puzzling and paradoxical.

Neusner espouses a theory of radical discontinuity between Bible and rabbinic literature, such that the rabbinic movement comprises a separate religion from biblical religion. I see no such radical discontinuity, though of course considerable development has taken place in the evolution of rabbinic Judaism from the Bible. Very often, when the rabbis seem to introduce concepts that are foreign to the Bible, it is possible to show that in fact these concepts derived from close attention to the biblical text. The rabbis systematise, and sometimes arrive at surprising results from their process of exegesis, but they do not innovate in any radical sense.

An issue also arising in the context of the Red Cow enables Neusner to assert once more his theory of discontinuity. This is the Mishnah's statement (Parah 7:9) that anyone taking part in the Red Cow rite who engages in any work unrelated to the rite thereby renders the whole rite invalid (*pasul*). Neusner sees this law as expressing the desire of the rabbis to relocate cleanness and holiness outside the Temple. For (he argues) the distinction between extrinsic and intrinsic work existed before this law was instituted only in a Temple context. On the Sabbath, the slaughtering of animals was permitted in the Temple, but not outside it, since the continuation of the Temple sacrificial service was considered to override the laws of the Sabbath. 'On the Sabbath-day labor is prohibited. But the cult must be continued. How? Labor intrinsic to the sacrifices required on the Sabbath is to be done, and that which is not connected with the sacrifice is not to be done.' By introducing a distinction that is peculiar to the Temple, the Red Cow rite, despite its perform-ance outside the Temple, is raised to the level of a Temple sacrifice, and so requires conditions of cleanness. The rabbis, with their new concept of outside purity, have transformed the Red Cow rite into a rite of cleanness, thus validating their own programme of replicating the purity of the Temple priesthood in the Jewish home.

This argument, however, is invalid.[3] The distinction between intrinsic and extrinsic work in the context of the Sabbath in the Temple has a meaning that has nothing to do with our present concern with the preparation of the Red Cow. Extrinsic labour is forbidden in the Temple on the Sabbath simply because it is forbidden anyway. The dispensation relates only to those actions that are necessary to continue the sacrificial service. Moreover, if the priest officiating in the Temple misinterprets the dispensation and performs work not covered by the dispen-sation, he commits a sin which must be expiated by repentance and a sin-offering. But the sacrifice which he has offered on the

---

[3] For fuller treatment of the topic, see Maccoby (1990), pp. 60–61.

Sabbath remains a valid offering, since the work he put into it *was* covered by the dispensation. In the case of the preparation of the Red Cow, the situation is entirely different. If the priest performs extrinsic work during the preparation (i.e. work not necessary for the preparation itself), he makes the preparation invalid, and it all has to be done again. On the other hand, he has not committed any sin and does not have to repent or bring a sin-offering; he has just wasted everybody's time. Clearly any extrinsic work performed during the sacrifice of the Red Cow affects the sacrifice itself, not just the moral record of the officiating priest.

Why is this? It is certainly not because the rabbis wished to invest the Red Cow rite with Temple purity, or to turn the area where it was performed into 'sacred space'. It was simply that the rabbis, reading the scriptural text very closely, interpreted it to mean that the Red Cow rite required total attention on the part of the officiating priest. Scripture includes some striking and unusual phrases in its instructions, saying ' . . . and he shall slaughter her *before him* (v. 3), and 'and he shall burn the Cow *before his eyes*' (v. 5). The meaning of the italicized phrases, in rabbinic interpretation, is that the priest must perform these operations with full attention (see Sifre ad loc. and b. Yoma 42a). Such phrases are not found in Scripture in relation to any other cultic acts.[4] Confirmation that this is indeed the thinking of the rabbis on the matter comes from the nature of the extrinsic acts which invalidated the Red Cow rite. Examples are showing someone the way, or removing food to a place of safety (M. Parah 7:9). These would not be reckoned as 'labour' at all in a context of the Sabbath. They do qualify, however, as acts that divert the attention from the matter in hand. Further confirmation is that even the performance of an extrinsic 'labour' does not count as such if it is performed absent-mindedly (b. Hullin 32a). It is not what is actually done that counts, but the extent to which it distracts the person from the performance of the Red Cow rite.

Neusner's attempt to explain the ban on extrinsic acts as a

---

[4] See the discussion in the *Talmudic Encyclopaedia* (Hebrew), under the heading *heseh ha-da'at*, vol. ix, pp. 556–8.

rabbinic transference of Temple procedure to the outside thus fails. The ban is perfectly explicable in terms of the rite itself, and shows no gulf of discontinuity between the Torah and the rabbis in their conceptualization of the Red Cow rite. The most one could say is that the authors of the Torah may not have intended by the phrases 'before him' and 'before his eyes' to prescribe a unique kind of attention, as the rabbis thought. But this is a matter of exegesis, not radical reform. The rabbis always had their eyes on Scripture, and were concerned to interpret it, not to subvert it.

In particular, the rabbis preserved the paradoxical nature of the Red Cow rite, even though they were puzzled by it. They were in fact far more faithful to the text of the Bible than the modern commentator Jacob Neusner, who simply ignores the elements of purity in the biblical text, and explains the mixture of cleanness and uncleanness in the rabbinic form of the rite as arising accidentally at a late date, through the rabbis' desire to introduce elements of cleanness where before there was only uncleanness.

Something that *is* a post-biblical, Pharisaic and rabbinic issue is the conflict with the Sadducees on the question of exactly how ritually clean the officiating priest had to be. The Sadducees insisted that the priest had to be fully clean, i.e. if he had been defiled by, say, a dead 'creeping thing', it was not sufficient for him to undergo purification in the ritual pool, he had to wait until the evening before becoming eligible to officiate at a Red Cow rite. The Pharisees, however, and after them the rabbis, said that purification in the ritual pool was sufficient, and the priest did not have to wait until the evening to officiate.[5]

The condition of a person who has bathed, but awaits final evening purification is known in the rabbinic literature as *tebul*

---

[5] Neusner argued that this conflict between the Pharisees and the Sadducees was unhistorical (Neusner, 1977, pp. 131–33). The whole discussion on this issue, he argued, arose after the destruction of the Temple, and represents a difference of opinion between rabbis centred on Yavneh and later rabbis centred on Usha. Neusner's view was cogently criticised by Joseph M. Baumgarten, 1980, pp. 169–70. The issue was settled by the publication of the MMT document of the Dead Sea Scrolls, which showed conclusively that the matter was being debated between Sadducees and Pharisees in Temple times.

yom (literally, 'immersed that day'). Such a person was regarded as clean for secular purposes, or for eating Tithe, but was forbidden to touch holy foodstuffs (i.e. priestly food, or *terumah*, or sacrifices) or to enter into the Temple area further than the Court of the Gentiles (M. Kelim 1:5,8). The condition, therefore, was one of semi-purity, intermediate between the impurity before immersion and the full purity attained by awaiting the evening.

Why then did the Pharisees insist that a person in this condition could partake in the Red Cow rite? So sure were they of this, and so sure that the Sadducees were wrong in demanding total purity, that the Pharisees used to bring about deliberate defilement of the officiating priest (by bringing him into contact with a dead 'creeping thing'[6]) and then instruct him to bathe and officiate before the evening. This, apparently, was not because they thought such a state was obligatory, but because they thought it important to flout the opinion of the Sadducees that it was forbidden.

It seems rather strange that the Pharisees should have made such a parade of their disagreement with the Sadducees on this matter. It is understandable that they paraded their disagreement on the question of the cutting of the Omer on the Sabbath (see M. Men. 10:3), because their procedure in this matter, in their view, was obligatory, not merely permitted. But in the case of the Red Cow preparation, why make such a public display about something that was permitted but not obligatory? If a priest who was fully clean had been chosen to perform the rite, no law would have been broken; but instead a semi-impure priest was deliberately chosen just to show that, contrary to the Sadducees, such a priest was eligible.

One suspects that there is more to this than meets the eye. The insistence of the Pharisees suggests that the employment of a semi-clean priest was, after all, essential rather than just permitted. Partial confirmation of this comes from the circumstance that not only the officiating priest, but even the instru-

---

[6] According to the opinion of Maimonides.

ments employed in the burning, were deliberately rendered semi-unclean.

True, the Mishnah does give the reason as merely to flout the Sadducees. But this may be because at the time of the composition of the Mishnah, the true reason had been forgotten. We need not doubt that this was a definite topic of conflict between the Pharisees and the Sadducees – the MMT document (4Q394–398) confirms this. But the issue may have been more substantial than the Mishnah reveals. This may have been one of the many issues in which the Pharisees preserved an ancient tradition which was rejected by the Sadducees because the latter could not find any support for it in Scripture. The basic difference between the Pharisees and the Sadducees was on the question of the Oral Torah, which the Sadducees rejected. This meant that the Sadducees, as well as rejecting the reforms and new ordinances sponsored by the Pharisees, also rejected the ancient extra-biblical traditions which the Pharisees preserved (for example, the water-libation at Tabernacles, deriving from pre-biblical rain-making rites).

It may be, then, that the Red Cow rite is even more ambivalent that it appears in relation to purity and impurity. Not only does the priest change from a pure person to an impure person during the course of the rite; but he is deliberately put into a condition of ambiguous purity even before the rite begins. To this extent, we may agree with Neusner that the whole rite is performed in impurity; but the impurity is a marginal one, a transitional state on the way to complete purity. Thus when the priest is rendered impure by his performance of the rite, he descends from marginal to complete impurity. These subtleties of ambiguity suggest a wealth of meaning in the rite that long precedes the factional squabbles of the Pharisees and the Sadducees. Contrary to Neusner, who sees the whole rite (in its aspects of purity) as later even than the era of the Pharisees, we may suspect that the rite belongs to a time preceding even the composition of the Bible, a rite so primitive and redolent of pagan thinking that in the course of being adapted for Israelite religion, it developed a web of contradictions.

While in the preparation of the Red Cow ashes a deliberate

laxness of purity is cultivated by the deliberate part-defilement of the officiating priest, at another stage of the preparation an extreme of purity is demanded; this too contributes to the atmosphere of paradox surrounding the Red Cow. The preparation of the priest for his task of partaking in the Red Cow rite is characterized by an extreme care to preserve him from corpse-impurity or other seven-day uncleanness. He was kept apart from his household for seven days, just as the High Priest was kept apart for the service of the Day of Atonement. He was kept apart from his wife lest she should become menstruous and he become unclean for seven days. On each of the seven days of his separation he was sprinkled with water of purification (made from previous Red Cows). Moreover he had to be sprinkled by someone who had never in his life suffered corpse uncleanness, with water contained in vessels of stone, which were insusceptible to uncleanness. How could it be ensured that these sprinklers had never suffered corpse uncleanness? The Mishnah here tells an almost incredible story: that such people were reared from childhood in areas of Jerusalem built over rock, beneath which the rock was hollowed out 'for fear of any grave down in the depths'. These children collected the water in Siloam and were conveyed in special conditions of cleanness to the Temple Mount where they inserted the ashes from a jar in the Temple Court (M. Parah 3:2–3).

Why this extraordinary care for the sake of a priest who was going to be deliberately rendered unclean at the beginning of the rite? The precautions, it is true, are directed against the possibility of corpse-impurity, which would indeed render the priest invalid for the rite. Yet the concern for utter purity is at variance with the lack of concern for purity in the rite itself. The rabbis try to explain the matter on commonsense grounds by saying that since the Red Cow is valid if prepared by semi-pure people, special care had to be taken in case people should regard the whole rite as unimportant and purity-indifferent. Therefore the Sages decreed these special measures of safeguard against impurity. But again this explanation has an ad hoc air. Were these precautions indeed late rabbinic institutions, or do they derive from a pre-rabbinic, or even pre-biblical period?

On the one hand, the Red Cow rite is aimed at purification from the most serious impurity of all, corpse-impurity. It is therefore natural that extreme precautions should be taken to prevent the means of purification from contracting even a suspicion of impurity; otherwise all the subsequent purification for which the ashes would be used would be invalid. On the other hand, impurity is deliberately imported into the rite both biblically and rabbinically. How are we to explain this pervasive and systematic contradiction?

CHAPTER 9

The Red Cow and 'niddah'

A full explanation of the paradoxes of the Red Cow has been offered by Jacob Milgrom (1990, pp. 438–44; 1991, pp. 270–78). This theory does not ignore relevant biblical textual evidence, as does Neusner's theory. Milgrom assembles all the data in his usual admirable way; but the resultant theory is not fully satisfactory, for it does seem that the uniqueness of the Red Cow disappears under his treatment.

To give a preliminary example: Milgrom considers the vital question why the Red Cow is a cow. In all other sacrifices featuring the larger animals, the sacrifice is a bull. Only when the sacrifice is from the sheep or the goats can the animal be a female. Milgrom's answer to this question is that in this case alone we are looking for a supply of ashes to be mixed with water to function as a purification for corpse-impurity. A large animal is more suitable to provide a viable supply; on the other hand, the Red Cow is a sin-offering (or in Milgrom's terminology a 'purification offering') and these are always females. So for once the female purification offering is taken from the herd instead of from the flock.

I suggest, however, that we should be looking for a solution with wider explanatory force than this. Both the redness and the cowness of the Red Cow are striking features that should turn our minds in the direction of comparative religion, rather than Israelite priestly technicalities. The cow goddess in Egypt and India, and her precursor in prehistoric times, are relevant to the discussion of an area where, as Milgrom admits, Israelite religion shows continuity with far older cults.

Milgrom's theory of the Red Cow is as follows. He argues

that it is basically a 'purification offering' (*hatta't*). Like other such community offerings (as opposed to the private 'purification offering'), it is wholly burnt outside the Temple, causing those concerned with its burning to become unclean. The reason is that these offerings absorb the sins or impurities which they expiate and thus become full of uncleanness, which they transmit to the persons handling them. The expiating agent in the case of ordinary 'purification offerings' is blood, which is sprinkled on the altar to cleanse it from impurity caused by the sin (in Milgrom's general theory of the *hatta't*). In the case of the Red Cow, however, which is sacrificed outside the Temple, some drops of blood are sprinkled in the direction of the Temple, but most of the blood is burnt together with the rest of the cow, and this residual blood is the main ingredient that gives efficacy to the ashes; the redness of the Cow, indeed, symbolises the importance of this blood.

The Red Cow, on this theory, is little different from other sin-offerings, except that, when reduced to symbolic blood in the form of the mixture of ashes and water, it is sprinkled not on the altar but on the person who is to be cleansed. This is the archaic feature of the rite, which has survived from the primitive sin-offering, which magically purged the sinner without requiring from him personal repentance and cleansing of the altar.

To the objection that the ordinary sin-offering, which is not wholly burnt outside, is actually partly eaten by the priest without causing him to be impure (Lev. 6:26), Milgrom replies that this eating is itself a destruction of the sin-offering, equivalent in its effects to burning. The defiling effect does not occur, however, because the eating takes place inside the Temple, and the holiness of the Temple overrides the defiling effect. Similarly, the guide of the Scapegoat does not become unclean until he has gone out of the Temple precinct.

An aspect which Milgrom elides in this low-key approach is the startling expression which Scripture uses to designate the purifying water-cum-ashes. This is the expression *mei niddah*, usually translated 'waters of purification'. But the word *niddah* has been used in Leviticus with only one meaning, 'menstruation'.[1] What can it mean that the Red Cow's ashes, when mixed with water, are called 'water of menstruation'? Is this the greatest paradox of all, that the agent of purification from corpse-impurity is no other than menstrual blood, or its symbolic equivalent? Is this why the Cow has to be totally red, so that its ashes can function as the essence of redness, the menstrual paradigm? Menstrual blood is itself a great source of impurity in the system; but there are so many ambivalences of purity and impurity in the Red Cow rite that it is worth considering that menstrual blood could be both a major agent of impurity and (symbolically or unconsciously) the prime purifying agent counteracting the severest impurity of all.

Milgrom does not mention this possibility (nor does any other writer[2]), but he takes pains to prove that *niddah* here can only mean 'purification' (a view taken also by NEB, which translates Num. 19:9, 11 as 'water of ritual purification'). His note on Lev. 12:2 reads: '*niddah* occurs twenty-nine times in Scripture and is capable of three meanings: (1) 'menstrual impurity' (here and chap. 15); (2) 'impurity in general; abomination' (e.g. 2 Chr. 29:5; cf v 16); and (3) 'lustration' (Num. 19:9, Zech. 13:1)'.

It is understandable that *niddah*, meaning 'menstruation', should be used occasionally as a metaphor for defilement in general; this does not reduce the possibility that it has its root meaning in our present passage, especially in the context of the Priestly Code, which deals for the most part with actual rather than metaphorical defilements. But what is the case for the assertion that *niddah* can mean 'lustration'?

The first example cited is Numbers 19:9, which is the very passage in question, so cannot be cited in evidence about itself. The other passage is Zechariah 13:1, where the translation 'lustration' is very doubtful. AV translates it as 'uncleanness',

---

[1] The exception is that Lev. 20:21 uses the word *niddah* to express disapproval (in relation to the prohibition against marrying the widow of one's brother). The word here seems to express something that is strongly disapproved of, without being totally forbidden (for the prediction, 'they will be childless' suggests a relationship that is allowed to continue). Perhaps here the word has reverted to its root meaning of 'separation' (as AV suggests), meaning that such a couple will be ostracized. As an expression simply of strong disgust, one would expect *zimah* or *to'ebah*.

[2] I discussed the possibility briefly in my article 'Neusner and the Red Cow' (1990).

and NEB renders 'impurity'. The word order of the verse aligns the word with another pejorative expression, 'sin', and it is implausible to align it with the earlier part of the verse referring to a 'fountain'. The evidence for *niddah* as 'lustration' is thus exiguous, as far as the Hebrew Bible is concerned.

On the other hand, one could argue (as does BDB) that *niddah* here means 'impurity' in general, and the phrase 'water of impurity' simply means 'water for removing impurity'. It seems very strange, however, that the impurity of corpse-impurity should be designated, in a general way, by the use of a term that has a very specific meaning in the system of impurity, namely menstruation-impurity. Such a term could have a general meaning in a general context (as in II Chron. 29:5), but not, surely, in a specific context.

It is interesting that here Milgrom is at one with rabbinic tradition, which also wishes to translate *niddah* here as 'lustration'. The medieval commentator Rashi makes some desperate lexicological efforts in this direction, relating the word to Lam. 3:53 and Zech. 1: 21 (Heb. 2:4). The motivation is clear: the purifying waters must be rescued from any association with impurity.[3]

Suppose, however, we abandon such efforts, and allow ourselves to consider seriously the possibility that the purifying water actually bears the designation 'water of menstruation'.[4] How can this be?

I suggest that this is an ancient designation, stemming from prehistoric times, which the authors of the Priestly Code transmitted without understanding it. It is a witness to an era when menstrual blood was regarded with awe and reverence as having healing and purifying power.

There is indeed evidence that this was once the case. From

---

[3] Another translation offered is 'water of separation' (AV). This goes back to the basic meaning of *niddah*, which indeed means literally 'separation'. But why should this purifying water be called 'water of separation'? If it means 'separation because of impurity', again why use this very specific term as a general one? If it means 'separation *from* impurity', this is indeed an extraordinary reversal of meaning in a word that normally signifies a serious impurity.

[4] That this was the accepted traditional designation of the Red Cow water is confirmed by the almost casual introduction of the term in Num. 31:23.

ancient literature and from modern anthropological research, we can gather evidence of positive valuations of menstrual blood (alongside the more obvious negative valuations). For example, it was believed that the body of a child was formed out of menstrual blood, and that in another transformation it became the milk with which the child was suckled.[5] Such opinions could only produce feelings of awe towards this amazing substance on which all human life depended. That the same substance, when expelled from the female body without having accomplished its beneficent magic, should be regarded as defiling and dangerous, is hardly surprising, since it could never give rise to merely neutral feelings. Having such power for good, it must also have enormous power for evil when diverted from its proper purpose.

The surprising appearance of the expression *mei niddah*, water of menstruation, puts the Red Cow outside the confines of the priestly system of purity. It suggests we are dealing here, not just with a sacrificial animal, but with an incarnation of the Goddess, powerful for both good and evil. The goddess Isis-Hathor in Egypt was a cow-goddess, often portrayed with a cow's head. Her appearance with her child Horus in a cow-byre was the inspiration of the Gospel story of Jesus' birth in a manger. In India, the cow was the holy animal who embodied the feminine principle, immune from normal slaughter for food, yet the most potent of sacrifices, whose death had cosmic significance.

The Red Cow is a virgin. This too is redolent with mythic significance. The text tells us simply that the Red Cow must be one that has never borne the yoke (19:1), but the Mishnah correctly expands the euphemism to mean that she has never been covered by the male (M. Parah 2:4).[6] In the case of the

[5] 'According to the primitive view, the embryo is built up from the blood, which, as the cessation of menstruation indicates, does not flow outward in the period of pregnancy' (Neumann, 1972, p. 31. See also Briffault, 1927, vol. II, p. 444). Studying Trobriand islanders, Mark S. Mosko observes, ' ... spirit children travel to the Trobriands, enter the bodies and wombs of women of the same matrilineage *dala*, and combine with their menstrual blood (*buyai*) to conceive foetuses ... Human mothers thus contribute two components to their children in conception: substantial menstrual blood, and insubstantial spirit' (Mosko, 1995).

[6] This is the majority opinion; but Rabbi Judah thinks that the Cow is invalidated only

executed heifer (Deut. 21), whose features imitate the Red Cow, the expression is given more fully as one 'that has never been put to work or worn a yoke', and NEB correctly renders 'or mated', instead of the literal 'or put to work'.

As Erich Neumann has pointed out (1972, p. 267), the significance of virginity in primitive myth is not childless purity, but on the contrary female fecundity owing nothing to the male. In varieties of religion where the female was supreme, the male being overwhelmed and overawed by the female mysteries of procreation, sexual intercourse was not regarded (or perhaps deliberately ignored) as necessary for childbirth. Just as the female was subject to periodic mysterious bleeding owing nothing to the male and everything to the phases of the divine Moon, so she periodically went into the paroxysm of childbirth. These processes were conducted away from male eyes in the female compound, which only later took on an aspect of servitude, isolation and impurity. The word *niddah* undoubtedly means 'separation', but separation is a double-edged concept, as can be seen even in the word *qodesh* ('holiness'), which can have negative as well as positive connotations (compare also the ambivalence of the word *badad*, 'alone').

The total redness of the Red Cow has been interpreted by many commentators as symbolic of blood, but the expression *mei niddah* tells us what kind of blood. The colour red is multivalent: it can signify violence and death, when the emphasis is on blood-shedding, but also fertility and life when the main positive significance of blood is held in mind. Merely to use the actual blood of the Red Cow as a detergent would be insufficient. What is needed is a substance that contains the essence of the Cow in its femaleness and this is obtained by burning the Cow whole and mixing its ashes with 'living water', i.e. the active moisture of the Earth itself. The resultant mixture is menstrual blood not in its impure manifestation outside the body, but in its magical state within the female body, when it

if she is deliberately mated by her owner. He thus takes a more literal view of the requirement that the Cow must not be worked. Rabbi Eliezer allows even a pregnant Cow, on the ground that the embryo is part of the mother's body. These are theoretical views, while that of the majority is traditional.

works to form the child in the womb, and the milk in the breasts. Only a few drops of blood are drawn from the slaughtered Cow to sprinkle in the direction of the Temple – a gesture of reverence to the God of Israel. But all the rest of the blood that is retained in the body is identified with the special female blood found in no male, animal or human.[7]

The location of the rite is also significant. The whole rite takes place outside the Temple, even including the act of sacrifice. This makes it unique in the sacrificial system of Scripture, for the heifer of Deut. 21 is not really sacrificed but executed, and the other outside rite, that of the Scapegoat, is not a sacrifice at all, even in the rabbinic version, in which the animal is killed but in non-sacrificial fashion. Here we have a full sacrifice that uniquely takes place outside the Temple, as if it belongs to a different cult. The burning of the sin-offering bulls outside cannot be likened to this, for they are sacrificed within the Temple, and the outside burning of the ordinary individual sin-offerings is a mere tidying-up operation.

A comparison with Greek religion is instructive.[8] Certain sacrifices were performed outside the temple, and these did indeed belong to a different cult. They were sacrifices to chthonic deities, who were regarded as belonging to an earlier era, before the invasion of the Dorians with their Olympic cult of sky-gods.[9] The outside sacrifices to earth-goddesses were wholly burnt. Yet there was also some measure of amalgamation of the two religions. The outside sacrifices served an essential purpose even for those who normally sacrificed in the temple. They were especially resorted to in times of plague or

[7] While fear of menstrual blood is manifest in many cultures, there is also much evidence of attitudes showing reverence for menstruation. For the Hua belief that the female body is superior to the male, see Meigs (1990), pp. 102–03: Hua men imitate menstruation and believe that they can become pregnant. 'Lelet men believe that women possess the most powerful form of love magic using their menstrual blood' (Eves, 1995). Chris Knight, studying Australian aborigines, argues that males co-opted female menstruation to develop their own source of power, which is the synchronous flow of their own blood through gashing their penises and arms to enact their collective solidarity and power (Knight, 1991).
[8] See Burkert (1985), pp. 199–203, 'Olympian and Chthonic'.
[9] This historical pattern, however, is questioned by Burkert, who sees an opposition between sky-gods and earth-gods in all ancient religion, though different cultures placed their emphasis differently (Burkert, 1985, p. 201).

famine. The earth-goddesses and gods were primitive and irrational, and in times of prosperity and ease were little regarded. But when things went wrong, they had to be appeased.

The earth-goddess Demeter was worshipped by a procession and a cow-sacrifice in a festival known as Chthonia. 'In the mysteries the corn-giving goddess makes death lose its terror' (Burkert). The earth-deities were particularly concerned with death, for they evolved out of a cult of the dead. Whereas the sky-deities were immortal and remote from all consideration of death, the earth-deities represent the cycle of birth and death, and particularly the overcoming of death by rebirth. The sky-gods do not offer any hope of immortality to mankind, whom they require to accept their mortal status. It is from the earth-deities that the hope of immortality, or salvation, arises for mankind, who can participate in the deaths and resurrections of the deities themselves.

The Red Cow is the last vestige in the religion of the Israelite Sky-God of the earth-goddess. She is retained to cope with the impurity of death, which the Sky-God himself disdains to handle or approach. In the person of the Red Cow, the goddess gives herself to death, and overcomes it by being transmuted into a substance, the *mei niddah*, that is sovereign against death-impurity. There is here a kind of resurrection. The Red Cow, among its other claims to uniqueness, is the only sacrifice in Israelite religion which survives its death and is preserved, though in changed form. All the other sacrifices, on the contrary, are not allowed survival, and are subject to the law of *notar*, by which they must be destroyed by burning after their time of sacrifice or eating has elapsed (Exodus 12:10, 29:34, Lev. 7:17). The burning of the Red Cow, on the other hand, is not a destruction but a preservation, not unlike, in intention, the Egyptian mummification of the dead.

The sprinkling of the corpse-impure with the Red Cow 'blood' should therefore be compared with the lustrations of the mystery-cults, such as the *taurobolium* of the Attis cult, and the baptism of Christianity. These ceremonies were indeed baptisms of blood, literally in the case of Attis worship, and metaphorically in the case of Christian baptism ('washed with the blood of the lamb'). The ritual pool of Judaism had no such symbolism of blood and rebirth; it was merely a means of cleansing, leaving the person undergoing immersion as mortal as before.

With these considerations in mind, we may turn to a famous anecdote about Rabban Johanan ben Zakkai and find new meaning in it.

A heathen asked Rabban Johanan ben Zakkai, saying: The things you Jews do appear to be a kind of sorcery. A heifer is brought, it is burned, is pounded to ashes, and its ashes are gathered up. Then when one of you gets defiled by contact with a corpse, two or three drops of the ashes' mixture are sprinkled upon him, and he is told, 'You are cleansed!'

Rabban Johanan asked the heathen: 'Has the spirit of madness ever possessed you?' He replied: 'No.' 'Have you ever seen a man whom the spirit of madness has possessed?' The heathen replied: 'Yes.' 'And have you not seen what was done to the man?' The heathen replied: 'Roots are brought, they are made to smoke under him, water is splashed upon him, until the spirit flees.'

Rabban Johanan then said: 'Do not your ears hear what your mouth is saying? A man defiled is like a man possessed of a spirit. This spirit is a spirit of uncleanness, and Scripture says, *And I will cause the prophets of the spirits of uncleanness to pass out of the land* (Zech. 13:2).'

Now when the heathen left, Rabban Johanan's disciples said: 'Our master, you thrust off that heathen with a mere reed of an answer, but what reply will you give us?'

Rabban Johanan answered: 'No matter how it appears, the corpse does not defile, nor does the mixture of ash and water cleanse. The truth is that the rite of the Red Cow is a decree of the Lord. The Holy One, blessed be He, said: 'I have set down a statute, I have issued a decree. Thou art not permitted to transgress My decree.' (Pesiqta Rabbati, 14:14, tr. William G. Braude: see also Pesiqta Rab Kahana 4:7)

Rabban Johanan's answer to the heathen tries to rescue the Red Cow rite from the charge of sorcery (forbidden in Jewish law) and to bring it into the category of normal medical or psychotherapeutic practice. But this answer is regarded by his disciples as inadequate and reductionist. He therefore gives another answer: that there is really no answer. The law has been given by God, and we have to obey it even though we do not understand it. He even seems to be saying that there is no real impurity or cleansing involved: 'The corpse does not defile, nor does the mixture of ash and water cleanse.' This, if taken literally, would be an extreme of scepticism and formalism: the ritual is meaningless, but must be gone through as a mere act of obedience to God's decree. But Milgrom is probably right in explaining that what is meant is that the corpse does not defile in itself, but only by God's decree: there is defilement, but not by the intrinsic qualities of the corpse. Even this is a considerable intellectualization; a removal from the world of actual defilement which would have to apply not just to corpse defilement, but to the whole purity system. Indeed, this intellectualization is characteristic of the whole rabbinic treatment of impurity. It has often been remarked that in the rabbinic literature, there is no sign of disgust or fear at any of the impurities so objectively analysed. The atmosphere is like that of a medical textbook.

Nevertheless, the charge of sorcery was one which the rabbinic tradents (whether or not the story has been correctly attributed to Rabban Johanan ben Zakkai[10]) felt had to be faced. They evidently felt that there was something primitive about the Red Cow rite, and that it had something in common with procedures of sorcery. The aim of sorcery was to contact and make use of unclean powers of the earth; so that sorcerers were actually late and disreputable practitioners of an early form of religion. The biblical prohibition against sorcery did not imply disbelief in demonic or chthonic powers; indeed such powers are even confirmed in stories such as that of the witch of Endor. But they were excluded from the official religion of Israel far more strictly than from the Olympian religion of Greece.

Yet not entirely excluded: for the Red Cow rite represents a last, if much muted, appearance of the earth-goddess. The earth-deities were too emotionally powerful to be totally abolished. Their rites survive in much modified form, marked by

---

[10] The earliest source of the story dates from the fifth century CE, whereas Rabban Johanan ben Zakkai lived in the first century.

the indicator of impurity for participants. But since these rites had been conscripted into the worship of the Sky God, they could not be marked by impurity alone, but had to be endowed with a measure of purity too. This accounts for the mixture of impurity and purity that characterizes these transitional rites. Indeed, in the case of both the Red Cow and the Scapegoat, their main means for survival was to take a role in the purity system. Instead of bringing salvation from death and initiating their devotees into immortality, they brought the much lesser salvation of freedom from impurity. The sky-gods of Greece had no interest in procuring immortality for their earthly worshippers, who were required to know their place and not to indulge in the *hubris* of immortal longings. In return, the gods undertook to care for the earthly needs of their worshippers by ensuring good harvests and giving them good laws. Those not satisfied with this lowly status could turn to the earth-deities and their mysteries.

By abolishing the earth-deities so completely, Israelite religion upset the balance found in Greek religion. The banishment of the earth-deities set up mortals as lords of the earth. A cosmic status was awarded to humanity itself, as performing a role in the plan of the One Sky-God. By giving up all hope of being eventually transformed into gods, humanity could pursue a human programme. It was accepted that 'the heavens are the Lord's, and the earth he has given to the children of Adam'. It was also accepted that 'the dead cannot praise the Lord, nor those who have descended into silence'. Instead of being alternately subservient to both the Sky-God and the Earth-Mother, humans embraced the Land as their possession, by permission of the Sky-God, who was the lord of everything.

The Earth-Mother could not be entirely effaced, but she was reduced to a relatively humble role as the Red Cow, whose female blood was the antidote to corpse-impurity. Though she brought purity, her pagan origins were indicated by an admixture of impurity in her rites. Her ministrations were brought under the scrutiny and legislative power of the Sky-God, who sought to dominate her magic and reduce it to rules. This process reached its apex in the dictum of Rabban Johanan ben

Zakkai, who wished to dissolve all the inherent mystery of the Red Cow and ascribe her efficacy entirely to the legislating will of the Sky-God.

Our study of both the Red Cow and the Scapegoat points to an ambiguity in the very concept of impurity. Sometimes (though not necessarily always) impurity is a sign of a previous holiness, or purity. On further enquiry, we find this ambiguity in the heart of Temple worship in the procedure of purification. Sometimes it is hard to say whether a washing procedure is intended to wash away impurity, lest it should contaminate, or to wash away holiness, lest it sanctify (see, for example, Exod. 29:37, 30:29, Lev. 6:11,20, Deut. 22:9, Ezek. 44:19, 46:20).[11] The rabbinic system reduces sanctification by contagion to a minimum, but cannot obliterate it altogether (see the excellent discussion in Milgrom, 1991, pp. 443–56).

Another point that emerges is one of general methodology. When a religious procedure appears in a document redacted in a particular period, it is a mistake to explain everything in the document entirely in terms of that particular period. The Hebrew Bible is the end-product of a long process of development and struggle. It has a particular viewpoint, certainly, belonging to the period of final redaction, but that viewpoint has had to cope with materials and problems deriving from earlier periods. A text is not only of its own time; it retains traces of earlier times and indications of the struggle to transcend them. I am sure that the authors of the Priestly Document did not consciously decide, 'Let us include the Red Cow despite its associations with goddess-worship.' Nor, I am sure, did they

---

[11] For a study of this ambiguity, see A. Baumgarten (1993). This author makes some acute remarks, but his study lacks a historical dimension, i.e. he does not consider the effect on the purity system of the incorporation of features derived from an earlier, suppressed form of religion. He thus fails to note the significance of the performance of certain rites outside the Temple, except to say, 'They need to be burned outside the camp because they are so sacred, and burning them in the normal manner would introduce a higher degree of holiness into the camp than can be tolerated.' If this is so, why not burn these remains inside the Temple grounds? He goes on to say, 'The man who incinerates them needs to cleanse himself in order to remove the high level of sanctity (not impurity) he has acquired in the process, a degree too high with which to live in normal realms.' But the text speaks plainly of impurity, not sanctity. While the ambiguity of purity and impurity needs to be acknowledged, they cannot be simply equated in this way.

understand the implications of the expression *mei niddah*, which they included out of deference to traditional vocabulary. But they did have the problem of how to present a rite of great antiquity and popular support in such a way as not to subvert the monotheistic revolution in which they were engaged. Some modern structuralist and anthropological approaches to biblical texts seem to adopt a deliberately superficial method, rather as if archaeologists were to refuse to investigate anything but the uppermost stratum. Fortunately, the best qualified investigators in the field, such as Jacob Milgrom, do not, in general, support such an approach.

CHAPTER 10

Leprosy

Those who would like to interpret the ritual purity system in medical terms find their best evidence in the impurity of leprosy. Here is an impurity which is definitely a disease. Of the other forms of impurity only the *zab* and the *zabah* are in an abnormal state of health. But their condition is not usually regarded as infectious, so procedures minimising contact with them do not seem to have a hygienic purpose. In the case of lepers, however, many societies have isolated them in the belief, however exaggerated, that they are dangerously infectious. Some have seen corpse-impurity as a hygienic measure. Especially in hot climates and places where infectious diseases are rife, it has been argued, there is danger in contact with a corpse. But contact with a corpse is not forbidden except to the priests. Others are actually encouraged to take part in the necessary work of preparing the corpse for burial. The impurity of the corpse is evidently part of the protection of the Temple from impurities, not the protection of people's health.

But how serious and how infectious is leprosy? It must be said at once that the skin affections described in Lev. 13 are not leprosy in the modern sense of the term (Hansen's disease). Indeed, the symptoms described belong not to one, but to many, skin affections, all of which were lumped together under the Hebrew term *tzara'at*: psoriasis, favus, vitiligo and others. The only reason why the term 'leprosy' was used to describe these ailments is a confusion (probably not perpetrated until the ninth century CE by John of Damascus) about the Greek word *lepra*, which is used both in Septuagint and NT. *Lepra* does not mean 'leprosy', for which the Greek term is *elephas* or *elephan-*

tiasis, but skin diseases of various kinds. It is probable that leprosy proper did not exist in the Middle East at the time when Leviticus was composed. Milgrom therefore jettisons the word 'leprosy' in relation to Leviticus, and uses the term 'scale disease', arguing that what is in common in all the skin diseases covered by *tzara'at* is the formation of scales on the skin, which, by falling off, give the impression that the body of the affected person is withering away.

It seems then that the 'leprosy' or *lepra* of Leviticus is not such a serious disease after all, and, unlike true leprosy, is not life-threatening. Nor is it infectious to any high degree (the infectiousness of true leprosy has also been much exaggerated). Nevertheless, *lepra* was much feared, and could blight a person's life. Some modern accounts by sufferers from psoriasis (John Updike, Denis Potter) show us the social and physical torments caused by such unsightly illness. The Bible too testifies to the horror aroused by it. When Miriam spoke against her brother Moses, she was afflicted by 'leprosy', and Aaron pleaded on her behalf, 'Let her not be as one dead, of whom the flesh is half consumed when he cometh out of his mother's womb' (Num. 12:12). This comparison between the 'leper' and the corpse is no doubt crucial for the place the former occupies in the ritual purity system. Even though, objectively, *lepra* is not a wasting-away disease like true leprosy or ebola, it gives the sufferer a deathly appearance, and this is enough to place him in the category of a living corpse. Many of the ritual purity features of the leper echo those of the corpse-impure, if not even of the corpse itself. Aaron's speech conjures up an even more horrifying comparison, to a dead child born with incomplete flesh. The 'leper' is one who is torn away from life in untimely fashion like a stillborn child.

Of all the impurities, 'leprosy' is the only one that is visible and frightening. This may be the reason why the 'leper' is banished from the camp, and also why he must cover his face and cry, 'Unclean, unclean.' This is not because of fear of infection. Many diseases were known to be far more infectious, but were not included in the ritual purity system. All the provisions in Lev. 13 concern matters of impurity and purifica-

tion, not of disease and cure. The priest is not at all concerned
with curing the disease, but only with preventing it from
spreading impurity to the Temple. When we do find concern
with healing, it is the province of the prophet (such as Elisha
and Naaman) not of the priest. When the prophet tells Naaman
to bathe in the Jordan, this is not a purification procedure
(which can take place only after healing has occurred) but a
miraculous cure. In any case, as the rabbis insisted, the purification procedures (which comprise far more than mere bathing)
apply only to Jews; non-Jews may suffer from 'leprosy' and
require healing, but they convey no impurity and require no
purification.

The outward humiliation and shame of 'leprosy' may
account for the fact that it is the only ritual impurity that is
regarded as a punishment for sin. This we see in Scripture in
the case of Miriam, but also in the case of Gehazi (II Kings
5:20–27), and of King Uzziah (II Chron. 26:16–19). Yet even in
Scripture it is not regarded as invariably the result of sin, for
Naaman is accused of no sin, and is indeed a highly sympathetic
character. In Lev. 13 itself there is no trace of this moralistic
approach. 'Leprosy' is just something that happens to people
(or cloth, or houses).

In the Bible, even where 'leprosy' is associated with sin, there
is no hint that this is an invariable connection. 'Leprosy', being
an unpleasant thing, is regarded as one of the modes of punishment available to God, like floods, famines and earthquakes. It
is included in the curses which describe the baleful results of
failing to observe the commandments of the Torah, but to say
that 'leprosy' can be a punishment is a very different thing from
saying that it is always a punishment. Thus there is little
justification from the Bible for the idea that compassion for
'lepers' was misplaced, since they were suffering what they
deserved.

The sins described as being punished by 'leprosy' were somewhat varied. In the case of Miriam, it is not quite clear whether
her offence is her criticism of Moses' treatment of his wife, or
her failure to give due reverence to his supreme prophetic role.
In rabbinic literature, the sin of Miriam is taken to be *lashon ha-*

r'a, or slander, and homiletic attempts are made to show some connection, linguistic or structural, between the offence of slander and the punishment of 'leprosy'. Here the rabbis depart widely from the scriptural data, which display no intrinsic connection between any particular sin and 'leprosy', but only an occasional use of a dreaded sanction, for offences as varied as Miriam's insubordination, Gehazi's greed, and Uzziah's presumption.

For the priestly authors of Lev. 13, however, 'leprosy' is not a matter of sin at all, but only of impurity which might threaten the sanctity of the Temple. Even the attitude of the rabbis, who connect 'leprosy' with the sin of slander, does not contradict the general rule that impurity is not sinful. For the moralistic approach of the rabbis is aetiological only; they are concerned with the cause of 'leprosy', not with its effects, which are considered non-moral, like other impurities. A person may have committed a sin (slander) and thus have been punished with 'leprosy', but the 'leprosy' itself was not sinful, but only an impurity. Thus in the Mishnah, the rabbis are able to consider the multiple laws of 'leprosy' in a very detached manner, like scientists analysing a physical phenomenon. Actually, even the rabbis do not consistently regard 'leprosy' as the result of the sin of slander, since they sometimes speak of it as the result of infection, as when they advise people not to place themselves in a position where the wind is blowing from the direction of a 'leper' (Lev. R. 16:3). One has the impression that the alleged connection with 'leprosy' is merely a peg on which to hang a number of homilies against slander, a deadly social evil.

In Leviticus, the non-moral nature of 'leprosy' is shown by the fact that it can affect fabrics and houses as well as humans. It is a kind of fungus that causes discoloration. Someone who enters a house that has contracted this fungus becomes unclean, but only for one day, so the impurity is not of the severest kind (for someone entering a 'tent' containing a corpse becomes unclean for seven days). Strangely, nothing is said about impurity caused by touching a human 'leper' – only that the 'leper' himself is banished from the camp. But the rabbis fill this

gap by analogy, arriving at the conclusion that someone touching a leper incurs a one-day uncleanness. They deduced also
that a 'leper' conveys uncleanness by carrying. These deduc-
tions are plausible, since it is hardly likely that a 'leper', unclean
enough to be excluded from the camp, would not convey
uncleanness by contact and carrying.

A rabbinic conclusion that is not so obvious, however, is that
a 'leper' conveys uncleanness to persons and objects under the
same roof, even without actual contact, just as a corpse does in
a 'tent'. Milgrom sees in this the reason why the 'leper' is
excluded from the camp, and he concurs wholeheartedly with
the rabbis in seeing this aspect as deducible from the scriptural
text itself. This is an arguable point, and the whole topic is so
complicated that I reserve it for separate treatment (see chapter
12).

The 'leper' himself does not have a fixed term of uncleanness,
since his purification depends on when or whether he becomes
cured. As long as he remains in the grip of his malady, he
remains unclean. In this he is similar to the *zab* and *zabah*, who
cannot hope for purification as long as their malady persists.
But once pronounced clean by the priest, after periodic examination, the 'leper' has a fixed period of seven days and a
purification procedure rivalling, in its complication, that of the
corpse-impure (see chapter 11).

Lev. 13, however, confines itself at first to defining the
symptoms of 'leprosy' and the role of the priest in examining
them. The different kinds of skin affections that come under the
term *tzara'at* are outlined.

As soon as a suspected case of 'leprosy' occurs, the priest has
to be called to diagnose it. What he looks for is whether the
discoloration is 'deeper than the skin', whether the hair within
the discoloration has turned white, and whether the affection is
spreading or static. He has to consider that the discoloration
may not be 'leprosy' at all, but merely a scab. A separate section
deals with sudden baldness, which if accompanied by discoloration of the bald patch, may be 'leprosy'. If the priest is doubtful,
he is required to delay the diagnosis by 'shutting up' the person
for seven days, and then, if things are unchanged, for a further

seven days, when, if spread has still not taken place, the person is to be declared clean, as suffering from a mere scab. Even so, if spread subsequently takes place, he must be pronounced unclean after all.

What is meant by 'shutting up' the suspected 'leper'? What is his status, in the ritual purity system, while he is 'shut up'? It seems that the suspected 'leper' was confined to his home, and that his ritual purity status was that of someone suffering a one-day uncleanness, for, even though pronounced clean, he must wash his clothes before becoming pure (v. 6). If retrospectively free from 'leprosy', why does he have to wash his clothes? This must be the effect of the suspicion itself, which is regarded as causing a lesser impurity. But why does he have to be confined to his quarters, a requirement not made even for the serious impurity of the *zab* and *zabah*? This must be because, if a diagnosis of 'leprosy' is eventually confirmed, he will have to be isolated 'outside the camp'; so, even while only under suspicion, his isolation or quarantine must commence, though in a less extreme form.

The role of the priest in all this is curious. Instead of being an official of the Temple, performing the sacrifices, he is called upon to be a diagnostician, for which purpose he must leave the Temple and make house-calls among the people. No diagnosis of 'leprosy' is valid unless it is made by a priest. Yet the priest is not brought into the diagnosis of any other complaints, even when they involve ritual impurity, as in the case of the *zab* and *zabah*. The role of the priest in diagnosing 'leprosy' seems to be a remnant of older practices, when the priest was a kind of shaman or witch-doctor, who was called in to apply magical remedies for disease. The priest in Judaism has no such role. The prophet occasionally acted as healing shaman, but also the services of the ordinary professional doctor were recognised (Exod. 21:19). In later years, even expertness in recognising the symptoms of 'leprosy' no longer belonged to the priest. The rabbis claimed the right of diagnosis for themselves, giving instructions to the priest, who was required only to say the words of confirmation or disconfirmation (though of course if the priest happened to be a rabbi too, he could perform the ceremony of diagnosis on his own).

One of the diagnostic rules is surprising: if the person examined is discoloured from head to foot he is declared clean (v. 12): 'it is all turned white, he is clean'. White is the colour of leprosy, as Scripture attests elsewhere (Exod. 4:6, Num. 12:9, II Kings 5:27), yet turning completely white exempts one from uncleanness! Various explanations have been given for this by medieval and modern commentators, but the rabbis regarded it as a paradox, inexplicable as the mysteries of the Red Cow. They take Scripture to mean that even if the person had previously been declared unclean, but his discoloration spreads to cover his whole body, he must then be declared to be clean (M. Negaim 8:1). But there is no need to see perverseness or mysticism here. Probably total whiteness was regarded as a disease of albinism that was distinct from the disease of 'leprosy'. Even though the patient had been previously declared unclean, the subsequent spread of the whiteness throughout the body had revealed him to be suffering from albinism, not 'leprosy'.

The expulsion of the 'leper' from the camp certainly shows the horror aroused by this disease, which altered the appearance of the sufferer so drastically. Only the 'leper' undergoes this degree of social exclusion. But what does this expulsion actually amount to? Does it mean that it was forbidden to others to come to the help of the 'lepers' by supplying them with food, shelter and clothing? Were they left entirely to their own devices? There is little evidence about this in the scriptural period (in the rabbinic period the isolation was not practised, and the 'lepers' were not sent out of towns or cities; see p. 146). Something may be gleaned from the incident of the lepers in II Kings 7. Here the lepers, in hunger, debate whether to enter the besieged city, which was in the grip of famine, or risk entering the war-camp of the Syrians, where they might be killed as enemies. They decide on the latter (which they find empty of soldiers and full of food), but they take for granted that they would not have been repelled from the city had they decided otherwise. Clearly, the needs of a starving person take precedence over the law of the exclusion of the leper, just as in later rabbinic theory.

Indeed, there is no reason to conclude from the leper's exclusion that others were forbidden to talk to him or supply his needs, as long as such social contacts took place outside the camp (which means, in times later than the wanderings in the wilderness, outside the city). After all, even physical contact with a 'leper' caused only a one-day uncleanness to the person contacting him, and this could easily be removed by washing in the ritual pool. The requirement that the 'leper' should 'dwell alone' (13:46) means that he must not share living-quarters, or (as the rabbis interpret it) meals, with anyone except other 'lepers', but this does not preclude contacts necessary to his survival.

The requirements of the 'leper' to tear his clothes, keep his head bare (Milgrom: 'dishevelled'), cover his upper lip and cry, 'Unclean, unclean!' (13:45) seem more related to expressing grief over his predicament than with avoiding human contacts. This ritualised grief is very similar to that prescribed for mourners.[1] Torn clothes, dishevelled hair and covered face are all characteristics of mourners (see Ezek. 24:17, 21 for the covered face). Even the cry of 'Unclean, unclean!' is interpreted by the rabbis as a cry of despair, rather than as a warning to others to avoid uncleanness or infection. 'He thereby informs others of his sorrow so that they can pray for him' (Sifra, ad loc., b. Niddah 66a). Other rabbinic passages, however, give the more obvious interpretation that the cry is a warning not to incur uncleanness from the sufferer (b. Mo'ed Qatan 5b). The question is, however, why this cry is not prescribed for others who are equally unclean, according to the table of impurities: the corpse-impure and the *zab* and *zabah*. The probable answer is that this cry is a survival from a more primitive period when the 'leper' was feared as the possessor of an evil spirit which could harm other people on whom the 'leper' breathed. This fear survived as a folk-belief even into Talmudic times: 'R. Yohanan said: It is prohibited to go four cubits to the east of

[1] See Feldman (1977), p. 39

a leper. R. Simeon b. Laqish said : Even a hundred cubits. They did not really differ: the one who said four cubits referred to a time when there is no wind blowing, whereas the one who said a hundred cubits referred to a time when the wind is blowing' (Midr. Lev. Rabbah 16:3).

There is a remarkable similarity, in social effects, between the ancient belief in demons of disease and modern belief in germs, bacilli and viruses. Both lead to socially sanctioned avoidance of the sufferer by others, and both can result in praiseworthy efforts by the sufferer himself to warn others of possible danger. This selfless attitude is given legal or ritualized shape in the requirement that the 'leper' should cry out giving warning of his condition. To reduce this to a cry of despair, or an entreaty for sympathy and prayer, shows an advance in the social status of the 'leper', and a reduction of his ostracism, but is also in some way a reduction of his moral status as one who, even in extremity, thinks of others.

The expulsion of the 'leper' from the camp and the requirement that he should live alone also indicate the fear that his condition arouses: his disease may attack those too close to him. The same fear is shown in the curses found in Middle Eastern culture threatening 'leprosy' to enemies or to those who break a treaty they have signed. Yet this fear is no longer active in the position of the 'leper' in the ritual purity system. He has been divested of horror by being considered only in the light of defilement, not substantive threat. Only in the narrative references to 'lepers' outside Leviticus do we see the plight of the 'leper' in a more personal, human frame of reference. Here we find 'leprosy' as a fate to be feared and bewept. At the same time, we see it as a punishment for sin, an aspect not mentioned in the priestly code.

A further objectification of 'leprosy' is effected in the priestly code by its treatment of 'leprosy' as occurring in buildings and fabrics. It is interesting that the first verse dealing with the 'leprous' house tells us that the 'leprosy' is put there by God: 'When ye be come into the land of Canaan, which I give to you for a possession, and I put the plague of leprosy in a house of the land of your possession . . .' (13:34). 'Leprosy' is put there by

God, not by demons. This implies that all the varieties of 'leprosy', not merely that of a house, are God-given. The phrase is gratuitous and insistent, as if the authors of the priestly code are struggling with the remnants of a demon-theory. The whole treatment of 'leprosy' has this atmosphere of struggling theories. Just as in the treatment of the Scapegoat we find a palpable vestige of demon-theory in the mention of Azazel, so in the treatment of 'leprosy' a matter-of-fact concept of impurity struggles with a tendency to relapse into primitive fear of dark, inexplicable forces.

In the treatment of fabrics and houses, we find an even more matter-of-fact approach, rather like that of a borough surveyor or municipal health authority. Concern is shown for avoiding precipitate measures that might result in undue loss to householders. If the malady has not spread too far, the destruction of only a limited part of the fabric will do. When the priest enters the suspected house, he is to tell the householder to take out his furniture in advance of the diagnosis (14:36), to avoid making it unclean.

Yet in the midst of all this practicality, an unrealistic, almost surrealist note is being struck. For if 'leprosy' is such a serious matter, how can it be bypassed in this way? Is there a real impurity, or does everything depend on the pronouncement of the priest? Removing furniture in advance of the priest's pronouncement surely does not clear the furniture of impurity if it has been situated in an environment that has now been pronounced to be 'leprous'. But no; if it is removed early enough, it escapes the 'leprosy'.

This anticipates even more non-realist interpretations of 'leprosy' by the rabbis. Since Scripture speaks only of houses in the Land (14:34), houses outside the Land do not come under the rules of 'leprosy' at all. Since the Torah is addressed to Jews, non-Jews cannot suffer from 'leprosy' – that is, if they show the symptoms described, they do not become unclean. We arrive, with regard to leprosy, at the same conclusion that was pronounced by Rabban Johanan ben Zakkai in relation to corpse-impurity: 'The corpse does not defile, nor does the Red Cow purify.' The whole topic of 'leprosy' becomes a system of arbitrary rules, having no relation to health or hygiene (whether defined in terms of demons or germs). We are experiencing here a phenomenon characteristic of Israelite and Jewish religion – emancipation from primitive fears through the elaboration of rules. The abolition of demonic powers and the award of all power to one source, God, meant that all diseases and impurities were sent by that source, who alone could say how one should deal with them, in relation to possible defilement of his Temple. Monotheism was in one way a leap into rationalism, since it abolished at one blow the propitiation and magical manipulation of multifarious supernatural powers; in another sense, however, monotheism did not prepare, as demon-worship and magic did, for the exploration and manipulation of nature by science.

Yet the system of 'leprosy', as we find it in Scripture, shows strong traces of its origin in primitive fear. More than any other form of impurity, it is treated from the standpoint of isolation. The impurity consequences of touching a 'leper' are not even mentioned, and have to be deduced by the rabbis. It is as if the isolation of the 'leper' is regarded as so complete that physical contact with him is hardly envisaged. But, with the rabbinic completions, the ritual-purity details may be outlined as follows.

The leper himself is a Father of Uncleanness. He must withdraw from the camp (city), and live and eat alone, or with other 'lepers'. He must undergo periodic examination by a priest, who pronounces his impurity, or (if he is cured) his resumption of purity.

Persons or vessels which touch him suffer a one-day uncleanness. Anyone who carries him or moves him (even without touching him) also suffers a one-day uncleanness.

A habitation in which the 'leper' lives, or into which he enters becomes unclean. All persons or vessels within it suffer a one-day uncleanness.

A house or garment that becomes affected by 'leprosy' may be pronounced only partly affected. In the case of a house the unclean part is removed outside the camp to an 'unclean place'. In the case of a garment, the unclean part is removed and burnt. If wholly affected, the house must be wholly removed, or the garment burnt.

Persons or vessels within a 'leprous' house suffer a one-day uncleanness, and wash their clothes. However, vessels may be removed before the priest's inspection.

The purification of the leper

The procedure for the purification of a 'leper' is described in Lev. 14:1–32. It rivals in complexity the procedure for the purification of the corpse-impure, which it resembles in some respects, though it contains nothing quite so startling as the Red Cow. In some respects, it is even similar to the ritual of the Scapegoat.

Once the 'leper' is declared clean by the priest, his purification begins the same day with a bird-sacrifice. Two birds are taken, one to be killed and the other to be set free (like the two goats of the Day of Atonement). But the sacrifice does not take place in the Temple, but outside the camp, where the 'leper' has been pronounced clean by the visiting priest (v. 3). Involved in the ceremony are cedarwood, hyssop and a thread of scarlet wool, ingredients also involved in the Red Cow ceremony. Running water is required, as in the case of the 'executed heifer'. Another feature, the shaving of the cured 'leper', recalls the procedure of the purification of the Nazirite who has become defiled (Num. 6:9).

One of the birds is killed, in an earthenware vessel over the running water. The living bird, together with the cedarwood, the scarlet thread and the hyssop are dipped into the blood of the sacrificed bird, and this blood is then sprinkled by the priest seven times over the cured 'leper', whom the priest now pronounces clean. The living bird is now let loose into the open field.

The cured leper now must undergo further cleansing. He washes his clothes, shaves off all his hair, and immerses himself in the ritual pool. After that, he may enter the camp, but is still not completely clean. He must still stay out of his house for seven days. On the seventh day, he shaves off all his hair again, and again washes his clothes and his body, and at last is completely clean.

But the rite has still not ended, for he must conclude it by a sacrifice on the eighth day. This takes place in the Temple. The sacrifice consists of three lambs (two male and one female), together with a meal offering and oil. The priest then takes some of the blood of the first animal sacrificed, which is called an *asham*, or 'trespass offering', and puts it on the right ear, thumb and big toe of the cured 'leper'. He then sprinkles oil with his finger seven times 'before the Lord', and then puts some of the oil on the right ear, thumb and big toe of the cured 'leper', and the rest on his head. The second sacrifice is called a *hatta't*, or 'sin-offering', and the third an *'olah*, or burnt-offering; then follows the meal offering. The priest is thus described as 'making atonement for him'. After the meal offering, we come at last to the pronouncement, ' . . . and he shall be clean' (v. 20). An addendum, however, tells us that if the person to be purified cannot afford three lambs, he can make do with one lamb and two birds, which will also serve as trespass offering, sin-offering and burnt-offering.

Throughout the purification sacrifice the emphasis is on 'atonement' for trespass and sin, and one wonders about this emphasis for a person who has contracted a distressing illness. This is no problem for the rabbis, who, on the whole, link 'leprosy' with various sins, especially that of slander. But Scripture itself does not make this link in general, and particularly not in Leviticus. Even where other scriptural texts show 'leprosy' as a punishment for some sin committed by some individual, this is not represented as an inevitable link; 'leprosy' may often be just a misfortune. Why then is Leviticus so insistent on the atoning character of the purification sacrifices of the 'leper'? The same question may be put (perhaps with even greater force) about the woman who must bring a 'sin-offering' after childbirth (Lev. 12:7), and about the *zab* (Lev. 8:15) and the *zabah* (Lev. 15:30).

The fact that the cured 'leper' brings a 'sin-offering' and also

a 'trespass offering' (*'asham*, normally brought to expiate sacrilege) fuels the rabbis' tendency to ascribe 'leprosy' to slander
and other sins. In the case of the parturient woman, one rabbi
was forced to the fanciful explanation that every woman, while
in the pain of childbirth, swears that she will never again have
intercourse with her husband, and the 'sin-offering' is an
expiation for this (Rabbi Eliezer, criticised, however, by Rabbi
Joseph, b. Niddah 31b). Other fanciful explanations are offered
for the sin-offering of the *zab* and *zabah*.

The fact is that the 'sin-offering' (*hatta't*) is more correctly
translated 'purification offering', as Milgrom proves abun-
dantly. It is therefore suitable for inclusion in a purification
ceremony for a severe impurity. Even when brought to expiate
a sin (transgression of a negative commandment), it is required
only when the transgression is unwitting. Its function, therefore, is not to wipe away sin, but to effect reconciliation
between the unwitting sinner and God (here Milgrom would
disagree, see p. 175). A gap has opened up between the unwitting sinner and God, not because he is guilty of actual sin, but
because by some unfortunate accident or negligence, he has
broken a commandment. This gap is closed by the *hatta't*, and
the closing of the gap is called *kippur* (atonement). There is no
such atonement for a deliberate sin, which must be annulled
by repentance and reparation, before it can be atoned. When
a severe impurity is suffered, another kind of gap opens up
between the sufferer and God, because the sufferer is excluded
from holy areas and foodstuffs. When eligible to return, he
must therefore first repair the gap by a reconciling offering. It
is like a gift offered to a king by a courtier returning from a
long journey.

The *'asham* of the cured leper is rather harder to account for,
since this offering is usually for the sin of sacrilege, i.e. wrong
usage of holy things. This offering is not made by the parturient,
zab or *zabah*. The explanation may be that this offering marks
the extra severity of the leper's impurity. He has been excluded
not only from holy areas, but even from his familiar surroundings. This extra offering is required to close a larger gap. The
third offering, the *'olah* (burnt-offering) has no connotation of

either sin or gap-closing, and it may be simply a thank-offering, to celebrate the return of the 'leper' to society.

An interesting point in the purification of the 'leper' is the use of shaving as a method of purification. This also occurs in other contexts: the purification of the Nazarite who has incurred impurity, and even in the dedication ceremony of the Levites. Yet in the legal code, shaving is forbidden to all Israelites and especially to priests (Lev. 19:27, 21:5). This prohibition is confined to the face and head, yet in the shaving of the 'leper', the head is certainly included, and this would appear to be a breach of the negative commandment. The simple answer is that shaving is normally prohibited precisely because it is prescribed specially for extraordinary purification. This is not an unusual move in the scriptural code. For example, it is forbidden to make the mixture of substances in the anointing oil and in the incense for normal use (Exod. 30:31–38). Similarly, the mixture of wool and linen is forbidden for normal use (Deut. 22:11) because it is specially prescribed for the garments of the priests and the hangings of the Temple. The Mishnah says that the shaving of the 'leper' must be performed with a razor, and no other implement is valid. This is precisely the implement that is forbidden for normal use in everyday shaving, a precept observed by Orthodox Jews to this day.

The main drama of the purification of the 'leper', however, is the picturesque ceremony of the two birds. Despite its drama, it has very little purifying effect, because the main burden of impurity remains to be removed by the subsequent ceremonies of shaving and immersion. This suggests that the bird-ceremony, as Milgrom argues, is a survival of a much older form of purification, retained to please the common folk, who clung to pagan ceremonies (Milgrom, 1991, p. 837–8). Milgrom also argues that the main features of the ceremony stem from a desire to banish the impurity afar. The impurity is transferred first to the sacrificed bird, and then (by blood-sprinkling) to the living bird, which is then released so that it can carry the impurity to some far-off land. This bird has to be a wild bird, for a tame one, such as a pigeon, might come back, bringing the impurity with it.

I agree about the primitiveness of the rite, which takes place, like the almost equally primitive rites of the Red Cow and the Scapegoat, outside the camp. I am inclined to disagree, however, about the purpose of the rite in terms of banishing impurity afar. The parallels which Milgrom adduces from other Middle Eastern cultures of the releasing of birds carrying impurities all relate to one bird, or if to more than one, all are released. The most dramatic feature of the two birds in the 'leprosy' rite is that one is sacrificed, and the other released. We should look for parallels to this double dramatic pattern, and mere examples of birds released to carry away pollution, or, more commonly, sickness, are not to the point.[1]

For parallels with a ceremony of two birds or animals, one sacrificed and the other released, one must look elsewhere. The most obvious parallel is in Scripture itself in the ceremony of the Scapegoat on the Day of Atonement. There are two goats, one of which is sacrificed, while the other is sent off alive to the desert. Are these simply two ways of doing the same thing? If sins are expiated by sacrifice, why send them off into the desert too? Scripture evidently feels the difficulty, for it provides an explanation in terms of division of labour. The sacrificed goat atones for the sins of pollution performed within the Temple (by priests and non-priestly sacrificers), while the live goat atones for the moral sins of the whole people. The question remains, why not two sacrificed goats? What is the significance of the two modes of expiation, combined into one striking ritual by the ceremony of drawing of lots? To draw lots as to which goat would be sacrificed, and which sent away to the desert, suggests that some important decision is being made. What does it matter which goat is chosen for sacrifice and which for banishment? In the case of the two birds, no lot-drawing is prescribed; but the ceremony of the Scapegoat may supply missing details, throwing light on both ceremonies.

---

[1] The parallels cited in Mesopotamian and Hittite rituals include a *Namburbi* ritual in which a male bird is released before the Sun god, Shamash, 'to the east'; in another similar ritual, an incantation is recited, 'May the evil of this bird cross over [the mountain]'. Sometimes a bird is only mentioned, not actually released: e.g. 'May my headache fly like a dove to the west' (Thompson 1971, p. 186).

Moreover, there are other features of the bird rite that require more explanation than commentators seem to acknowledge. The use of cedar, hyssop and scarlet thread, echoing their use in the Red Cow rite, invites enquiry into the meaning and poetry of this collocation of elements. The Scapegoat too involves a scarlet thread, though not cedar and hyssop. Why?

Is there a parallel to the rite of the Scapegoat in Mesopotamian ritual? Here again, the parallels that have been adduced are unsatisfactory. Milgrom cites the Babylonian New Year festival, when the priest wipes the sanctuary walls with the carcase of a ram, which is then thrown into the river. 'Thus the same animal that purges the temple impurities carries them off.' It is an innovation of the Hebrew priestly code, according to Milgrom, to separate the two functions (purging and carrying off) into two animals: this 'reveals how Israel transformed an ancient exorcism' (1991, p. 1042). 'Hence it can be inferred that the Azazel goat was originally a discrete elimination technique that was artificially attached to the sanctuary purgation in order to focus on Israel's moral failings rather than on the sins and impurities that polluted the sanctuary' (p. 1069). This explains the doubling of the goat as an artificial result of Israelite preoccupation with sin rather than, or in addition to, pollution; the unity of the rite is demolished. To be consistent, Milgrom ought to explain the doubling of the birds in the 'leprosy' purification in a similar way; but here there is no differentiation between the functions of the two birds; both equally serve the purpose of purification, so that one of them seems otiose. Surely an explanation would be preferable in which there is good reason, and the same reason, for the doubling of both birds and goats, and for their different roles, one to be sacrificed and the other to be banished.

The true parallel, as I suggested earlier, is not with Babylonian rites but with even older sacrificial ceremonies, which survive not in any priestly code, but in the form of myth. These are not animal, but human sacrifices. We find disguised references to them in the story of Cain and Abel, and (outside Israelite religion) in the stories of Osiris and Set, Baal and Mot, Romulus and Remus, Balder and Loki, and others. A human sacrifice is performed, but the community is unwilling to accept the guilt of performing the bloody deed, which is therefore transferred to a figure who, after performing the necessary deed, is banished to the wilderness alive.

A human sacrifice could serve many purposes. One type was the foundation sacrifice, when a young man, sometimes royal, was killed to act, after death, as tutelary deity of a new city or tribe. The story of Romulus and Remus is a disguised version of a sacrifice of this kind; disguised as the result of a quarrel, because later generations did not wish to admit that their ancestors had practised human sacrifice. The Cain and Abel story is another foundation myth; Cain, after his expiatory wanderings (similar to Romulus' banishment for purification) founds a city. Again, the sacrifice is disguised; this time as a murder. Other human sacrifices were aimed at averting disaster, such as a siege or a plague. Some aimed at procuring a good harvest, as in the story of Balder, betrayed by Loki. Some aimed at procuring salvation or immortality for initiates; these later took imitative, rather than actual form – the death of the salvation man-god was enacted by initiates. But the role of the dark betrayer or slayer was preserved even in these mystery rites – Set in the cult of Osiris, Judas in the cult of Jesus. For initiates had to be preserved from consciously expressing their desire for the death of the sacrifice; they mourned as if dismayed by the foul deed that brought salvation, and three days later greeted resurrection and salvation with incredulous joy. The performer of the foul deed could thus be disowned; sent off into the desert with a curse upon his head, though, because of the inestimable service he had performed for the tribe, he retained vestiges of honour, and in some versions was even received back into the tribe at a later date as leader, having purged his sin.

The Hebrew rite of the Scapegoat, sent off alive into the desert, having been chosen by lot for expulsion instead of death, has always captured the imagination of poets and artists, who have sensed here some profound secret of suffering. The poets and artists, I believe, have seen further than the scholars. The rite is indeed one of the deepest poignancy. The plight of the Scapegoat represents a very ancient and yet perennial mode of coping with guilt – not just the guilt attendant on sinning, but the guilt arising from our ways of expiating sin. Sin is expiated by sacrifice, in earlier times human sacrifice, but who will expiate the guilt of sacrifice itself? The answer is a ritual in which one victim sacrifices his life, while the other sacrifices his soul by taking upon himself the deed of blood which brings salvation to the tribe. He himself must not die, indeed must bear a charmed life, but is condemned to wandering, whereby he carries away the curse that would otherwise adhere to the tribe itself.

In Israelite sacrifice in general, sacrifice-guilt is absent, largely because of the validating myth of the aborted sacrifice of Isaac, by which human sacrifice was abolished and animal sacrifice substituted.[2] In Greek sacrifice, guilt was never absent, as was shown by what Burkert has called 'the comedy of innocence' (Burkert, 1983, p. 42), by which the sacrificer absolved himself of the guilt of murdering an innocent animal. This absolution was usually obtained by imputing some fault to the animal. In the Bouphonia ceremony at Athens, the sacrificial animal was tempted to eat holy grains from the altar; the sacrifice was thus interpreted as a punishment for the sacrilege committed by the animal. This was in addition to the better-known imputation of guilt to the sacrificial knife, which was put on trial, found guilty and thrown into the river. The trouble, however, with imputing guilt to the sacrificial animal is that this lessens the value of the sacrifice itself. The victim in every sacrifice should be perfect, and, if possible, willing. More effective, then, would be to impute blame to the sacrificer, whom the community can then disown (Maccoby, 1982).

The puzzling drama of the two goats can best be understood as a late version of a rite in which humans, not animals, were involved. Two human beings stand before the priest, who casts lots to decide which is to die and which is to perform the sacrifice. Even the choice of the Sacrificer is removed from the responsibility of the community and its representative, the

---

[2] Milgrom argues, however, in a brilliantly worked out theory (pp. 704–13), that the prohibition against ingestion of blood springs from guilt about the killing of animals for sacrifice and food.

priest, but removed into the domain of chance or fate. Thus one more 'distancing device' is brought into play, one which often plays a role in such rites; the victim died by accident. Having been chosen, the Sacrificer kills his victim. He then receives the curse of the community, and departs to the desert, where he must wander for the rest of his life. Like Cain, he may be given a talisman identifying him, so that noone will kill him.

The two birds of the leper purification repeat the theme. One is sacrificed, and the other is sent to fly away, but without the casting of lots. In the absence of the casting of lots, another device would be needed to supply the element of chance, fate or accident. This element is supplied, I suggest, by the combination of cedar, hyssop and scarlet thread.

Milgrom explains the cedar as a symbol for blood, since one variety of cedar has a red colour. There is no evidence in the text, however, that red cedar was essential for the rite. As for the hyssop, Milgrom explains that this was included simply because it was a useful instrument for sprinkling (as shown in the case of the Passover lamb, Exod. 12:22). The scarlet wool thread clearly symbolized blood, which is the colour of life and therefore of purification. More to the point, however, is the *contrast* between cedar and hyssop. Solomon, in his poems, 'spake of trees, from the cedar tree that is in Lebanon even unto the hyssop that springeth out of the wall' (1 Kings 4:33). The cedar and the hyssop are at the two extremes of the vegetable kingdom. To include them in one ceremony, together with a woollen thread representing the animal kingdom, is to summon the whole of nature to participate in the sacrifice.

Again one must turn to myth and legend for understanding. The Norse story of Balder, though remote from Middle Eastern influence shows the psychological process at work. When the god Balder dreamt of his imminent death, the goddess Frigg took an oath from all beings and substances on earth, animal, vegetable and mineral, that they would not harm Balder (prose Edda, *Gylfaginning*). They all gave this undertaking, so the gods now regarded Balder as invulnerable. But Frigg had made a mistake; she neglected to require an oath from the mistletoe, thinking it insignificant. This mistake brought about the death of Balder, through the machinations of Loki.

Strangely, a similar legend arose about Jesus. All the vegetable kingdom swore not to harm him, with the exception of the cabbage. For this reason his enemies, unable to use wood, were forced to crucify him on a giant cabbage stalk.[3]

These legends show nature refusing to cooperate in the human sacrifice so necessary for salvation. But they also reflect a possible scenario in which nature does cooperate and therefore participates in the blame. The complicity of all nature is secured in the sacrifice: all the universe is guilty, but not the community. In fleeing to the desert, the sacrificer becomes a creature of the wild, a part of nature; thus the sacrifice becomes a natural event, what we would call an 'accident'.[4] In the bird sacrifice of the leper, the live bird has to be a wild one. This is not just to ensure that it will not return, bringing back its burden of impurity (Milgrom). It is to make wild nature complicit in the sacrifice.

In two Israelite sacrifices, the leper purification and the Red Cow rite, the cedar and hyssop feature together with the scarlet thread. This reminiscence or trace of ancient human-sacrificial procedure remains attached to rites performed outside the Temple, and, in the case of the birds, retaining little connection with the Temple. The two greatest pollutions, the corpse and leprosy, still have the aura of fear of the demonic characteristic of pre-Israelite sacrifice. Only sacrifice could appease these fears; but only the cooption of nature or fate, and the removal of responsibility from the community through the services of a wild, disowned individual as sacrificer, could make such necessary violence supportable.

The purification of the 'leper' is one of those points in the

---

[3] This legend, found in the Jewish medieval compilation *Toledot Yeshu* is probably derived ultimately from a Christian source (see Krauss, 1902).

[4] This same desire to involve the natural world in responsibility for the sacrifice can be seen in the otherwise inexplicably naïve blame cast on the sacrificial knife, in the Bouphonia ceremony. In the sacrificial death of Neoptolemus, a man called Machaereus was said to have committed the 'murder' with a sacrificial knife. This is a complex of 'distancing devices'. The sacrifice is commuted into a murder, following a brawl, and the sacrificial knife is personified under the name Machaereus, the Greek for knife being *machaera*.

priestly code where primitive preoccupations characteristic of paganism survive vestigially, in tension with a new monotheism which is striving to banish both the fear of demons and the stirrings of guilt even within the holy.

CHAPTER 12

Corpse and leper: an excursus

Contamination at a distance through empty space is found in two similar modes in rabbinic law: in relation to a corpse, and in relation to a 'leper'.[1] In both cases, the presence of the source of impurity within an enclosed space causes the contents of the space to become unclean even when untouched by the source of impurity. There are, however, some intriguing differences between the impurity effects caused by a corpse in a 'tent' (*'ohel*) and those caused by a leper in a 'habitation' (*moshab*). Is it possible to see a rationale in these two contrasting patterns? In particular, why does the law of 'overshadowing', characteristic of corpse-impurity, have no place in the law of leper-impurity?

The law of overshadowing is different from the law of the tent. Overshadowing takes place in the open air (or within a solid block of stone, earth or other material), not in an enclosed space. Its meaning is that if a person or vessel is situated vertically above or below a corpse, or piece of a corpse, then that person or vessel becomes contaminated. This contamination has no spatial limit. It operates only vertically: anything situated to the side of the corpse, even if only a foot away, is unaffected.[2]

In a tent, or enclosed space, as we have seen, contamination affects even persons or objects not vertically above the corpse, provided that they are situated somewhere in the same enclosed area or tent, but the movement of contamination in an upward direction goes only as far as the ceiling of the tent. Thus the

[1] Contamination through empty space, on a smaller scale, also occurs in the case of a dead 'creeping thing' that falls into the space of an earthenware vessel (Lev. 11:33).
[2] See M. 'Ohalot 6:6, 7:1–2, 9:13,14,16, 10:6–7, 12:6–7, 15:1,3,7.

141

ceiling functions not only to spread the contamination to everything beneath it, but also to protect anything above it. Downwards, however, the floor of the tent does not protect. Anything situated below the corpse lying in the tent becomes contaminated if the earth below is uninterrupted by hollow spaces. If there is a hollow area, such as a cave, at some distance below the corpse, then this acts as a tent, and anything in the hollow area is protected from outside contamination by its roof.

In chapter 3, I discussed how these results were arrived at by exegesis of the biblical passage about the corpse in the tent (Numbers 19: 14–16). I disagreed with the judgment of Jacob Neusner, 'If we started with Scripture [on the tent] and asked what it taught, we should never, *never*, discover even the simplest datum of rabbinic law [on the ten].' On the contrary, I argued, rabbinic law on the tent (which Neusner has to agree was derived from the pre-rabbinic period) comprises an elegant if imaginative meditation on the relevant biblical verses.

In summary, the rabbinic doctrine starts with the question, 'Why do persons and objects within a tent containing a corpse become unclean even though they are not touching it?' The answer is that a corpse has a unique power of contaminating at a distance through empty space. The question then is, 'How strong is this power?' Is it merely strong enough to fill a tent? Or is this power so strong that it would continue unchecked in the absence of a tent? The answer given is that the power is indeed so strong that it would continue unchecked if not stopped by the tent. The tent is thus conceived as a device for containing and limiting an otherwise unstoppable power.

Thus overshadowing represents what happens to corpse-impurity if it is not limited by a tent. This power, though strong, does not operate in every direction: otherwise nothing would be protected from it, not even the Sanctuary. If unchecked, it operates infinitely in an up-and-down direction. If checked by the ceiling of a tent, it cannot travel upwards any more, but is deflected in such a way as to fill every part of the tent, and thus contaminate every person or object in it. Thus within a tent, the power spreads sideways as well as upwards; though the natural behaviour of the force, if unimpeded, is to act only in an up-and-down direction.

In the case of the 'leper', however, the enclosed space within which his impurity acts through empty space is not called a 'tent', but a 'habitation' (*moshab*). The habitation, just like the tent, is defined by its ceiling or roof, as is shown by the Mishnah passage: 'If a man unclean (from leprosy) stood beneath a tree and one that was clean passed by, he becomes unclean: if he that was clean stood beneath the tree and he that was unclean passed by, he remains clean; but if he [that was unclean] stood still the other becomes unclean' (M. Neg. 13:7). The impurity is transmitted simply through being under the same covering (the branches above), even if there are no walls. Yet there is also a difference. The leper, unlike the corpse, has to establish his 'dwelling' in the habitation by, so to speak, settling down in it. A fleeting passing presence is not enough for this.

Biblical text-proof for the contaminating power of a leper through space within a habitation is far weaker than for that of a corpse in a tent. There are no explicit verses about the leper assigning him this power, as there are about the corpse. The rabbinic view is derived from what seems a flimsy interpretation of the words, 'Outside the camp shall his habitation be' (Lev. 13:46): 'His habitation is unclean' (Sifra). This is interpreted to mean that not only does the leper spread contamination throughout his own habitation, but if he enters another's habitation, he causes it to be contaminated throughout, just as a corpse introduces impurity throughout any enclosed space into which it is carried. It would seem, then, that the enclosed-space-contamination of the leper is modelled on that of the corpse, and is a rabbinic development, perhaps based on the accepted idea that leprosy is a living death (see Numbers 12:12, Aaron's plea for Miriam).

Yet much can also be said to the contrary. Even if post-biblical, the leper's enclosed-space-contamination is pre-rabbinic, as evidenced by Josephus, who writes, ' ... and [Moses] declares that such as either touch them [lepers], or live under the same roof with them, should be esteemed unclean' (Contra Apionem, 1:281). Since Josephus thinks that this is a biblical precept, it must be at least already traditional in his time.

Moreover, it can be argued plausibly that this is in fact a biblical precept, despite the flimsiness of the rabbinic proof-text. Jacob Milgrom has argued this strongly, urging that the law that the leper must reside outside the camp cannot be understood on medical grounds but only on the basis that he conveys impurity to those who share habitation with him, unlike other conveyors of impurity, such as the *zab/zabah*. 'People might be under the same roof and be unaware of it and then enter the sanctuary or eat sacred food.' (Milgrom assumes here, quite correctly, that to incur or cause ritual impurity is not in itself a sin.)

Milgrom also claims (1991, p. 843) that Lev. 14:8b (' . . . and he shall dwell outside his tent for seven days', referring to the 'leper' in his days of purification) points to a danger of contamination of sacred food or objects, such as donations to the sanctuary, by 'overhang'. (He is actually not the first to offer this interpretation of this verse, see Joseph Melkman (Michman) in *EJ*, 'Leper'.) This verse is interpreted differently in the rabbinic sources, so here we have a case of modern scholars finding more biblical confirmation of a rabbinic law than the rabbis themselves were able to find.

To these arguments it may be added that the law of the leprous house has already created the idea that the empty space of a house can be full of leprous infection, just as the empty space of a tent can be full of corpse infection (see Lev. 14:46). If a clean person entering a leprous house can become unclean, it is not a surprising extension that a leprous person entering a clean house makes the contents of the house unclean.

It remains true, however, that there is no very explicit text to support the enclosed-space-contamination of a leper. It seems probable, therefore, that this very natural extension of biblical law arose in the Second Temple period and later became part of rabbinic law, too authoritative to be regarded as rabbinic, and therefore supported by a somewhat flimsy proof-text.

There was a strong incentive to make the leper similar in his mode of infection to the corpse, not only because of the scriptural analogy drawn between the two, but also because of the similarity between their modes of purification. The use of cedarwood, hyssop and scarlet, and sprinkling, occur in both rites and in no other cleansing procedure (Lev. 14:6–7 and Num. 19:6, 18).

Yet the legislators drew short of making the identification between corpse and leper too complete. One reason for this is that Scripture itself makes clear that corpse-impurity is far more virulent than leprosy-impurity. A person who touches a leper suffers uncleanness only until the evening, while a person who touches a corpse, or even a person or vessel that has touched a corpse, suffers a seven-day uncleanness (M. Kel. 1:4). The only respect in which leper-impurity is regarded more severely than corpse-impurity is the banishment of the leper from the camp. Actually, a corpse is treated with surprising leniency with regard to exclusion from holy zones. Unlike the other major categories of impurity, a corpse is not excluded from the Temple Mount, but only from the Temple area itself (b. Pes. 67b).

A person entering a tent in which lies a corpse is unclean for seven days, while a person entering a leprous house is unclean only until the evening. This marked difference in virulence had to be taken note of in the legislation about the leper's habitation. Leprosy-impurity could not be thought of as having the universe-wide up-and-down thrust (or 'cleaving') of corpse impurity. It was strong enough to affect persons or objects within a habitation, but outside a habitation it had no contaminating effect through empty space, but only by touching or carrying.[3]

We may gain information about the nature of leper-contamination in a habitation by considering two passages in the Mishnah. The first is the following:

If a leper enters a house every vessel therein becomes unclean, even to the height of the roof beams. R. Simeon says: Only to a height of four

---

[3] Actually this is the majority opinion: there is one opinion, that of R. Simeon, that leprosy also causes impurity through overshadowing, but to a limited extent. See Tosefta Neg. 7:3.

cubits. The vessels become unclean forthwith. R. Judah says: Only if he stayed time enough for to light a lamp. (M. Neg. 13:11)

It seems from this that a habitation, just like the corpse's tent, has to have a roof. Yet surprisingly, there is a difference of opinion as to whether the contamination within this volume of space reaches as far as the ceiling. R. Simeon thinks that anything above the height of four cubits, even though under the same roof as the 'leper', does not become contaminated. The plausible reason given for this by the commentators is that the area above four cubits (six feet) cannot be regarded as 'inhabited'. Since Scripture explicitly restricts the area of contamination to the leper's habitation, any area that cannot be regarded as inhabited (except by a giant) must be excluded. R. Simeon's view is a minority one and did not become halakhah. Yet it is most revealing, for it shows how weak the impulse of leper-contamination was considered to be. Even if (in accordance with the majority opinion) it reaches to the ceiling, it does so, as it were, with its last gasp, not, as in the case of a corpse in a tent, in a surge of upward motion which only the ceiling can restrain. Again the operation of leper-contamination is slow compared with that of corpse-contamination. A 'leper' entering a habitation does not contaminate it immediately, but only when he has stayed long enough to establish his presence as more than fleeting, at least according to R. Judah. Again, his view is a minority one, but its respectability underlines the far weaker force of leprosy as opposed to corpse-contamination. A corpse does not have to establish its credentials as a visitor. It does not inhabit its tent, as the 'leper' inhabits his habitation.

The second passage is the following:

When he enters a synagogue they must make for him a partition ten handbreadths high and four cubits wide. He must enter in first and come forth last. (M. Neg. 13:12).

It may be asked why a leper was allowed in a synagogue if he was banished to 'outside the camp'? The answer is that in rabbinic theory, the leper was excluded only from walled cities whose walls dated from the time of Joshua (M. Kelim 1:7 and Arak. 9:6). It is probable too (as Tosafot on b. Ber. 5b suggests) that since other laws concerning walled cities apply only when the Jubilee is in operation (b. Arakh. 29a), the law of exclusion of the leper too was obligatory only in the period when the Jubilee was observed. This would mean that, in majority rabbinic opinion at least, there were no cities from which lepers were excluded from the beginning of the Second Temple period onwards.

It may be asked further how the partition erected in the synagogue for the leper was supposed to work. How can this partitioned area be regarded as a habitation, since it has no roof, and its walls are too low? Surely the ceiling of the synagogue acts as a common ceiling both for the 'leper' and for the other congregants, placing them all in a common habitation, so that leprosy-impurity will be conveyed to all. Even if the partitioned area could be regarded somehow as a separate habitation, does not the Mishnah declare that a leper's habitation situated inside another habitation makes all under the larger roof unclean (M. Neg. 13:6, majority opinion)?

The simple answer is that a synagogue does not count as a house in rabbinic law (b. Yoma 11b). This is true also in relation to the law of *mezuzah* : a synagogue, not being inhabited by any individual, but by the whole community, does not come under the definition of a house for which a *mezuzah* is required. Similarly, a synagogue is not a house in a context of leprosy (e.g. it cannot become a leprous house). Consequently, a 'leper' may enter a synagogue without conveying impurity to the other congregants. Nevertheless, the duty of isolating the leper must be obeyed, so an area is partitioned off for him. In Geonic times, even this observance was abandoned, and lepers were allowed into synagogues freely (*Sha'arei Teshubah*, no. 176).

It may be asked further why the house into which a leper enters rendering all within unclean is not given the minute definition which is applied to the tent in which the corpse lies. What if the house consists of several rooms? Do they all combine to make one house, or is the leper's impurity confined to the room which he enters? In the case of the corpse, the answer is elaborated in terms of 'apertures' (*halonot*) of minimum size, communicating between one room or space and another, while no such theory is applied to the 'leper'. The reason is: a 'leper' is a whole human being, while a corpse may be a small portion of a corpse. A tent may be as small as a cubic handbreadth, while a house's minimum is four-cubits cubed, the space of human habitation. Consequently the discussions about a 'leper' in a house turn on what is the total definition of a house, and apertures are irrelevant. Discussions do develop about whether the upper room or the wings are included in the definition, but the abstract considerations of the tent and its apertures are irrelevant. This makes the law of the 'leper' entering a house much simpler than the law of a corpse situated in a tent, even though certain aspects of discussion remain in common (the question of objects inside containers within the contaminated space).

To sum up, the law of the 'leper' in a habitation does show some development in rabbinic times, but its main principles are pre-rabbinic, perhaps even biblical as Milgrom argues. As in the case of the law of the corpse in the tent, rabbinic law is not arbitrary, but proceeds on the basis of biblical exegesis deriving from the pre-rabbinic period. The law of the 'leper', though showing some striking similarities to that of the corpse, is far more lenient, because the legislators, despite their tendency to regard the 'leper' as similar to a corpse, never forgot that the 'leper' is in fact a living being, who may even be cured eventually of his disability, and whose power of contamination is biblically far less than that of a corpse.

CHAPTER 13

Ritual purity in the New Testament

There are a few overt references to ritual purity in the New Testament, but most of the ritual purity aspects which scholars have read into the text are non-existent. For example, there is no basis for the idea that Jesus' association with sinners and tax gatherers was opposed by the Pharisees on ritual purity grounds. The text does not say so, and it would not make sense to say so. The vast majority of Jews were not expected to be in a state of ritual purity except at festival times, when they entered the Temple area. Only a tiny minority of Jews, known as *haberim*, or Associates (see Appendix A), made a special undertaking to keep themselves in a state of ritual purity, as an exercise in piety and in order to perform the service to the community of separating the priestly dues (*terumah*) from the crop without causing them defilement.[1] It was not a sin to be in a state of ritual impurity: in fact, it was often a duty. Some of the most respected members of the Jewish community were members of burial societies, which, without pay, looked after the corpses of the dead and prepared them for burial. Such people dedicated themselves to impurity, just as the *haberim* dedicated themselves to purity, and with equal sense of service and general approval.

The sinners and tax gatherers with whom Jesus associated, with the aim of inducing them to repent, were real criminals, not just unwashed. The tax gatherers, for example, formed the Jewish part of the infamous Roman tax farming system. They were gangsters, working for the Roman tax farmers who had

---

[1] See the important article by Solomon J. Spiro, 'Who was the *haber*?', 1980.

bought the right to levy unlimited taxes. With the support of the Roman occupying forces, they extorted from the populace by violence and threats money and goods to the point of bankruptcy. Jesus hoped to bring even such desperate characters to repentance, but the Pharisees had legitimate doubts about this project. Jesus, however, was engaged in an apocalyptic messianic campaign, and such campaigns, in Jewish history, have always been accompanied by extraordinary efforts to induce repentance.

A passage in the Mishnah has misled some commentators into thinking that the tax gatherers were regarded as especially unclean. The passage says that if a householder returns home and finds his house has been rifled, he must consider whether this has been done by a burglar or by a tax gatherer. If by a burglar, he must consider all items visibly disturbed by the intruder to be unclean; if by a tax gatherer, he must consider all the contents of the house without exception to be unclean (M. Toh. 7:6). We are concerned here with a Jewish burglar and a Jewish tax gatherer; and the reason for the difference is simply that a tax gatherer touches everything. He is making an assessment for purposes of levying tax, and he is concerned with everything in the house; while the burglar is concerned only with items which he finds suitable and convenient to steal. It should be pointed out also that the Mishnah is talking about a householder who is a member of the *haberim,* and is therefore dedicated to ritual purity; an ordinary person would not have to care about whether the contents of his house have become wholly or partially unclean.

A New Testament passage into which ritual purity considerations have been wrongly imported is the story of the Good Samaritan. Many commentators have said that the reason why the priest and the Levite did not come to the rescue of the wounded man was that they were afraid of jeopardizing their ritual purity. If the wounded man were to die, they would come into contact with his corpse and incur corpse-impurity. This explanation is wrong on every possible count. Only a priest, not a Levite, is forbidden to incur corpse-impurity, and even he is not only permitted, but obliged, to lay aside his purity if in a situation where there is danger to human life. Even if the wounded man were dead, not just in danger, the priest would be obliged to handle his corpse in order to give it decent burial, a duty that far transcends ritual purity considerations.

Why then did the priest and the Levite fail to come to the aid of the wounded man? Simply because they were too lazy, or, more probably, too cowardly, to do so, the bandits who had robbed the man being still in the vicinity. The moral of the story is not about ritual purity but about love of one's neighbour. The priest and the Levite failed to fulfil the commandment to love their neighbour, whereas the Samaritan did fulfil it. The moral is that it is not rank or respectability that confer merit, but behaviour. The Samaritan, one of a community regarded with contempt as heretics, did what the priest and Levite failed to do. This is not an anti-Jewish story, but in fact belongs to a genre of Jewish stories found in rabbinic literature about good deeds performed by non-Jews. An example is the story about Damah ben Netinah (y. Pe'ah, 1:1), the Gentile of Ashkelon, whose respect for parents put the Jews to shame. This method of putting the Jews on their mettle by praising the good deeds of non-Jews is found in Scripture too (e.g. Malachi 1:11).

The text of the story of the Good Samaritan says nothing about ritual purity, yet commentators could not resist introducing it. The reason is a strong propensity, on the part of many Christian commentators, to overestimate the importance of ritual purity in Judaism and to portray Judaism as a religion of formalism and ritual, as opposed to the free operation of the spirit in Christianity.[2]

A determined attempt to introduce ritual purity considera-

---

[2] A typical example appeared in the Sunday Times, December 21, 1997. Karen Armstrong, a writer on religious topics, was reported to have said in an interview: 'Luke introduces the presence of shepherds who were regarded as outcasts and unclean because they did not observe kosher laws.' Shepherds and goatherds were, in fact, in bad reputation in the first and second centuries, not because they were more unclean than others, or because they ate forbidden foods, but because they grazed their flocks on crops, and were therefore regarded as robbers (b. Sanhedrin 25b). Impurity laws had nothing to do with this, and in any case people were not despised for being in a state of impurity. The most likely reason for the appearance of shepherds in Luke's story of the Nativity of Jesus is that they appeared in a very similar way in the Nativity of Mithras.

tions into a New Testament pericope is by a Jewish commentator, Jacob Neusner (1976). He argued that the saying of Jesus, 'First cleanse the inside . . . ' (Matthew 23:25–26) is related to a rabbinic purity law (contained in the Mishnah) which states that a cup or vessel, defiled on the outside, remains undefiled on the inside. This rabbinic law makes the inside of a cup primary: for a cup defiled on the inside is wholly impure, while if defiled on the outside it remains pure on the inside. So Jesus, Neusner argues, appears to be agreeing with the rabbis, for he too is saying (in a metaphorical context of hypocrisy) that the inside is more important than the outside. But this is a puzzle, Neusner urges, for why should Jesus be arguing against the Pharisees when he agrees with them? Neusner's solution is that the Pharisees of Jesus' day must have had a different doctrine about insides and outsides of cups from the Pharisees (or rabbis) who wrote the Mishnah. The Pharisees of Jesus' day must have thought outsides more important, while the rabbis of a later date had come round to Jesus' view that insides were more important. Neusner then goes into complicated textual arguments to show that we can deduce from the Mishnah itself that a change of view took place between Jewish authorities of the first and the second century on the subject of the ritual purity of the inside and outside of a cup.

This argument is totally confused. Jesus is not disputing with the Pharisees about which is more important in ritual purity contexts, insides or outsides. He is attacking hypocrisy, which may be defined as being different on the outside from what one is on the inside.[3] Hypocrisy lends itself to metaphors about things that look beautiful or clean on the outside but are dirty on the inside: for example, a whited sepulchre. When Jesus elsewhere likens hypocrites to whited sepulchres, he is not proposing any change in the laws or customs of burial. He is not saying, for example, 'Please discontinue this custom of covering

---

[3] A rabbinic expression about hypocrisy is that a person's 'inside should be like his outside' (*tokho ke-varo*); see b. Berakhot 28a, b. Yoma 72b. Metaphors for hypocrites are 'white pitchers full of ashes' (b. Ber. 28a), 'one who has no court, but makes a gateway for his court' (b. Yoma 28a), and many others. Jesus' attack on hypocrisy was a common rabbinic theme, and was couched in rabbinic terms.

graves with white paint because it gives an image of hypocrisy.'
Metaphors are not proposals for social or legal reform. They
use social facts, well known to the audience, in order to give a
vivid image. A cup that has been washed on the outside but is
still dirty on the inside is a vivid image of hypocrisy, and a
speaker who uses this image is not aiming at any programme
for the reform of cup-washing in the area of ritual purity.

Moreover, there are many good reasons to argue that Jesus is
not talking about ritual purity at all, but about ordinary cup-
washing such as takes place after a meal in order to ensure that
clean cups will be available for the next meal. The ritual law
about the inside and outside of a cup, to which Neusner refers,
is not about washing. Whether a cup has been totally defiled, or
defiled only on the outside, there is only one remedy, and that is
to wash the whole cup in the ritual pool. Ritual washing on the
outside only is totally unknown in biblical or rabbinic law. The
ritual law in question is about demarcation, not about washing.
It is a law to the effect that contaminated liquids touching a
vessel on the outside cause the outside, but not the inside, of the
vessel to become unclean. This means that the contents of the
vessel, if any, remain clean. But as for washing, no distinction
between inside and outside is ever made, and therefore Jesus,
talking in terms of washing, cannot have had any ritual purity
demarcation law in mind, but must have had in mind a context
in which there is an important distinction between washing the
outside only and washing the whole cup – namely the context of
ordinary kitchen cleanliness.

Further, there is good reason to suppose that in Jesus' time,
the ritual law that distinguishes between the inside and the
outside of a cup did not even exist. This law was enacted among
the Eighteen Decrees that were probably made in 66 CE
(b. Shabbat 13b and 14b). The only ritual purity law distinguishing between the inside and outside of a vessel that existed
in Jesus' time was the biblical law about earthenware vessels
(Lev. 11:53), but these had to be broken, not washed, if contaminated, so Jesus, talking in terms of washing, could not have
had them in mind. Anyway, an earthenware vessel cannot be
clean on the outside and unclean on the inside. If touched on

the outside by a source of impurity (even a corpse), it remains entirely clean; if touched on the inside by, say, a 'creeping thing', it becomes entirely unclean. Even an ordinary vessel (as envisaged by the Eighteen Decrees) can never be clean on the outside and unclean on the inside, only the reverse. So there is no ritual purity analogue to Jesus' metaphor of the cup with a clean outside and an unclean inside.[4]

All the complications of ritual purity which Neusner (and other commentators before him) have sought to introduce into Jesus' simple homily are irrelevant, and are examples of the tendency of New Testament scholars to import ritual purity considerations where the text is much better understood without them. Jesus was talking not about ritual purity but about ordinary cleanliness. Even in this, he was not doing anything original. Jewish culture was not obsessed with ritual purity to the point that it was unable to distinguish it from ordinary cleanliness.

For example, we are told that certain muddy pools were declared to be suitable for ritual purification, but, after bathing in them, people used to have an ordinary bath in 'drawn water' in order to achieve ordinary cleanliness (b. Shabbat 14a). This shows that ritual purity was not identical with cleanness; to be muddy did not rule out being ritually pure. The two conditions 'pure' (*tahor*) and 'clean' (*naqi*) were not confused in rabbinic law, even though, at times, ignorant people may have confused them.

Further, in the last resort, hygienic cleanliness has a higher place in rabbinic law than ritual purity, since concern for averting danger to health takes priority over ritual laws (*hamira sakanta me-isura*, 'danger carries more weight than prohibition', b. Hullin 10a, and frequently). This is not to say that rabbinic conceptions of hygiene coincide with those of modern science. The rabbis were concerned with possible harmful, poisonous substances inhering in foodstuffs, rather than with the dangers to health of mere dirt. When they did show concern about

---

[4] For further details see Maccoby (1982). An incompetent attempt to criticize this article was made by John C. Poirier in *Journal of Jewish Studies* (Poirier, 1996). See my rejoinder to this (Maccoby, 1997).

insalubriousness, their tendency was animistic (e.g. they thought that privies were haunted by evil spirits which could be exorcised by hand-washing after use of the privy). But they were also concerned about the avoidance of dirt itself from the standpoint of human dignity; it was important to have cleanly habits and to avoid disgust, because the human body was a temple, and was made in the image of God.[5]

New Testament passages about washing, therefore, should not be unthinkingly referred to the ritual purity system. They may be simply about washing, in the modern secular sense, though in rabbinic Judaism even this kind of washing had religious significance, not as part of the ritual purity system, but as promoting health or dignity. An example is the passage about the washing of hands, which has been regarded as unquestionably a matter of ritual purity. This instance is not quite so clear-cut as the matters discussed above. I would argue, however, that this too is not a matter of ritual purity, but of hygiene.

The incident, as described in Mark 7, is as follows:

1. Then came together unto him the Pharisees, and certain of the scribes, which came from Jerusalem.
2. And when they saw some of his disciples eat bread with defiled, that is to say, unwashen, hands, they found fault.
3. For the Pharisees, and all the Jews, except they wash their hands oft, eat not, holding the tradition of the elders.
4. And when they come from the market, except they wash, they eat not. And many other things there be, which they have received to hold, as the washing of cups, and pots, brasen vessels, and of tables.

The Mishnah also records that a certain rabbi, Eliezer ben Hanok, 'criticised the ritual cleansing of hands', and was therefore excommunicated (M. Eduyot 5:6). This, however, was in the second century CE. It is puzzling to find such criticism from Jesus in the first century, because it seems clear that the

---

[5] 'Once when Hillel the Elder left his disciples, they said to him, "Whither are you going?" He replied, "To do a pious deed." They said, "What may that be?" He said, "To take a bath." They said, "Is that a pious deed?" He said, "Yes, for if the man who is appointed to polish and wash the images of kings which are set up in the theatres and circuses receives his rations for doing so, and is even raised up to be regarded among the great ones of the kingdom, how much more is it obligatory on me to polish and wash my body, since I have been created in the divine image and likeness" ' (Lev. Rabbah, Behar, 34:3).

ritual washing of hands was not required for laymen by Pharisaic law in that period. Its institution is ascribed by the Talmud (b. Shab. 15a) to the time of the Eighteen Decrees (about 66 CE). The hygienic washing of hands, however, was part of all ancient etiquette, Jewish and non-Jewish (as well as of modern etiquette), and this can be found in Jewish sources at a date much earlier than the ritual washing prescribed in the Mishnah tractate *Yadayim*. It makes sense to describe this hygienic washing as 'a tradition of the elders'.

The similarity between Jesus and Eliezer ben Hanok on this issue is thus only apparent. The ritual washing of hands to which Eliezer ben Hanok objected was a late refinement of the ritual purity system by which a person's hands were held to be unclean even if his whole body was ritually clean. A special washing was thus prescribed for the hands only. There was no pretence that there was any scriptural authority for this washing. It was held that ritual hand-washing had been instituted for priests only and for *qodashim* (sacrifices) only by King Solomon, that this had been extended by Hillel and Shammai for *terumah* (priestly food from the crops), and that the Eighteen Decrees had extended it to laymen. The offence of Eliezer ben Hanok was thus not the flouting of an ancient tradition, but the rejection of a recent rabbinical ordinance which he regarded as unjustified and tiresome. That is why the disciplinary procedure of excommunication was thought appropriate.

Handwashing of a ritual kind, accompanied by a blessing, is performed by Jews before eating bread even today. This is undoubtedly a ritual washing, yet it cannot be said to be for the purpose of attaining ritual purity. For in the absence of the ashes of the Red Cow, all Jews are in a state of corpse-impurity. By the rules of ritual impurity, hand-washing would have no effect on this, or on any of the other kinds of impurity, in addition to corpse-impurity, to which a Jew is liable, and which, in Temple times, he would occasionally wash off by visiting the ritual pool. So present-day hand-washing before bread is merely a token performance, having no validity in the ritual purity system. It is what is called a 'remembrance of the

Temple' (*zekher la-Miqdash*), an exercise in piety in remembrance of times when ritual purity meant something.

Such token hand-washing must have been practised even in ancient times, after the destruction of the Temple and after the supply of Red Cow ashes gave out. The hand-washing described in Mishnah Yadayim, however, is not of this token kind; it is a real ritual purity washing (of rabbinical status), additional to the attainment of ritual purity in the biblical sense.

The hand-washing described in Mark, however, cannot have been either the rabbinic and supererogatory practice described in the Mishnah (instituted just before the destruction of the Temple) nor the token hand-washing practised at some period after the destruction of the Temple. Yet it is described as a 'tradition of the elders'. What kind of hand-washing was this?

I suggest it was a hygienic hand-washing, which was indeed a tradition of the elders in the sense of being a time-hallowed prescription of good manners and hygiene. Similarly today, hand-washing before meals is universal in decent society as both traditional etiquette and as a commonsense hygienic precaution.

The authors of the Gospels, however, may have not quite understood this. They observed Jews of their own day to perform a ritual hand-washing, and extrapolated this to Jesus' day. They then assimilated it (in an aside) to the washing of pots and pans. This latter indeed in Jesus' time might have been performed in the interests of ritual purity (though not necessarily, for washing of pots and pans might have been performed in order to render them free of leaven in preparation for Passover; or to render them free of particles of meat to make them usable for milk dishes). Luke even represents a Pharisee as complaining that Jesus (not the disciples as in Mark and Matthew) did not wash his whole body before eating (Luke 11:38).

It is most interesting, however, that the Gospel writers, despite their intention, have transmitted words of Jesus on the subject of hand-washing that put it into the realm of hygiene rather than of ritual purity (Mark 7):

15. There is nothing from without a man, that entering into him can defile him: but the things which come out of him, those are they that defile the man . . .

18 ... Do you not perceive that whatsoever thing from without entereth into the man, it cannot defile him;

19. Because it entereth not into his heart, but into the belly, and goeth out into the draught, purging all meats? [Thus he declared all foods clean: NEB, see also RV]

20. And he said, That which cometh out of the man, that defileth the man.

21. For from within, out of the heart of men, proceed evil thoughts, adulteries, fornications, murders,

22. Thefts, covetousness, wickedness, deceit, lasciviousness, an evil eye, blasphemy, pride, foolishness:

23. All these evil things come from within, and defile the man.

All this is irrelevant to questions of ritual impurity. Noone ever claimed that the purpose of ritual purity was to prevent impurities from entering the body. On the contrary, it was held that ritual impurity never penetrates beyond the surface of the body (see p. 59, on the problem of why a woman becomes unclean through an act of sexual intercourse). Even impurities incurred through eating forbidden food do not cause impurity to the interior of the body, only the exterior. So why is Jesus so concerned about whether the interior of the body may be defiled by eating with unclean hands? His answer is that any impurities that enter the body are expelled by the natural process of purgation. This is a physical process, which might indeed be efficacious in purging the body of harmful or poisonous substances, but is irrelevant for the purgation of impurity that never reaches the belly.

We must also consider what, in the ritual purity system, is the purpose of hand-washing before eating, or, for that matter, washing the whole body in the ritual pool. It is not in order to protect the body of the eater, but to avoid contaminating the food. This is clearly the case when the food is holy, i.e. *terumah* and *qodashim*. But it is also, though less obviously, the case when the food is not holy (*hullin*). Non-holy food of the Land of Israel was considered to have sufficient holiness to need protecting from defilement when the eater was a member of the Associates (*haberim*), whose whole undertaking, in fact, was worded 'to avoid defiling ordinary food'. Most people did not make this undertaking, and could therefore eat ordinary food while in a state of impurity. But the common practice, performed even by non-Associates, of washing the hands before ordinary meals was not only 'a remembrance of the Temple', but also a gesture of respect towards the practice of the Associates. In view of this, Jesus' remarks about hand-washing as intended to protect the body are totally irrelevant.

The answer must be that Jesus was not talking about ritual purity, with its concern for the protection of food from defilement. He was dealing with the possibility of harmful substances reaching the interior of the body. This might come about through eating with unwashed hands, which might have been busy with harmful substances such as germs, or their equivalent in ancient medical thinking. Such a concern was important in Pharisaic thinking, and is quite distinct from concern with ritual purity. And what Jesus is saying is that this Pharisaic fear of harmful substances is wrong, because the body is equipped by God with mechanisms for dealing with harmful substances by expelling them. In other words, Jesus was objecting to concern for hygiene, not to concern for ritual purity.

It was actually part of the thinking of one group of the Pharisees, the Hasidim, that concern for hygiene showed culpable lack of faith in the protection of God. The Hasidim, who included such figures as Hanina ben Dosa and Honi the Circlemaker, believed that it showed little faith to take thought for the morrow or to take precautions about dangers to health and life. Jesus' saying, 'Take therefore no thought for the morrow' (Matt. 6:34) is entirely in Hasidic style, and is paralleled by the saying of Eliezer ben Hyrcanus, 'He who has bread in his basket, but says, 'What shall I eat tomorrow?' belongs to those who lack faith' (b. Sotah 48b). That Jesus was a member of the Hasidic group of the Pharisees has been argued by more than one scholar.[6]

---

[6] For example, Vermes (1973). Vermes, however, makes the mistake of proposing that the Hasidim were in serious conflict with the mainstream ('legalistic') Pharisees. This, he argues, explains the Gospel conflict between Jesus and the Pharisees. The rabbinic evidence, however, is that, though there was some tension between mainstream Pharisees and the Hasidim, this never amounted to serious conflict. Vermes himself seems to have abandoned his theory in later writings, though without explicit acknowledgment of a change of view.

The anti-hygienic views of the Hasidim are shown, for example, in their refusal to accept the rabbinic dictum that liquids left uncovered in the open at night should be thrown away, because of the danger that a snake may have supped and left its venom (M. Terumot 8:4 and y. Ta'anit 23a). Hanina ben Dosa himself was bitten by a scorpion, while deep in prayer, but the scorpion it was that died. He carried the dead scorpion into the synagogue and said, 'This shows that it is not the scorpion that kills, but sin (b. Berakhot 33a).'[7] Mainstream Pharisees, however, while admiring the Hasidim for their faith and charismatic powers, did not recommend such behaviour for ordinary people, for whom they laid down sensible precautionary rules, applying their dictum: 'One should not rely on a miracle.' On the recommendation of Rabbi Eliezer to take no thought for the morrow, they commented drily 'Many tried to follow Rabbi Eliezer's example, but few succeeded.'

Jesus, then, was following a respected, though minority trend when he rejected the hygienic rule of hand-washing before meals. He thought that such rules showed lack of faith, especially at a period of history when God was about to intervene by inaugurating the messianic age. Jesus' reference to the process of bodily metabolism as guarding the body from ill effects from food shows that he cannot have been referring to ritual purity washings, which were never claimed to protect the body from physical damage. Jesus' reference, in particular, to the internal regions of the body take his discourse far away from ritual purity considerations, which concerned only the surface of the body.[8]

---

[7] Vermes (1973), p. 73–74, misinterprets this incident as showing indifference on the part of Hanina towards ritual impurity: ' ... he even went so far as to carry the unclean carcase of a snake' (p. 81). Even if the carcase of a scorpion or snake conveys uncleanness (very doubtful), there was no prohibition against touching it, only against subsequently entering holy areas without purification. Vermes gives other instances of alleged Hasidic indifference to ritual purity. One of them is that the Hasidim 'sneered at the Mishnaic rule forbidding the use of liquids kept in an uncovered vessel by night' (M. Ter. 8:4). But this was not a ritual purity rule at all, but a rule of hygiene. The Hasidim did oppose hygienic rules, but as for ritual purity laws, they not only did not despise them, but were meticulous about them far beyond average observance.

[8] Some difficulty was evidently felt even in ancient times about Jesus' remarks on the internal mechanisms of the body in an allegedly ritual purity context, for a note was added to the text (Mk. 7:19) saying that Jesus was here permitting all foods to be eaten

Modern commentators, belonging to a society which takes hygienic washings for granted, could not believe that Jesus was actually advocating unhygienic practices, and therefore assumed without question that Jesus was denouncing ritual purity. Yet we know that Jesus was not an opponent of ritual purity, for he is recorded as urging the leper, whom he had cured, to undergo the prescribed purification procedure (Mark 1:44: '... show thyself to the priest, and offer for thy cleansing those things which Moses commanded ...'). This is indeed one of the few genuine references to ritual purity in the New Testament, as opposed to the many spurious references that have been adduced.[9]

Apart from this, there are some interesting passages in the New Testament that are relevant to our theme.[10] Mary's visit to the Temple after the birth of Jesus was certainly an observance of ritual purity law, since 'the days of her purification' are mentioned (Luke 2:22), and also her sacrifice of two turtledoves (in accordance with Lev. 12:8). Yet Luke's story (not found in the other Gospels) shows some puzzling features. He says that Mary brought the infant Jesus with her 'to present him to the Lord, as it is written in the law of the Lord, Every male that openeth the womb shall be called holy to the Lord' (Luke 2:22–23). This is

(as correctly translated by RV and NEB). This switch from ritual purity to the topic of forbidden foods was not part of the original text, as all modern scholars agree, but it does show that later editors felt something wrong with the text as it stands, if interpreted as concerned with ritual purity.

[9] A recent instance of the genre is Poirier and Frankovic (1996). This article attempts to establish a ritual purity context for Paul's recommendation (1 Cor. 7:5–7) to spouses to refrain from sexual intercourse 'for a season' for purposes of prayer. The authors relate this to the Jewish requirement (in the rabbinic period) for ritual washing after intercourse before engaging in study or prayer. The authors also find relevance in the rabbinic view that Moses, after fulfilling the duty of propagation, abstained from intercourse altogether because his constant dialogue with God necessitated continual ritual purity. Nothing in the article, however, establishes that Paul had ritual purity considerations in mind. His recommendation was on grounds of mental and spiritual concentration, not purity. The rabbinic washing before study or prayer did not involve any cessation of sexual intercourse, since morning washing could be followed immediately by study or prayer. Paul does not adduce the example of Moses for his own celibacy, which he regards as a 'gift' and as spiritually valuable in itself; whereas Moses, in the rabbinic theory, did not value celibacy in itself, but regarded it as a necessity in a situation similar to continual attendance in the Temple.

[10] For an interesting treatment of the whole topic, see Booth (1986).

also said to be 'the custom of the law' (v. 27). However, there was no such law of bringing a new-born infant, even a first-born son, to the Temple at the time of the mother's purification. This aspect seems to be an invention of Luke's, designed to lead up to his picturesque story of Simeon.

The later Christian ceremony of the Churching of Women is based on both features of Luke's story. 'The prayers indicate that this blessing is intended solely for the benefit of the mother, and hence it is not necessary that she should bring the child with her, nevertheless, in many places the pious and edifying custom prevails of specially dedicating the child to God' (Catholic Encyclopaedia, 'Churching of Women'). The distinction made here between what is obligatory and what is optional seems to reflect awareness that Lev. 12 does not require the child to be brought to the Temple for purification, since the child acquires no impurity by being born. Of course, the ceremony of the Churching of Women is not concerned with purification itself, but only with thanksgiving, but it is based on Luke's story about Mary, which is an uneasy combination of two separate themes: the purification of a woman after childbirth, and the 'redemption' of the first-born son, which actually does not take place in the Temple (Exod. 13:13).[11]

The curing by Jesus of the woman with a running issue (Matt. 9:20–22 and parallels in Mark 5 and Luke 8) has given rise to some incorrect interpretations. The woman's affliction has ritual purity associations, for this is the condition of the *zabah*. But the Gospel story concerns the healing, not the purification, of a *zabah*, and no impurity or purification aspects are mentioned in the text. Some have sought to import such aspects by saying that Jesus showed his freedom from ritual purity observance by evincing no horror at being touched by a woman suffering from impurity; or that the secrecy with which the woman touched Jesus shows that she feared he would recoil from touching her. These exegeses show unawareness of the fact that ritual impurity, whether primary or secondary, was not

---

[11] There may be some influence too from the story of Hannah and her dedication of Samuel to the Temple service (1 Sam. 1:24–28). Samuel, however, had been weaned, and his dedication was a unique event, not 'the custom of the law'.

a sin, and that anyone handling a sick person for the purpose of bringing about a cure was regarded as engaged in a holy activity far outweighing any considerations of ritual purity.

A few other occurrences of purity require little comment. John 2:6 mentions that wine was kept in stone jars, to avoid impurity, since stone was insusceptible to impurity. Acts 21 mentions that Paul was required by James to show his loyalty to Judaism by defraying the expenses of Nazirites seeking purification, and by purifying himself before entering the Temple with them.

When one has discounted all the spurious efforts to find ritual purity in the New Testament, one is left with remarkably little. This provides evidence that first-century Judaism was not obsessed with ritual purity in the way often represented. Even when Jesus is shown reproving the Pharisees for their meticulous observance of minutiae of the law, neglecting 'the weightier matters of the law, judgment, mercy and faith', ritual purity is not mentioned: instead Jesus mentions 'tithe of mint and anise and cummin' (Matt. 23:23).

Ritual purity disappeared from Christianity under the formula (which took some time to achieve definition) that Christians were bound to keep the moral precepts of the Torah, but not the ritual ones. This is a formula that Jews had no quarrel with: for it had always been Jewish doctrine that non-Jews had no obligation to keep the ritual laws.

The practice of holy water in the Church cannot be traced to Judaism, because the sprinkling of holy water, sanctified by special blessings, was regarded as having miraculous effects. The water of the *miqveh* produced purification but was never blessed and had no miraculous power. The ritual pool had no exclusive power of purification, for immersion in a river or the sea would do. The Christian holy water can be traced to origins in pagan temples, not to Judaism.

Again, the Christian practice of baptism is not really of Jewish origin. A convert to Judaism did indeed have to undergo immersion. This was probably a rabbinic institution to remove a rabbinically ordained impurity imposed on Gentiles (see p. 10), or possibly a rite of inauguration. John the Baptist and

Jesus, prophesying the coming Messiah, did practise baptism, but not as it was later understood in Christianity, as a rite of salvation and assurance of immortality. They baptised Jews as a symbol of repentance in preparation for the coming messianic age, an earthly kingdom of freedom, peace and prosperity.[12] Christian baptism, on the other hand, as practised in Pauline Christianity, resembled the *taurobolium* of Attis-worship, an initiation into mystery and a symbolic death and rebirth into immortal life (Romans 6:4–5).

[12] This baptism functioned as a renewal of the Sinai covenant, which had been inaugurated by baptism (Exod. 19:10). Note also that the inauguration of the priests (Lev. 8:6) was marked by baptism, even though no previous impurity had been incurred.

CHAPTER 14

Milgrom on purity in the Bible

Jacob Milgrom, in his treatment of ritual purity (Milgrom, 1991), makes use of biblical, rabbinic and Near Eastern material with impressive control. His views on the relationship between the biblical and rabbinic systems, therefore, deserve close attention, especially as they have found wide acceptance and show signs of becoming an orthodoxy.

His overall view is almost the opposite of that of Jacob Neusner. While Neusner thinks that in the Bible ritual purity is required only in the proximity of holy foods and areas (Neusner, 1973, p. 65), Milgrom thinks that the Bible requires purity even outside holy areas, because the very existence of impurity (if unduly prolonged by failure to seek prompt purification) affects the Temple from a distance, causing it defilement. While Neusner thinks that rabbinic legislation extended the scope of ritual purity by requiring it in the home, Milgrom thinks that the effect of rabbinic legislation was to narrow the scope of ritual purity by confining it to the Temple.

The above statement of the views of Milgrom and Neusner is a useful first approximation, but requires some qualification. Milgrom does not think that every form of impurity is equally defiling: the milder forms (i.e. one-day impurities) do not defile the Temple (p. 1051); yet he argues that continued failure to correct them by immersion causes even the milder forms to acquire more virulence. Further, Milgrom does not deny that some observance of ritual purity in the home is found even in rabbinic legislation; but this is still practised in the interests of Temple purity (by preventing the transfer of impurity to priests and other people intending to enter the Temple); or, if this is not the case, it is supererogatory and practised only by specially dedicated people, not regarded as obligatory for the masses; or, in the case of purity observances that are widely practised, are only token or symbolic performances of no great moment. Similarly, Neusner does not deny that supererogatory ritual purity observance existed even in biblical legislation, especially in the law of the Nazirite.

While Milgrom is often able to demolish Neusner in discussion of both biblical and rabbinic legislation, his own views on the biblical theory of ritual purity are open to criticism. He seems to be in the grip of a compelling and picturesque construction which he elaborates in brilliant style, but for which, in the end, adequate evidence is lacking.

His most remarkable innovation is his theory that even the prohibitions of the Torah which are not concerned with matters of ritual purity (e.g. the prohibition against theft) carry an aspect of ritual defilement, for while they do not defile persons or vessels or foodstuffs, they defile the Sanctuary altar, which needs to be purified from these sins by the offering of the *hatta't*, or 'purification sacrifice'. Milgrom thus much extends the scope of the theme of defilement to include all prohibitions (but not positive injunctions, since no *hatta't* is prescribed for the neglect of these).

Both Milgrom and Neusner are agreed about one thing: that there is great lack of continuity between biblical and rabbinic legislation on ritual purity. The fact that they disagree so radically about the direction of the discontinuity – Milgrom opting for rabbinic liberalisation, while Neusner opts for rabbinic stringency and obsessionalism – points to the possibility that they are both wrong in opting for discontinuity. The possibility needs to be explored that the biblical and rabbinic systems of purity, while showing development, are, in general outline, continuous rather than discontinuous: that, ironically, Milgrom, the biblical specialist, is wrong about the Bible and right about the rabbis, while Neusner, the rabbinic specialist, is wrong about the rabbis, and, despite his many questionable interpretations, right about the Bible.

Milgrom's thesis is based on a plausible reading of certain

biblical verses, combined with comparative study of ancient Near Eastern religion. One biblical verse, for example, reads, 'Whosoever touches the dead body of any man that is dead, and does not purify himself, defiles the tabernacle of the Lord' (Numbers 19:13). This appears to mean that he has defiled the holy place by the mere fact of not taking the correct steps to become clean, whether he actually enters the holy place or not. The rabbinic understanding of the verse, however, is that he has defiled the holy place only if he enters it without purification. Milgrom takes the view that this rabbinic interpretation is a late rationalization of the biblical law, which is essentially non-rational, for it postulates a polluting substance emanating from the unpurified person by which the Temple is defiled from a distance. Yet Milgrom agrees that the existence of impurity does not *immediately* contaminate the Temple; this is caused only by the prolongation of impurity beyond the time allowed for undergoing purification. Thus Milgrom disagrees with those who have understood the verse ('whosoever touches ... defiles') to mean that impurity is itself sinful. He argues (quite correctly) that there is no biblical justification for such a view, since impurity arrives involuntarily as a result of unavoidable life-events (death of a relative, sexual intercourse, menstruation, etc.). Instead, he takes the view (more controversial) that *prolongation* of ritual impurity is sinful. Since prolongation occurs, however, only by human decision (or indecision), Milgrom has to conclude that the defilement of the Temple is never caused by non-human sources of impurity (corpses, carcases, or even bodily fluids such as semen or menstrual blood), but only by human beings who have failed to take the necessary steps to purify themselves after contact with these sources.

Milgrom reinforces this reading by comparative study. He points out that in Babylonian, Egyptian and Assyrian religion, the gods residing in the shrine are thought to be threatened by evil spirits which are given added power by ritual pollution. Acts of ablution and purification of polluted objects thus drive away the harmful spirits and protect the gods. In Israelite religion, he argues, this concept has been changed in accordance with monotheistic belief. Pollution no longer involves evil spirits, for God is omnipotent and cannot be harmed. Instead, pollution becomes a miasma that threatens not God but the Temple; if the Temple becomes irremediably polluted, God will no longer reside in it and will depart, with disastrous consequences to Israel. The pollution arises from human sin, so the need for purification arises only from human action, or (in the case of neglected impurity, human inaction). Humans have taken the place of evil spirits as the threat to the shrine. Since humans are imperfect, the shrine is continually being polluted, but God will remain in it as long as the pollution remains below a certain level. The purpose of the purification sacrifices (wrongly called 'sin-offerings') is not to cleanse or atone for humans (who have their own modes of purification and atonement, by ablutions and repentance) but to cleanse the Temple itself, the chief cleansing operation being the yearly Day of Purification (wrongly called 'Day of Atonement').

Before examining in detail the texts on which Milgrom bases his thesis, let us consider in general whether it is likely. Let us take first the question of delayed purification. Milgrom is saying that merely to remain in a state of impurity for any length of time is sinful in the biblical system. Having incurred impurity, a person is obliged to carry out the prescribed purification procedure at the first possible moment, or otherwise he will be guilty of the sin (according to Milgrom the greatest of all sins) of adding to the pollution of the Temple. If through some oversight he fails to carry out this procedure at the correct time, he must expiate this negligence by carrying out the necessary personal purification and then bringing a purification offering in the Temple in order to repair the harm he has done to the Temple by his delay.

According to this thesis, the observant Israelite must have been in a constant state of anxiety about ritual impurity. Every moment he remained in a state of ritual impurity had dire consequences for the whole Israelite community, since the accumulating miasma, increasing the contamination of the Temple, made more likely the departure of God from his protecting role. Since it was quite easy for a person to become ritually impure unawares (through contact with a dead creature, or walking over a grave, or even treading on the spittle of an unclean person), he would have to carry out purification rites every day just to be sure.

One may ask how the 'miasma' actually works. Milgrom is far from clear about this. He is certain that the miasma arises from human beings, not from the contaminating objects themselves. Thus the mere existence of dead rodents or even dead human beings does not cause any addition to the Temple's contamination, but once a human being has touched one of these contaminating objects, and failed to seek purification at the first opportunity, he becomes a suppurating source of miasma which flies through the air and attaches itself to the Temple like iron filings to a magnet.

People suffer from impurities for which they bear no blame because the impurity is itself an act of God, or an indispensable part of everyday experience. Often impurity arises from an act that is actually praiseworthy: for example, caring for the disposal of a corpse, or performing an act of marital intercourse. If we are to say that the impurity of a blameless person is not miasmic and has no deleterious effect on the Temple, but the same impurity becomes miasmic as soon as a person fails to take advantage of the first possible opportunity to remove it, then what we are really saying is that impurity itself has no effect, but only disobedience. It is not the impurity that is miasmic but the disobedience of failing to remove it at the proper time.

Indeed, the very term 'miasma' loses its meaning when one tries to visualise Milgrom's thesis in tangible terms. He wishes to preserve the idea of impurity as a kind of gas that swirls round the Temple contaminating its air. The gas arising from serious impurities, and from deliberate sins, penetrates further into the Temple interior than the gas arising from less serious impurities, and from unwitting sins. But if impurity is thought of in this way, it is hard to understand why impurity operates only when a sin of disobedience has occurred. Miasma makes sense in a context of real impurity, not in a context of mere obedience.

We need to develop a theory of ritual purity and impurity that makes a clear distinction between impurity and sin, and defines the conditions under which impurity can turn into sin. We need to know what exactly is meant by defiling the Temple, and what are the limits of this concept, as opposed to a theory in which every forbidden act without exception is defined in terms of defiling the Temple.

The great difference between the rabbinic interpretation of the Bible and Milgrom's is that the rabbis did not think of impurity as acting at a distance (except vertically, see pp. 7 and pp. 16–18). Impurity could be imparted by contact or close proximity. Thus it was an offence for a person in a state of impurity to enter the Temple (how far he might enter the Temple complex depended on the seriousness of the impurity). But it was not a contamination of the Temple to be in a state of impurity while at a distance from it. Consequently, there was no urgency in the matter of removing one's minor impurity. In the case of major impurities, there might be some urgency, but not because of distance-pollution of the Temple, but because of other considerations: a leper had to expedite his purification so that he might return to the community, and a pelvic discharger so that he (she) might resume normal intercourse; the corpse-impure, so as to avoid conveying impurity to priests. As far as minor (one-day) impurities were concerned, a person could go around in a state of impurity most of his or her life, only taking pains to achieve purity when engaging in some religious activity demanding total purity, such as entering the Temple to perform a sacrifice, or handling holy food.

On Milgrom's thesis, it is hard to see why it should be specially offensive to enter the Temple while in a state of impurity. Since impurity acts at a distance, it is just as offensive to be impure outside the Temple as in it. Yet there is no question that the Torah contains a special injunction not to enter the Temple while unclean (see Lev. 12:4). It is stated in II Chronicles 23:19 that Jehoiada set porters at the gates of the Temple to prevent anyone who was unclean, for whatever cause, from entering. What was the need for this, if the Temple was affected even by the uncleanness of people who did not set foot in it?

As for transgressions of the prohibitions of the Torah, the rabbinic view is that these have no defiling effect at all. They are moral lapses which must be repented in due measure whether they are deliberate or merely negligent. The offering of a *hatta't* ('sin-offering') is part of a process of 'atonement' or reconciliation with God, not a detergent for the altar, which does not need to be cleansed.

Milgrom acknowledges that the rabbinic system of impurity is a logical development of the biblical system. Since the Bible has eliminated the pagan rationale of impurity – the hostility of evil spirits – and made impurity reside only in humans, the logical next step was to eliminate the magical distance-operating miasma emanating from humans and make ritual purity laws a matter of legal observance. If there is no miasma, ritual impurity can only operate by close contact. Milgrom indeed suggests that this development precedes the rabbinic period by many years. The Bible itself, however, he contends, is still in the miasmic phase. However, it is not easy to see how miasma is an improvement on evil spirits, and it may even be thought worse. At least evil spirits have a personal aspect and can be confronted and defeated by both gods and humans. A miasma, on the other hand, is an impersonal force, resembling the impersonal Greek *ananke*, before which both gods and demons were helpless. Milgrom himself likens the miasma to electromagnetic forces. A miasma is thus hardly distinguishable from an evil spirit, except in being more inexorable. True, Milgrom conceives the miasma as not actually threatening God, but as, so to speak, disgusting him. He removes himself from the shrine not because he has been overcome by the miasma, but because he is offended by it. The result, however, is the same: God has been compelled to withdraw in the face of a non-moral, evil power.

Let us turn now to the texts which, according to Milgrom, make his interpretation inescapable. These texts may be grouped under the various propositions of Milgrom's thesis.

Proposition 1. *That to remain in a state of impurity is itself a sin.*

But if he wash them not, nor bathe his flesh; then he shall bear his iniquity. (Lev. 17:16)

COMMENT Here the rabbis interpret the verse as elliptical (omitting 'if he should enter the Temple or eat holy food'). Milgrom's case for the sinfulness of remaining unclean depends heavily on refusing to interpret such verses elliptically. But does he himself totally eschew elliptical interpretations? His treatment of the following verse suggests not:

Of their flesh shall ye not eat, and their carcase shall ye not touch; they are unclean to you. (Lev. 11:8)

This verse has often been quoted to prove that even to incur impurity is sinful (since it seems to make the touching of the carcase of a forbidden animal just as sinful as eating it). Milgrom, however, does not take this view. He asserts that the words 'and their carcase shall ye not touch' should not be interpreted literally (p. 653), adding '... touching the carcase of a quadruped is not subject to any penalties unless the purificatory ablutions are neglected'.[1] The question is, however, why Milgrom limits so severely this option of not taking verses quite literally. Other verses which appear to say that it is sinful to be, or remain, unclean, because this causes pollution to the Temple, may also be elliptical (omitting the clause, 'if you should happen to enter the Temple'), as the rabbis think.

Proposition 2. *That states of human impurity affect the Temple from a distance.*

And you shall separate the children of Israel from their impurity, so that they shall not die in their impurity by their contamination of my tabernacle which is in their midst. (Lev. 15:31)

COMMENT Milgrom remarks, 'The impurity can be incurred anywhere in the camp; it need not be brought into the sanctuary. If this verse refers to all the pericopes in chaps. 11–15, it includes not only the major impurities whose sacrificial requirements imply that the sanctuary has been polluted, but even the minor impurities, such as eating carcases (chap. 11), which,

---

[1] Milgrom also suggests, however, that this may be a prohibition without a penalty, a sort of 'fence' to the law. But even in rabbinic practice, laws enacted as a 'fence' were not without penalty, even though of a lower severity. This seems to be a rather desperate expedient, on Milgrom's part, to avoid saying 'This verse is elliptical', realising that such an admission may damage his case elsewhere, where he rejects rabbinic interpretations based on elliptical constructions.

however, turn into major impurities if their purification is neglected.' But all this depends on a questionable translation. *betame'am* can mean 'when (if) they contaminate', rather than 'by their contamination' (AV), or 'through their impurity' (Milgrom). If the meaning is conditional, Milgrom's theoretical edifice collapses. The verse is saying to the Israelites that they will die in their impurity *if* they contaminate the Tabernacle by entering it. This is how the rabbis understood the verse.

Whosoever toucheth the dead body of any man that is dead, and purifieth not himself, defileth the tabernacle of the Lord. (Numbers 19:13)

COMMENT Again, Milgrom takes the verse quite literally, not allowing for any ellipsis, such as 'if he should enter it'. But we may even grant, in this case, that there are grounds for the fear of defiling the Tabernacle even without entering it: by touching a priest, who then enters the Tabernacle, unaware of his defilement, or eats holy food. Such considerations do not require a theory of miasmic defilement of the Temple from afar.

But the man that shall be unclean, and shall not purify himself, that soul shall be cut off from among the congregation, because he hath defiled the sanctuary of the Lord. (Numbers 19:20)

COMMENT Again, a wholly literal reading yields Milgrom's result that failure to purify defiles the sanctuary even at a distance. But such a literal reading is not necessary. Again, this verse deals with corpse-impurity, so that even if speedy purification is being urged, this may be for reasons other than distance-defilement of the Temple; the concern may be for indirect defilement of the sanctuary through unwitting defilement of priests.

GENERAL COMMENT ON BIBLICAL ELLIPSIS

Milgrom stigmatizes elliptical interpretation as 'eisegesis', yet there are clear cases of elliptical expression in Scripture. For example, the passage on vows (Lev. 5:4) prescribes a 'graduated sin-offering' for someone who makes a vow and forgets it. But the passage omits what we might regard as an essential clause,

namely, 'if he breaks his vow'. On the face of it, we might think
that the graduated sin-offering is required by someone who
makes a vow whether he keeps it or not. This shows that the
biblical style actually permits the omission of such a clause. It is
taken for granted that a vow does not raise any problem unless
it is broken, so this does not need to be stated. This being so,
there can be no valid argument on grounds of eisegesis in the
matter of impurity either. Scripture states that expiation is
necessary if impurity occurs, but omits to add 'if the impure
person touches sancta'. The omission is merely parallel to a
similar omission in the case of vows. Actually, Milgrom himself
does not avoid 'eisegesis'. For example, he gives a great role to
delay as deciding whether a state of pollution is sinful or not, but
is not able to adduce a single text in which the concept of delay
is explicitly mentioned. In many verses in which the unwary
might think that impurity itself is being characterized as sinful,
Milgrom has to assume the ellipsis, 'if purification is delayed'. If
this ellipsis is allowed, why not the further ellipsis, 'if he enters
the sanctuary'?

I conclude that Milgrom's case is not proved, insofar as it is
based on verses that, taken literally, appear to attribute pollution of the Temple to impurities arising outside the Temple.
  Nevertheless, I concede that some explanation is required for
the apparently categorical and absolute tone of the verses cited
above. It seems to me that Milgrom's theory of miasmic defilement of the sanctuary began with contemplation of these verses,
and was then elaborated into a developmental theory covering
the history of ritual impurity, starting with Mesopotamian rites,
continuing with the diverse biblical systems of the Priestly Code
(P) and Holiness Code (H), and concluding with the rabbinic
system. Further, he found it necessary to include in his theory a
new and original conception of how the 'sin-offering', or as he
renames it, 'the purification offering' (*hatta't*), works, and this
new theory entails that not only delayed purification but even
moral sins cause defilement to the Temple. This is a remarkable
and comprehensive theory, which is in fact a great advance on
preceding theories, which postulated a considerably greater gap

between the biblical and rabbinic systems of purity. Milgrom is, in a way, showing continuity between biblical and rabbinic thought. He is denying that the rabbis had to overcome an earlier view that ritual impurity was sinful in itself; instead, he argues that, biblically, only *remaining* in a state of impurity longer than necessary was sinful. Yet the gap he leaves is still a huge one, and, to explain why remaining impure is sinful, he has to postulate that impurity, in some sense, was a miasma (though not a demonic one) that affected the sanctuary from afar. I shall be offering, however, in the next chapter, an alternative theory which accepts (on one redactional level of the text) a biblical imperative to seek purification as soon as possible, but without involving the unlikely idea of a miasma created not by demonic influence but by human disobedience.

Proposition 3. *That the purpose of the 'purification offering' (hatta't) is to cleanse the Temple, not to atone for the offerer.*

And he slew it; and Moses took the blood, and put it upon the horns of the altar round about with his finger, and purified [*vayehatt'e*] the altar, and poured the blood at the bottom of the altar, and sanctified it, to make reconciliation upon it [*lekhaper 'alav*].' (Lev. 8:15)

And he shall make an atonement for the holy place [Milgrom: he shall purge the adytum], because of the uncleanness of the children of Israel, and because of their transgressions in all their sins: and so shall he do for the tabernacle of the congregation, that remaineth among them in the midst of their uncleanness. (Lev. 16:16)

Much of the weight of Milgrom's argument lies in his third proposition. For if it is true that the purpose of the so-called 'sin offering' is not to atone for the sin of the offerer, but to cleanse away the pollution which his offence has created in the Temple, and which still remains there even after the sin has been purged by repentance, restitution or outside purification procedures, then it becomes plausible that transgression of prohibitions just as much as delays in purification produce a pollution which gravitates to the Sanctuary altar.

Milgrom's arguments for his Proposition 3 are reinforced by philological analysis of the verbs *hatt'e* and *kapper*, showing that they have the meaning of 'to cleanse' rather than to 'atone', and of the prepositions used together with these verbs, showing that the cleansing action is directed towards one or other of the two altars, not towards the offerer. This analysis of the language concerning the *hatta't* at the altar is the real ground of Milgrom's inclusion of non-purity sins in his theory, for he offers no other evidence that sins such as theft, or eating leavened bread on Passover, have any defiling effect on the Sanctuary (on the separate question of defilement of the Land, see chapter 16).

We must consider carefully the philological arguments which form Milgrom's main armoury. He argues that the language used in connection with the sin-offerings shows a primary concern with Temple-pollution and that the offerings were intended to cleanse the Temple, not to atone for the sins of the offerers. In particular, he argues that the ritual of the Day of Atonement (more correctly, he urges, the Day of Cleansing) displays how far each separate kind of pollution penetrates into the Temple, and how the object of the yearly ritual itself is to cleanse each area of the Temple in turn from the type of pollution which it has suffered during the course of the past year. Having laid down this basic philological argument, he can then turn back to the verses which say that ritual impurity causes impurity to the Temple and insist that these verses must be taken in a literal sense as pointing to a direct influence on the Temple from a distance by all humans affected by impurity, which they have failed to cleanse away. The non-literal interpretation found throughout the rabbinic literature that these verses mean only that an unclean person pollutes the Temple when he enters it and touches objects within it must be regarded, Milgrom argues, as a later watering-down of biblical doctrine. He goes on to argue, on the basis of his theory of the *hatta't*, that even the transgression of (negative) commandments not involving ritual purity (e.g. the law against theft) contribute to the miasma defiling the sanctuary, which thus requires purgation, even after repentance, and restitution to the person wronged.

Verbs Milgrom first argues that the verbs used in connection with sin-offerings have the sense of 'to cleanse', not of 'to atone for'. This argument, however, is not conclusive for his purpose, since verbs meaning 'to cleanse' may be used metaphorically to mean 'to cleanse a person's soul of guilt or sin', and may therefore have a meaning very like that of 'to atone for'. The possibility remains, especially in relation to the verb *kapper*, that diverse meanings and usages exist depending on the context.

Prepositions More powerful is Milgrom's argument about prepositions. He argues that whenever 'cleansing' verbs are used in relation to sin-offerings, the prepositions used show that the cleansing operation is directed towards the altar, not towards the offerer. This argument reinforces the meaning of 'to cleanse' rather than 'to atone for', since the altars can hardly be said to need atoning for.

Sometimes, Milgrom shows, the cleansing verbs are not followed by prepositions at all, but govern the altar as direct object. These examples are, he argues, the clearest proof that cleansing is directed towards the altar. An instance is:

Moses took the *hatta't* blood with his finger put [some] on the horns around the altar, decontaminating [*wayehatte'*] the altar. (Lev. 8:15)

The prepositions *'al* or *b* when following a verb of cleansing, and governing an object, not a person, Milgrom argues, have the same force as a direct object. When these prepositions are used in relation to the altar, they refer to the cleansing of the altar, not of the offerer. Instances are:

... and he poured the blood on to the base of the altar, and he sanctified it, to cleanse it. (*lekhapper 'alav*) (Lev. 8:15, continuation)

When, however, the meaning required is 'on behalf of' a person, the preposition used is either *'al* or *be'ad*, the difference being that *'al* refers to persons other than the subject of the sentence. Persons are never the direct object of cleansing verbs. Instances are:

And Aaron shall bring the bullock of the sin-offering, which is for himself (*lo*), and he shall make atonement for himself (*ba'ado*) and for (*be'ad*) his house, and shall kill the bullock of the sin offering which is for himself (*lo*). (Lev. 16:11)

However, enquiry shows that the use of prepositions is more

flexible than Milgrom allows. For example, the preposition *be'ad*, which Milgrom wishes to confine to the meaning 'on behalf of', relating to persons, can even be used in relation to the sins themselves: (Exod. 32:30) ' ... perhaps I will be able to atone for (*be'ad*) your sin'. Moreover, the verb *kapper* does not have to be followed by a preposition or even a noun, but may be used absolutely ('to bring atonement'), e.g. II Sam. 21:3: 'With what shall I atone?' (Here the preposition *b* is clearly instrumental.) Consequently, when Scripture says, for example, *vekhipper 'alav*, which Milgrom translates 'he shall cleanse it [the altar]', this could equally mean, 'he shall cleanse him [the offerer]' or 'he shall cleanse [absolute] by means of it [the altar]'. The use of prepositions in Hebrew, as in English (consider the endless variety of uses of the preposition 'for'), is too slippery to be made the basis of the 'surprising' argument (as Milgrom himself calls it) that the sin-offering does not atone for sin but acts as a 'detergent' for the altar.

Let us focus, however, on a crucial text to test the force of Milgrom's contention that the *hatta't* is brought not to atone for the sinner, but to cleanse the altar of the contaminating effect of his sin.

When a ruler has sinned ... through ignorance ... or if his sin, wherein he hath sinned, come to his knowledge, he shall bring his offering ... and the priest shall make an atonement for him as concerning his sin [Milgrom: 'shall effect purgation on his behalf for his wrong], and it shall be forgiven him. (Lev. 4:22)

This text begins, 'When a ruler has sinned', and ends 'concerning his sin, and it shall be forgiven him.' On any straightforward reading, the 'sin' mentioned at the end of the text is the same as the 'sin' mentioned at the beginning. In other words, the purpose of the offering is to clear the sinner of his sin. In Milgrom's view, however, the offering is not to atone for the sin originally committed, for that has already been atoned for by repentance (or in the case of a sin concerning impurity, by the appropriate purification procedure), but for the additional sin of causing pollution to the altar, and the whole purpose of bringing the offering is to cleanse the altar. It is this sin, not the original offence, for which he is now being 'forgiven'.

This is an implausible reading of the sequence of the text. The plain meaning is that the offering atones for the sin, not for its contaminating effect. If it be objected that an unwitting sin needs no repentance, the simple answer is that even unwitting sins have an aspect of negligence which requires repentance. To have committed a forbidden act, even by accident, produces both horror and guilt in the performer; and these feelings are alleviated by the bringing of the sin-offering. The offerer is comforted by the announcement of the priest that he has been forgiven; the breach that has opened up between the unwitting sinner and God is healed. Milgrom's view depends to some extent on his understandable conviction that an unwitting sin requires no expiation; but this is to underestimate the sense of guilt aroused even by unwitting sins. Further, one may ask, if unwitting sins do not require expiation, why do they defile the altar? There is an inherent improbability in Milgrom's formulation (p. 256), 'The inadvertent offender needs forgiveness not because of his act per se [which] is forgiven because of the offender's inadvertence and remorse, but because of the consequence of his act. His inadvertence has contaminated the sanctuary, and it is his responsibility to purge it with a *hatta't*.' If God forgives the sin, why should he insist on its defiling consequence?

It remains, however, to consider those texts in which the verb *kapper* is followed not by a preposition but by 'the altar' or 'the holy place' as direct object. Surely Milgrom is right in saying that in such cases we are concerned not with 'atonement' but with 'cleansing', and that the aim is to rectify pollution of the sanctuary by the sins of the people?

The main texts here are the inauguration of the sanctuary by Moses, and the ritual of the yearly Day of Atonement. It is undoubtedly true that in these cases it is the sanctuary that is being cleansed. But in the case of Moses' inauguration (Lev. 8) there are no sins to be expiated, for the sanctuary has just been built, and could not have accumulated defilement from the people's sins. The cleansing of the altar, then, is an inaugural ceremony, like the immersion of the priests.[2]

Similarly, the yearly cleansing of the Temple on the Day of Atonement is a renewal of the inauguration. In this case, however, there are defilements to clear away. But it is quite unnecessary to explain these defilements in terms of miasma. In the course of a year, it is impossible that the Temple has escaped defilement through the operation of the sacrificial services themselves. Priests or Israelites must have entered the sacred precincts while in a state of impurity, whether knowingly or (more probably) unknowingly. This is how the rabbis explained the part of the yearly service that relates to the removal of impurity from the sanctuary, and their explanation covers the data at least as well as a theory of contamination from afar. Milgrom's view is that the purification of the Temple from impurities was the earlier concept of P, for which the Day of Atonement was a Day of Cleansing. It was the later concept of H that the day was also concerned with the absolution of sins, and these two concepts lie uneasily together in the final redaction. Even if this analysis is correct, we are not constrained to adopt Milgrom's view that the cleansing operations were necessary because of accumulated miasma attacking the sanctuary from outside.

I conclude that grammatical analysis does not compel us to adopt Milgrom's thesis. Wherever the sin-offering is concerned, the atonement is easily explained as relating to the sin of the offerer, rather than to the defilement of the altar. Where the removal of defilement from the altar is undoubtedly concerned (in cases where the verb *kapper* is followed by the altar or other sancta as direct object), the subject-matter is inauguration or renewal of the sanctuary, not the expiation of individual or communal offences. The verb *kapper* has more than one meaning: sometimes it means 'to cleanse' and sometimes it means 'to atone', depending on the context. The classic text about the atoning power of the blood sprinkled on the altar is the following: (Lev. 17:11) 'For the life of flesh is in the blood;

---

[2] Another striking example of the use of *kapper* with sancta as direct object in an inaugural context is Ezekiel 43:20,26.

and I have given it to you on the altar as a ransom for your lives; for the blood it is that ransoms by means of the life.' Milgrom explains (p. 710) that this refers to *shelamim*, and the blood expiates the spilling of animal blood. But the verse seems to have a broader meaning: that the sacrificial blood of all sacrifices (including the sin-offerings) has an atoning power because it is the life of the animal that is offered. Blood may sometimes operate as a 'detergent', as Milgrom proposes, but not always, and in the case of the *hatta't* it is the atoning power that matters.

CHAPTER 15

From demons to ethics

Milgrom is aware of the need to provide some historical justification for his theory of the discontinuity between biblical and rabbinic notions of how impurity reaches the sanctuary. In his own view, the discontinuity is not large; yet, objectively, it is considerable, the Bible having the miasmic view of impurity impinging on the Tabernacle from all areas of the camp, while the rabbis think that no impurity can arrive at the Tabernacle unless some impure human individual brings it there.

Milgrom's theory is in some ways more congenial to the modern mind than that of the rabbis. For Milgrom provides an evolutionary scheme, by which we can see how demons evolved into ethics, while the rabbis provide a static scheme in which there is no development from the scriptural to the rabbinic system.

The demons, Milgrom argues, are not actually in Scripture, but they lie in its background, and occasional hints (such as the mention of Azazel) provide traces of a previous demonic theory of pollution which the priestly authors are endeavouring to overcome. Milgrom considers that the P document represents an enormous advance on ideas of demonic pollution, but has not quite emancipated itself from them. Previous Mesopotamian fears of temple-pollution derive from an active belief in demons, which were thought to threaten the Temple and even the god. Such evil forces, threatening to invade the temple from outside, had to be diverted by procedures of exorcism and cleansing. P has got rid of the demons, and denies that there is any threat to the omnipotent God. But in place of the malevolent demons, there are human beings, whose sins threaten to pollute the sanctuary and so offend God that he will remove his protection in disgust. And human sins assail the sanctuary from afar in the form of a miasma that has many of the characteristics of the previously held demonic forces. Yet this shift from demons to humans as the source of pollution is a shift towards the ethical sphere, in which evil resides in the heart of man not in hostile supernatural forces.

The rabbis, however, Milgrom acknowledges, got rid of the miasma. In their system, as applied exegetically to the biblical text, there is no danger to the sanctuary from afar either from delayed purification from impurity or from unexpiated sins. The historical question that now arises is when the biblical system ceased, and when the rabbinic system began. Milgrom thinks that we must look to the intertestamental period for this important development rather than to the rabbinic period itself. But he has not been able to find any sign of his postulated miasma system in intertestamental literature. Instead, he relies on alleged traces of it in the rabbinic system itself.

For example, he quotes the saying of Rabbi Simeon (M. Shevuot, 1:4): 'They [the communal sin-offerings] are all brought to make atonement for uncleanness of the Temple and its Hallowed Things.' This, Milgrom asserts, shows that Rabbi Simeon retained the old tradition that the sin-offerings cleansed not their offerers, but the Temple itself. Milgrom, of course, is aware that, in context, this saying of Rabbi Simeon's does not mean this. It is referring to impurities caused to the Temple by people entering it inadvertently in a state of impurity. Rabbi Simeon is saying that those who infringe Temple purity, if they become conscious of their offence, can be atoned for by an individual sin-offering; but if the perpetrators never become aware of their offence, atonement is made for them through the communal sin-offerings offered at festival times. There is nothing here to suggest that the purpose of the sin-offering is to cleanse the Temple itself rather than to bring atonement to the offenders. Nor is there anything to suggest that the pollution being atoned for occurred outside the Temple, affecting it from a distance.

Milgrom, however, relies on the idea that the rabbinic literature, though it contradicts his reading of the biblical texts, preserves an unconscious knowledge of the older interpretation. Thus Rabbi Simeon, though subscribing to the rabbinic view that the sin-offerings atone for the offenders, and that the offences referred to occurred inside the Temple, preserves a form of words that is redolent of an older, pre-rabbinic view. But this remains a subjective re-interpretation of Rabbi Simeon's words.

Intertestamental literature, so far from corroborating miasmic theory, appears to show continuity with the rabbinic view. Philo, for example, refers, in his account of the sacrifices, to the need for purity in these words ('On those who offer sacrifice', III): 'It is necessary, therefore, for those who are about to go into the temple to partake of the sacrifice, to be cleansed as to their bodies and as to their souls before their bodies.' This says plainly that ritual purity was required of those entering the Temple, not for those going about their business outside the Temple. Philo, writing at about 40 CE, knows nothing about an obligation to remove one's impurity at a distance from the Temple, because of the 'aerial' miasmic properties of ritual impurity.

The Dead Sea Scroll sect did indeed place great store on ritual purity in areas outside the Temple, but certainly not because they wished thereby to avoid remote contamination of the Jerusalem Temple, which they regarded as hopelessly polluted by a degenerate priesthood. Their concern with ritual purity was a spiritual exercise valued for its own sake, or perhaps motivated by their belief that their own community constituted a substitute Temple, serving as such until the restoration of a proper Temple in Jerusalem by the Messiah. The ritual purity devotees (*haberim*) of the Pharisees and rabbinic movement were again formed for the exercise of supererogatory piety, not for the sake of preserving the Temple from pollution (see Appendix A). In biblical times, the institution of the Nazirite (which survived also into rabbinic times) expressed a similar use of ritual purity as a form of supererogatory piety, and nothing in the Bible suggests that the Nazirite aimed to protect the Temple from pollution by cultivating purity in areas outside it.

The total silence of the post-biblical literature on the subject which Milgrom regards as so important in the Bible is surely significant. But there is even evidence in the (admittedly later) biblical literature that ritual impurity was not regarded as an objective, palpable miasma, but merely as a set of rules which could be set aside occasionally, when more important considerations intervened. This is the striking case of King Hezekiah (II Chron. 30), who decided that, because of special circumstances preventing the people from achieving ritual purity in time for Passover, the ritual purity rules could simply be waived, and the Temple rites performed in a state of impurity. Milgrom gives surprisingly little consideration to this incident, which surely shows an attitude towards ritual purity very similar to that of the rabbis.

It may be possible, however, to construct an evolutionary theory showing some measure of development from the biblical to the rabbinic system without recourse to miasmic ideas or to the violent gap postulated by Milgrom, which he cannot fill by any intertestamental evidence of gradual change. We may do this by considering the definition of the 'camp'.

THE DEFINITION OF 'THE CAMP'

Milgrom points out (1991, pp. 316–17) that while persons suffering from certain impurities are excluded from 'the camp', there is considerable inconsistency, even within the P document, about the definition of the limits of 'the camp'. Yet Milgrom does not consider how this insight affects his theory of the miasmic threat to the Tabernacle. If, according to one strand of P, the whole camp is a holy area from which impurity must be excluded, then there may be good reasons for requiring speedy purification without introducing any notion of aerial contamination of the Tabernacle from a distance.

Milgrom draws particular attention to Lev. 15:31 and Num. 19:13, 20, which show clearly, as he thinks, that the concern is about the sanctuary, and that this concern exists even when the contaminated person is not actually in the sanctuary but at a considerable distance from it (though apparently if the person is

outside the camp altogether, there is no concern, because the
impurity flies only through the air of the camp itself). He argues
that when the contaminated persons were sent outside the
camp, there was no concern, but once the law was changed,
allowing the contaminated persons (except the *metzoraʿ*) to
remain in the camp, there was concern that they should seek
earliest purification.

But if, at one time, the whole 'camp' (not just the sanctuary)
was regarded as holy, then it is understandable that, when this
view was reigning, to remain in a state of impurity was regarded
as undesirable. Even minor impurities would need to be washed
off quickly, not because such delayed impurities accumulated
and formed a miasma that flew through the air until it reached
the sanctuary, but because they polluted a holy area (the camp)
just by staying where they were. I would therefore postulate the
following developmental scheme:

Stage 1 This stage is found in the Bible in an older stratum of P.
At this stage, the 'camp' was defined as entirely holy, as
constituting, in fact, the outer grounds of the sanctuary. Consequently, verses which forbid defiling 'my Sanctuary' (*miqdashi*)
or 'my tabernacle' (*mishqani*) referred to the whole camp. This is
why, at this stage, the corpse-contaminated and *zab* and *zabah*
were excluded from the camp, which was too holy to endure
their presence. Those suffering minor impurities, however, were
allowed to remain in the camp, but required to seek early
purification because of the holiness of the camp, not because
their impurities attacked the sanctuary miasmically.

Stage 2 The camp was divested of holiness. Only the sanctuary
and its surrounds were to be regarded as holy. Verses forbidding
defiling 'my sanctuary' and 'my tabernacle' now referred to the
actual sanctuary (and its outer grounds) alone, but were allowed
to stand in the text without the now necessary additional clause
'if you enter it'. As a consequence of the reduced holiness of the
camp, the corpse-contaminated and *zab* and *zabah* were no
longer excluded from it. They were required to seek early
purification, however, so that others might not be defiled unwittingly and then enter the sanctuary. There was no contamina-

tion of the sanctuary from afar, and no miasma. The only danger was that they might enter the sanctuary itself, but this was unlikely. Those suffering minor impurities had no need to seek early purification, and could wait until they had occasion to enter the sanctuary.

NOTE This reconstruction differs from Milgrom's in making the permission given to the corpse-impure, *zab* and *zabah* to enter the camp an indication of general increased permissiveness, rather than an occasion for new severity.

Stage 3 (the rabbinic stage) This is substantially the same as Stage 2 of P, but adds certain refinements to the concept of the 'camp'. In rabbinic interpretation of the biblical data, there were three 'camps': the camp of God, the camp of the Levites and the camp of Israel, which was the outermost area.[1] In the camp of Israel, all impurities were permitted except that of the *metzora'*, or 'leper', who had to stay outside the camp until he was purified. In the camp of the Levites, parturients, menstruants and *zab/zabah* are excluded, but not the corpse-contaminated; while in the camp of God, corpse-contaminated are also excluded. These 'camps', originally referring to areas of the encampment in the Wilderness, were re-interpreted to refer to areas of Jerusalem. The sectarians of the Dead Sea Scrolls were more severe in their re-interpretation, ruling that the whole of Jerusalem was a holy area, thus returning to something like the view characterized as Stage 1 above.

The rabbis, of course, had no notion of contamination of the Temple from afar by reason of delay in seeking purification. They also had no idea of the sin-offering as functioning as a detergent for the altar. It may be useful here to outline what, in the rabbinic view, was the actual remedy for any contamination discovered to have occurred in the Temple. This is explained in M. Hagigah 3:8:

How did they enter upon the cleansing of the Temple Court? They used to immerse the vessels that were in the Temple and say [to the priests], 'Take heed lest ye touch the table and render it unclean.' For all the utensils that were in the Temple they had a second and a third

[1] See Rashi on Num. 5:2, based on b. Pes. 67a. See also Sifre ad loc.

set, that if the first contracted uncleanness they might bring a second in their stead. All the utensils that were in the Temple required immersion, excepting the altar of gold and the altar of bronze, for they were reckoned as like to the ground. So Rabbi Eliezer. But the Sages say: Because they were plated [with metal].

It is clear from this that in the practice of the Second Temple, the utensils of the Temple, if known to have been polluted, were dealt with in the same way as vessels outside the Temple that required purification. They were simply immersed in a ritual pool, or *miqveh.* Those features of Temple furniture that were fixtures were never immersed, because they were regarded as immune to impurity. Thus if the altars at which sacrifices were performed were touched by a person who had acquired an impurity, nothing needed to be done. We also learn from M. Hagigah 3:7 that after each festival, when the influx of pilgrims had ceased, there was a regular immersion of all the movable utensils of the Temple. This was done because it was likely that some cases of inadvertent pollution of Temple vessels had taken place among the festival throng.

This is a far cry from the position attributed by Milgrom to the biblical authors. According to this, Temple vessels, including and especially the two altars, were being continually polluted from outside the Temple, every time some Israelite, from Dan to Beersheba, incurred impurity and failed to seek immediate purification. The method of purification of these Temple vessels, and of the Temple itself, consisted of the application of the blood of the sin-offerings. To adopt the simple, commonsensical course of taking a Temple vessel to a ritual pool for cleansing is unthinkable in such a system of thought, where the incoming seeping miasma can be exorcised only by blood.

The question is whether it is really credible that biblical and post-biblical thought about the Temple are really so alien to each other. From a system in which the altars are a particular focus of concern, being continually daubed with purifying and salvific blood, to a system in which they are of no concern at all, being immune to ritual impurity, seems a change that defies the tempo of religious evolution.

THE GRADUATED SIN-OFFERING AS AN EXPIATION FOR DELAY

An important part of Milgrom's argument is his view that delay to seek purification causes defilement to the sanctuary by means of the accumulated clouds of impurity which thereby mass against the altar and other sancta. A difficulty, however, is that no such sin of delay is ever mentioned explicitly in the text. Milgrom deals with this difficulty by his treatment of the 'graduated sin-offering', as he calls it (Lev. 5:1–13). In rabbinic literature, this is called the 'ascending and descending sacrifice' (*qorban 'oleh veyored*), so-called because it varies according to the financial standing of the offerer, the best-off being obligated to offer an animal, while the worst-off need only offer a measure of grain.

In rabbinic thinking, this offering is not called a 'sin-offering' (*hatta't*), since Scripture seems to differentiate it clearly from the *hatta't*, which is described in Lev. 4. It is explained as expiating an offence that was caused not by negligence (e.g. forgetting that he was in a state of impurity) (as in chapter 4) but by total inadvertence (e.g. the offender entered the sanctuary in a state of impurity but did not know of the impurity until later). This most pardonable kind of 'unwittingness' still has to be expiated, but a lenient form of expiation, adapted to people's means, is allotted. This same form of expiation is allotted to the case of someone who swore falsely in a court of law that he had no evidence to give; this is a form of perjury that is not so bad as giving false witness against one's neighbour, yet requires expiation when the offender repents of his culpable failure to give evidence. Again, the same form of expiation is allotted to one who made a vow (affecting only himself) which he failed to keep through forgetfulness, but later became aware of. The rabbis thus regarded the 'ascending and descending offering' as a kind of sin-offering for minor sins. A difficulty, however, is that a similar type of graduated offering is prescribed by Scripture for the purification of a 'leper' and of a parturient woman; the rabbinic exposition does not explain this.

Milgrom does not accept the rabbinic theory of the 'ascending and descending offering', though he accepts that the same theory is to be found in Philo (*Laws*, 3.205). Milgrom does accept, however, the rabbinic view that the 'ascending and descending offering' is a distinct offering that must not be confused with the ordinary sin-offering. (Milgrom criticises acutely those modern scholars who make this confusion.)

Milgrom's view is that the 'graduated sin-offering', as he calls it, is precisely to expiate the sin which he has discovered in Scripture, that of *delaying* purification. This fills a gap in Milgrom's general theory, against which one might otherwise urge that this sin, so important in Milgrom's miasmic view, is nowhere explicitly mentioned or penalized.

Someone who has incurred impurity, but, by an oversight, has failed to apply the proper purification procedure, contributes thereby to the accumulation of impurity in the atmosphere, especially as such impurity becomes more virulent with every hour that passes without purification. The resultant contamination of the sanctuary can only be removed by an offering; and this is the 'graduated sin-offering'. This is not the same as an ordinary sin-offering because the latter expiates a breach of a negative commandment of the Torah, whereas a delay in purification breaks only a positive commandment (to seek purification) and there is no negative commandment prohibiting the incurring of impurity in the first place. The reason why the sin-offering is graduated is that the law applies to relatively minor matters, and therefore leniency is suitable.

Milgrom rejects the rabbinic explanation that the law applies to actual contamination of holy objects or areas by the simple argument that no such direct contamination is mentioned in the passage, which appears rather to be concerned with the state of personal impurity itself. 'The condition of "the pollution of the sanctuary and its sancta" by contact is plainly eisegesis; it is nowhere expressed' (p. 309).[2]

---

[2] Milgrom actually gives two other reasons for rejecting the rabbinic theory. (1) 'The direct contact of impurity with sancta is banned elsewhere (e.g. 7:20–21; 12:4; 22:3–7), where the punishment is entirely different: *karet*.' But these prohibitions refer to the *deliberate* defilement of sancta by contact, for which the punishment of *karet* is prescribed, while here we are explicitly told that the defilement is by unawareness or amnesia, for which not *karet* or an ordinary sin-offering, but a graduated expiation is

Milgrom's own view, however, involves a considerable degree of eisegesis. Nowhere in the passage is there any reference to the concept of *delay*. If we are going to take the passage solely at face value, we would have to say that the mere incurring of impurity is something that requires expiation, and Milgrom is well aware that this interpretation is impossible. Therefore he has to import the conception of delay – but if he imports something, why complain that the rabbis import something?

There is thus no *prima facie* objection to the rabbinic interpretation of the passage about the graduated offering as referring to one who defiled sancta while unconscious of his own impurity.

PURITY AND ETHICS

One of the greatest discontinuities between the Bible and the rabbis in matters of ritual purity, according to Milgrom, is that the Bible attributes ritual impurity to sins, while the rabbis do not. For in Milgrom's scheme, even the committing of moral sins adds to the miasma of impurity that attacks the sanctuary. It is not merely the failure to seek purification for states of impurity that creates the miasma, but also the disobedience involved in such sins as theft, murder, injustice or cheating, as well as non-purity ritual sins, such as eating on the fast of the Atonement, or wearing a garment made of a mixture of wool and linen. For these sins all involve the breaking of negative commandments, and this demands, when the sin is committed unwittingly, the bringing of a 'purification offering', as Milgrom terms it. Such sins defile the altar, in Milgrom's scheme, and the altar has to be cleansed of the impurity. If the sins are unwitting, they reach into the outer area of the Temple, but if they are deliberate, they reach into the innermost recesses of the Temple and can only be countered by the detergent procedures of the

prescribed. (2) 'Verse 3 speaks solely of those who are secondarily contaminated ... however, regarding contact with sancta no such distinction is made.' But, as Milgrom has himself earlier pointed out, the reason why primary sources, such as a *zab* or parturient, are not mentioned here is that a person who is a primary source of impurity must be aware of his/her own condition, while here we deal with those who are unconscious of their condition.

Day of Purgation, which aim at cleansing the stains from the inner altar.

The rabbis, on the contrary, hold that sins do not cause impurity. The only apparent exception is idolatry, the appurtenances of which were ritually defiling, but the rabbis freely acknowledge that this was not a scriptural but a rabbinic law, enacted to induce people to keep far from contact with idolatry. Even though certain biblical verses ascribe impurity to idols and idolatry, this was regarded as metaphorical only, like the assertions that evil deeds pollute the Land (see next chapter). Certain prohibited acts do cause impurity, but not specifically because of the prohibition but incidentally to the act: for example, the eating of forbidden food or cohabiting with a menstruous woman. In such cases, repentance for the act is quite separate from the need to undergo purification, and the incurring of impurity is not a sin but a consequence.

If Milgrom's concept of the *hatta't* is incorrect, as I have tried to show, the Bible is not guilty of confusing sin with impurity. For the function of the sin-offering (correctly so called) is not to wipe the altar clean from contamination, but to expiate the sin of the offerer. This is why the culmination of the offering is the declaration *venislah lo* ('and he will be forgiven').

CHAPTER 16

Ritual purity and morality

Ritual purity forms part of the code of holiness, by which the Israelites were set apart as a 'kingdom of priests'. Other parts of this holiness code are the rules about permitted and forbidden foods, the rules about the Sabbath and the festivals, the rules about the performance of sacrifices in the Temple. All these rules are laid down for Israelites alone. They are obliged to keep these rules, but non-Israelites are not obliged to keep them, and incur no blame for not doing so.

This sets up a somewhat paradoxical situation. The ritual laws are, in one sense, the most important elements in the religion; but, in another sense, they are the least important. They are the most important because they give the Israelites their identity; they are the least important, because the laws of morality, which Israelites share with the rest of humanity, take precedence over them. In every case where there is conflict between ritual and morality, ritual gives way to morality. This is true both in the biblical and the rabbinic context. The paradigm case for this is the incident when David and his men arrived at the shrine of Nob, and in dire emergency were fed the holy shewbread by the High Priest (1 Sam. 21:1–7). The Talmud treats this as a case of morality versus ritual; the shewbread was of the utmost sanctity, and could normally only be handled by the priests; yet the preservation of human life took precedence over all sanctities.[1]

---

[1] The incident is mentioned in the Gospels as part of Jesus' defence in the matter of the Sabbath corn-plucking. But here it is used merely to show that ritual prohibitions could be broken at the whim of an authoritative person. Behind this interpretation,

RITUAL LAWS AS A PRIESTLY OR MONASTIC RULE

It is clear in Scripture that non-Israelites are not required to keep the ritual laws, but are required to keep the moral laws. When non-Israelites are punished by God, it is always for non-ritual offences. The generation of the Flood is accused of corruption and violence (Gen. 6:11). The inhabitants of Sodom are accused of inhospitality, violence and injustice (Gen. 19). The inhabitants of Canaan are accused of incest (Lev. 18:24), and human sacrifice (Lev. 18:21). The inhabitants of Nineveh, to whom Jonah preached repentance, were guilty of 'violence' (Jonah 3:8). Nowhere is there any complaint that non-Jews ate forbidden food, or did not rest on the Sabbath or festivals, or failed to keep rules of ritual purity. On the other hand, when non-Jews are praised as virtuous (Job for example) their virtue consists in moral, not ritual, behaviour: generosity to the poor, love of one's neighbour, opposition to oppression and injustice.

Israelites are required to keep holiness laws, but this does not exempt them in any way from morality laws. The prophets inveigh continually against those who fail to understand that holiness laws are not a substitute for morality. Scholars have ceased to say that the prophets were opposed to ritual as such; it is now well understood that the prophets wanted the holiness code to be observed, but not at the expense of morality. Sacrifices of animals obtained through robbery or oppression were worse than no sacrifices.

Israelites are required to regard themselves as a nation of priests, and as therefore bound by a priestly code which is not binding on non-priests. An analogy here can be seen in the roles of priest and layman in the Catholic Church. Noone is obliged to become a priest, but having become one, a person must keep certain rules, such as the rule of celibacy. Entry to the priesthood here is purely voluntary, and because of the rule of celibacy no hereditary element is included. In Judaism, entry into the priest nation is voluntary insofar as the religion is open

however, lies an original story (hinted at by Matthew) in which Jesus was defending the corn-plucking on grounds of emergency. See Maccoby (1986), pp. 40–42.

to converts, but the hereditary element is strong, since one born an Israelite is automatically a member of the priest nation.

Catholic priests lead a particular community or parish, whereas the Jewish priestly role does not involve such a direct pastoral function in relation to the rest of humanity. It is therefore better, in some ways, to compare the role of the Jews, or Israelites, with that of the Catholic monastic orders, which pursue a separate life governed by a 'rule'. Again, entrance is voluntary, and non-entrance carries no stigma. The rule is defining, and yet not allowed to override common moral obligations. A Trappist monk takes a vow of silence, but if his silence were to endanger life, it would have to be broken, for his life of dedication does not replace his duty as a human being.

There are nowadays extraordinarily strong trends and motivations directed at obscuring and minimizing the distinction between morality and ritual in Judaism. Some are influenced by relativist and structuralist preoccupations, seeing the rules by which societies work as too arbitrary to be divided into areas labelled 'morality' and 'ritual'. Some are motivated by a reaction against antisemitism, seeing the accusation of ritualism levelled against Judaism as so much a matter of religious polemics that they feel it necessary to cultivate a tolerance and objectivity towards ritualism as a legitimate mode of religious experience (thereby begging the question of whether Judaism is essentially ritualistic). Some see the attack on Judaism as a disguised Protestant polemic against Catholicism, and thus to be resisted.

The fact is that the distinction between morality and ritual, however hard to justify philosophically, is basic in biblical and rabbinic Judaism. The attempts that have been made to develop a theology and morality of Judaism out of ritual data alone (e.g. by Jacob Neusner out of the Mishnah Order of Purities) are missing the point. These elements are intended to be subordinate and limited; they are not a coded philosophy, but just what they purport to be, rules for the conduct of a priestly society, in which a sense of constant attendance on God demands a protocol which in no way supersedes the demands of ordinary duties to neighbours, family and strangers. They do

form an important element in the philosophy of Judaism, but
the difficulty is to formulate this importance without either
exaggerating or belittling it.

The clue to a correct assessment is the distinction between
rules binding only on Jews, and those binding on all mankind.
The rabbis made this distinction explicit by their doctrine of the
Seven Noachic Laws, but the same distinction between a *lex
gentium* and the *lex judaica* is plain in Scripture too. However, the
line that is drawn between the two is not entirely coincidental
with that between morality and ritual. There is also a level of
morality that is enjoined only (as a mandated duty) for Jews. As
a priest nation, the Jews are expected to practise a moral code
that is supererogatory for non-Jews. For example, Jews must not
lend money to each other on interest; not that such lending is
regarded as immoral, for it is permitted among non-Jews, and
between Jews and non-Jews, but that the family tie between
Jews is to be regarded as so strong that all lending must be like
the lending that takes place between members of a family.
Lending between Jews is to be divested of its business aspect,
and made into an act of love and charity; a behaviour that
cannot be universalized, because to do so would bring world
commercial activity to a halt. Similarly, the laws of the seventh
year (when debts are cancelled) and of the Jubilee (when land
returns to its original owners) are legislated for Jews only, as
members of a Utopian society of love.

One consideration that is perhaps confusing is that, while the
Jews are a nation of priests, they contain within themselves a
caste of priests, the Kohanim, the descendants of Aaron. This,
however, is a priesthood that is not open to recruits or volunteers; the indispensable requirement is to be a descendant in the
male line from Aaron, the brother of Moses. Converts to
Judaism from outside nations become full Jews; but they can
never become Aaronite priests (though, of course, they can have
Aaronite grandchildren, if their daughters marry priests). But
the Aaronites are not priests in the manner of, say, the Catholic
priesthood. They do not have teaching authority, and do not
preach sermons or perform a pastoral role. These roles are
reserved for the rabbis. The role of the Aaronites is to perform

the sacraments: as if, in Catholicism, the priest performed the Mass and left all other priestly functions to others. There is diagreement among scholars how early in Jewish history this division of roles between priest and rabbi (or Sage) began. In Scripture, at times, the priests are sometimes given a teaching role (e.g. Deut. 17:9), and yet there are indications in Scripture too that the chief teaching roles were not confined to priests (the prophets, for example, beginning with Moses, were mostly non-priests). The Sadducees seem to have disagreed with the advancing teaching role of the rabbis, and to have wished to give teaching authority to the priests. But the democratic vision of universal education firmly entrenched in Scripture (Deut. 6:7) made it increasingly impossible to confine learning to one hereditary group. In the end, even the teaching authority (about 'leprosy', for example) which Scripture seems to give unequivocally to the priests was taken over by the rabbis (see p. 123).

An important limitation of the status of the priests is that they were never given a comparable role in the ritual purity system to that of the Brahmin priests in Hinduism. The priests are not rendered impure simply by contact with someone of lower caste. This is a point that has been stressed by Mary Douglas.[2] The ritual purity rules are the same for everyone, priest or non-priest. The sources of impurity are laid down (corpse, pelvic discharger, leper, 'creeping thing', etc.) and are the sole sources of impurity, irrespective of one's status in society. A priest who has been made unclean by one of these sources causes impurity to any non-priest with whom he comes in contact. The only difference is that a priest has to be more careful about avoiding impurity than a non-priest, because a priest comes into more contact with holy things and areas. Also there is one form of impurity (corpse-impurity) which a priest must avoid *ab initio*

---

[2] 'In so far as the Levitical rules for purity apply universally they are useless for internal disciplining. They maintain absolutely no social demarcation. It is true that only the priest can make atonement, and that the priest's dedicated food must not be eaten by outsiders, but the book insists over and over again that the poor and the stranger are to be included in the requirements of the laws; no one is excluded from the benefits of purification' (Douglas, 1993/94, p. 113).

(except in the case of a close relative or in case of emergency or if he finds a corpse needing burial).

The priests are thus a hereditary caste which is differentiated from other Jews by having a more severe ritual purity rule (in relation to corpse-impurity) and by having more frequent ritual purity obligations because of constant contact with holy foods and areas. The other special castes in the Jewish community are the *mamzerim* (children of incestuous or adulterous unions), the slaves, and people whose origin is from the Moabites, Ammonites, Edomites and Egyptians, nations mentioned in Scripture as suffering marriage disabilities of varying severity after conversion to Judaism. The latter group, however, had their disabilities removed by rabbinic decree.[3] These castes are not distinguished from other Jews by ritual purity considerations, only by marriage disabilities (i.e. there was a ban on their marrying into the higher castes for a given number of generations, or for ever). This means, for example, that even *mamzerim* or slaves are not debarred from entering the Temple and offering sacrifices, as were the Untouchables in Hinduism before the Gandhiist reforms. Rabbinic Judaism worked in the direction of abolishing the special castes (by freeing the slaves, and by allowing unpublicized and undetected *mamzerim* to go without enquiry) but there was no need for Gandhi-type reforms, since the ritual purity system had never been used as a means of differentiating between classes.

The conception of the Jews as a priest-nation, therefore, is not contradicted by the existence of a class of priests within their own community, since these are ceremonial priests only, who do not carry teaching authority. The Jews as a whole, however, are designated a nation of priests in another sense: that they have teaching authority for the whole world ('Out of Zion shall go forth the Law'), and that they observe purity rules because of their special proximity to God and his Temple. These purity rules, however, only mark their priest-status; they are not a substitute for the laws of morality which apply to all

---

[3] For a fuller description of these castes, see Maccoby 1996, pp. 74–81.

mankind (though certain moral refinements too are required of the Jews as a seal of their status as a dedicated group).

DEFILEMENT OF THE LAND

Another matter that has tended to obfuscate the all-important distinction between morality and purity in Judaism has been the special status of the Land. Certain texts say that wrong behaviour on the part of the Israelites pollutes the Land, which will therefore spew them forth unless the sinners repent (Lev. 18:27–28, 20:22). This has often been taken to mean that what is wrong about this wrong behaviour is precisely that it causes pollution to the Land, which is holy. If this interpretation were correct, we would have to conclude that there is no concept of morality in Judaism at all, only of pollution and its purification.

But this interpretation is incorrect, because it puts the cart before the horse. The Land is polluted because the behaviour is wrong; not the behaviour wrong because it pollutes the Land.

Consider the Canaanites. They, we are told, polluted the Land and are therefore being thrown out of it before the Israelites (Lev. 18:27), who are warned that they will receive the same treatment if they do not improve on the performance of their predecessors. Does this mean that the behaviour complained of is only wrong for people inhabiting the Land? In that case, why did God complain of the behaviour of the generation of the Flood, who did not inhabit the Holy Land, or of the inhabitants of Sodom or Nineveh? It appears that certain things are wrong even if the Land is not involved. Indeed, certain things are wrong (injustice, for example) even if the perpetrator is God himself (Gen. 18:25). Wrongness and rightness, then, are not functions of the Land, but a characteristic of the behaviour of rational beings everywhere.

How then does the pollution of the Land come into the matter? The generation of the Flood, and the inhabitants of Sodom and Nineveh, were not threatened with ejection from their lands. This is because their lands were not holy. The threat of ejection is in addition to other punishments allotted to wrongdoing, and it applies only to inhabitants of the Holy Land, Jewish or non-Jewish. To behave badly is wrong, but to do so in a holy area is even more wrong (since it adds insult to the holy area to the wrongness of the deed), and merits ejection from the holy area.

But how are we to understand the concept of 'pollution' as it applies to the Land? How, in particular, does this kind of pollution compare with the pollutions mainly considered in this book, which arise from the sources of ritual impurity, and give rise to various procedures of purification?

The answer given by most enquirers has been that pollution of the Land is a metaphorical, not a real pollution. This, in my opinion, is the correct answer, but doubt has been thrown on it recently, so the matter merits further consideration.

By saying that moral sins cause pollution to the Land in a metaphorical or figurative sense, it is meant that this pollution cannot be 'cashed' in terms of location in a system of graded impurities or procedures of purification. To say that a moral sin (for example, murder or idolatry) is polluting or defiling is like saying it is 'disgusting'; that too is a metaphor, taken from the realm of mouldy food, or filthy surroundings, which may affect a person physically by taking away his appetite or producing a reaction of retching. A metaphor involves two terms, one of which supports the epithet literally, while the other supports it only by transfer or likeness. In Scripture we frequently find serious sins characterized as 'abominations' (*to'ebah*) or as 'detestable things' (*shiqutz*), words which primarily denote physical repugnance. Such terms are metaphorical, and they are not essentially different from the characterization of sins as 'unclean' (*tame'*).

In a recent article, Jonathan Klawans has attacked the idea that sin, in Scripture, is defiling only in a metaphorical sense (Klawans, 1997). He agrees that sins such as murder and idolatry do not have ritual purity effects that can be remedied by normal purification procedures. Nevertheless, he argues, there is another kind of defilement which he calls 'moral defilement', which has its own special purification procedures. Moral defilement causes the Land to be desecrated, and the remedy for this is expulsion of the offending inhabitants, after which the Land becomes purified.

But this is to overlook some important aspects. It is clear that the Land becomes 'defiled' to the point of expulsion not by individual misdeeds, but by an accumulation of misdeeds such that the offender becomes the community at large rather than individuals. The Land can support individual misdeeds, especially if they are corrected by communal justice and action, but when uncorrected misdeeds accumulate to a certain point, the Land suffers nausea and 'vomits out' its inhabitants. This is not a matter of impurity, but of genuine moral depravity. When the Land is conceived as a kind of large animal that has a limited power of digesting disgusting food, this is surely a metaphor or image, to which a literary response is appropriate, rather than an attempt to fit the matter into a system of impurity. The metaphor is intended to convey moral disgust at deeds that are hated in themselves, not because of their alleged defiling effects. To literalize the metaphor is to reduce the moral disgust: as if to say, 'The reason why you must avoid these sins is because the Land has a delicate digestion.' It is precisely when a person is overwhelmed by moral disapproval that he is likely to use metaphors based on physical disgust. The whole passage is using literary, rhetorical methods to convey a feeling of moral repulsion.

The expulsion of the Land's inhabitants is not a purification but a (metaphorical) retching. The Land's inhabitants, too, are not purified by their expulsion, but only rehabilitated by their subsequent repentance. The expulsion itself is not a purification but a punishment.

Another dimension has been given to the matter by Milgrom's attempt to explain the defilement of the Land in terms of source criticism. Leviticus 1–16, most scholars now agree, belongs to the Priestly Code, while the rest of Leviticus belongs to the Holiness Code. According to Milgrom (who argues that the Holiness Code is the later of the two codes, and that in fact its authors are the redactors of the whole of Leviticus), different ideas on impurity can be found in the two codes, and the defilement of the Land is an exclusively Holiness concept.

According to Milgrom, only the Holiness code has a concept of Israel as a totally holy nation. The P document confines holiness to the Temple, its sancta and its officiants (p. 689). It is H only that threatens expulsion from the Land unless the whole programme of holiness is collectively observed, including the laws of forbidden foods and of ritual purity, as well as the moral laws against incest, adultery, murder and injustice. On this view, the threat of expulsion is something extra, not included in P, and in effect replacing the sanctions of P.

However, Milgrom seems to overlook the evidence that the threat of expulsion is tied to the concept of defilement of the Land in Leviticus only in connection with moral, not ceremonial, sins. Not even all moral offences are involved, but only those that are specifically sexual.[4] Only in Lev. 18 and 20 (both concerned with sexual offences) do we find mention of defilement of the Land combined with the threat of expulsion. In both chapters, the threat of expulsion and the concomitant accusation of defilement of the Land are tied to the previous expulsion of the Canaanites. The Canaanites were never required to keep ritual purity or dietary laws, and they were not regarded as a holy people, even though they lived in a holy land. Yet they were expelled because of their sexual sins, which belong to the category of behaviour forbidden to all mankind, but are considered especially heinous when committed in a holy Land.

We do indeed find the threat of expulsion in connection with other offences, both moral and ceremonial (e.g. Lev. 26:33, Deut. 4:26–27, 28:63–64), when these derelictions amount to an obstinate abandonment of the commandments: but in these Curses, the defilement of the Land is never mentioned.

The concept of defilement of the Land is found in connection with murder in Num. 35:33–34. Here no mention is made of

----

[4] Some confusion may have arisen because of Lev. 20:24–26, in which purity laws are mentioned. But this is not part of the previous passage denouncing the defilement of the Land by sexual offences. It is a separate exordium, reminding the Israelites of God's favour to them in giving them a land flowing with milk and honey and exalting them to priestly status, marked by a priestly code distinguishing between the clean and the unclean. These laws of the clean and unclean are not included in the previous list of offences causing defilement to the Land and expulsion.

expulsion, the subject being individual, not communal violence. Defilement of the Land is mentioned also in connection with the prohibition against leaving an executed corpse to hang overnight (Deut. 21:23), but again there is no reference to expulsion. Nevertheless, we may add murder and disrespect to the dead to offences defiling the Land. The list is still restricted to moral offences, and does not include ceremonial offences such as ritual purity violations, or even non-observance of sabbaths and festivals. In the case of non-observance of the sabbatical year, it is said that the Land will make up the number of sabbaths she has lost during the years of exile of the Israelites (Lev. 26:34). Here we do have a collocation of exile and injury to the Land, but the injury is not called 'defilement'. Defilement of the Land and expulsion come together explicitly only in relation to sexual offences.

Thus there is no contradiction between the Priestly Code and the Holiness Code. The Priestly Code demands priestly conduct from the community of Israel but not from the rest of the world. The Holiness Code adds that any nation, Israelite or non-Israelite, residing in the holy Land must face expulsion if the Land is desecrated by immoral conduct.[5]

The distinction between purity and ethics is made clear in Leviticus, not only in relation to sexual morality (which is the same for all human beings, Canaanites as well as Israelites), but also in other ethical areas. It has been regarded as a matter of wonder that Leviticus, which is mainly concerned with purity, contains a chapter in its heart which is concerned with basic morality. It is in Leviticus, of all books, that we find the injunction, 'Thou shalt love thy neighbour as thyself.' Mary Douglas has shown brilliantly, by structural analysis, that this chapter 19 is the centre of the book, being the fulcrum on which the whole structure of the book turns (Douglas, 1994). This tells us that there is some important relationship between ritual and morality, but it is easy to mistake the nature of this relationship.

---

[5] Milgrom states : 'Pollution for H is nonritualistic ... the polluted land cannot be expiated by ritual, and hence, the expulsion of its inhabitants is inevitable' (1991, p. 49). One wonders, if there is such a fundamental discrepancy between P and H, how Milgrom can argue that H is the redactor of P.

Mary Douglas herself sees her structural insight as a spur to the discernment of moral implications in the laws of purity themselves. Accordingly, she follows in the wake of a long tradition of homiletics in which moral lessons are inculcated through the dietary and purity regulations: birds of prey, for example, are forbidden as food, because violence is deprecated; insects are forbidden for food, on the other hand, to show that the poor and disadvantaged should be exempted from the perils of competition. To be forbidden has in one case a negative connotation, and in the other a positive one, but this does not matter as long as some moral lesson can be drawn (Douglas, 1993).

To Mary Douglas, the reason why Lev. 19 breaks out into explicit morality is that this chapter gives us the moral rationale of all the ritual details surrounding it. In that case, one may ask, why bother with ritual encoding at all? If one is able to articulate moral precepts in plain style, why does one need to convey them inarticulately by means of ritual? It is Douglas's view, in common with other anthropologists (following the lead of Durkheim and Lévi-Strauss), that a primitive tribe conveys its feelings about the world and society through its network of observances, whether in diet or initiation rites or ritual purity shunnings. This is probably true, and it is also probably true that such observances convey, like poetry, a more nuanced and subtly dialectical view of life and society than could ever be conveyed in the mere prose of philosophical discourse. Nevertheless, it seems strange that a tribe should attempt both methods simultaneously, evincing two different levels of societal expression. For it is characteristic of primitive society not to make an explicit distinction between ritual and morality; morality is expressed, and indeed only exists, through ritual.

The relationship between ritual and morality in Leviticus, and also in the rabbinic literature, as I have been suggesting throughout this book, is a different one. Ritual is about holiness, not about morality; yet it is also about morality at a second remove, for holiness is for the sake of morality. An anthropological approach that is appropriate for primitive tribes is not appropriate for Leviticus. Illuminating as such an approach to Leviticus is, or can be (since in the sensitive hands of Mary Douglas the method is used to rebut the usual charges of mindless, obsessive ritualism), it nevertheless fails to appreciate fully the level of consciousness, differentiating between ritual and morality, that is characteristic of Judaism at all periods.

Why then does Leviticus break out into overt morality in its central chapter? It is not to give us the ritual all over again, this time in plain language. It is to tell us what the ritual is *for*. The ritual marks out the Israelites as a holy people. But this holiness would be of little use if it did not result in a higher moral standard. This is what the prophets are saying; in effect, 'You, of all people, should know better.' But the priestly authors of Leviticus are saying the same thing, in their own way. 'All these ritual observances mark you out as a special, chosen, dedicated group. But what is the point of this dedication? So that you can be motivated by *esprit de corps* and sense of specialness to show the world what is meant by love of neighbour, love of justice, and abandonment of violence.'

We must look, therefore, in the ritual code for an intention of dedication and sense of holiness. I will not go into detailed consideration of the dietary laws here, but will only suggest as an example that the prohibition against eating birds of prey is motivated not by moral allegory, but by the consideration that such birds are miserable fare. One would not offer such a bird at the altar, for which only the best is good enough, and therefore it is also below the standard of eating required of a holy nation (like the insects banned later in the chapter). I am not suggesting that inadequacy as food is the sole consideration in the list of forbidden foods: there may well be a variety of reasons. A varied history lies behind the choice of permitted foods, and also, perhaps, an element of arbitrariness. The insignia of dedication may be almost anything; the important thing is that there should be insignia. Of course, there are limits here; while the insignia are not for the sake of morality, they should not, in a morality-based society, flout morality. Carrying a belt of scalps, for example, would not be in accordance with the spirit of a society basing its moral norms not on warrior pride but on love of one's neighbour. One motivation for the list may be asceticism. All dedicated, or even merely proud, communities impose dietary restrictions on themselves, and this may have a moral purpose of its own, namely to show an ascetic superiority to the lazy self-indulgence of the undedicated. But even this moral purpose is a function of vocation and dedication, not of basic morality itself. Even if one motive for the restrictions is guilt about eating animals (as Milgrom suggests), this is as much a priestly as a moral consideration, especially when we consider parallels in Hinduism. There is a moral penumbra surrounding even the precepts of dedication, but this should not be allowed to obfuscate the all-important distinction between ritual and morality.

In the case of ritual purity, it is even easier to see that the purpose is dedicatory, rather than directly moral. It all has to do with the Temple. It is simply the protocol for entry into the palace of the King. The priestly people of God is privileged to have his residence in their midst, and must consequently comport themselves in accordance with the prescribed etiquette. There is not a single precept of ritual purity that has anything to do with morality, except insofar as etiquette has a moral aspect of reverence and gratitude. The Israelites have this privilege of service in the portals of God, and must therefore be careful to wipe their feet before entering. Only instead of wiping their feet, they must cleanse their whole body of impurities which, outside the Temple, have no negative meaning. Those (i.e. the rest of mankind) do not have to concern themselves with this etiquette at all. It does not apply to them. They are not unclean in the special sense of Temple-uncleanness; only Israelites can incur this uncleanness, because only they are chosen house-servants of God.

But does this mean that the system of ritual purity is merely arbitrary rules instituted just for the sake of having rules? There is undoubtedly an element of the arbitrary in them, just as in the rules of any dedicated society, such as an army. Yet it is possible to discern a theme in these rules, one that derives from their function as dedicatory, not from basic morality or even basic cleanliness; if they were moral or hygienic, this would relegate all the rest of mankind to the status of the immoral and the unclean.

The theme is that of the cycle of birth and death (not merely of death, as Feldman and Milgrom have argued). Everything that is a feature of the cycle of birth and death must be banished from the Temple of the God who does not die and was not born. Not that there is anything sinful about birth and death, which are the God-given lot of mankind. But the one place in the world which has been allotted for the resting of the Divine Presence must be protected from mortality. When entering the Temple, one is entering the domain of eternity.

Thanatos and Eros are the keys to the system of ritual purity. The polluting quality of death is shown not just in the obvious case of the corpse, but in that of the 'leper', who is a living corpse. On the other hand, the polluting quality of generation is shown in the impurity of semen, of menstrual blood and of childbirth. In the pollution of *zab* and *zabah*, we find a pollution of sickness, which is also a sexual pathological condition. Other sicknesses, even when more obviously related to the danger of death, but which do not have this sexual component, do not cause impurity.

Yet this cycle of birth and death, which in Judaism forms the basis of pollution of the Temple, is itself an awesome object of contemplation that can give rise to religious systems. It is the basis of chthonic religion, in which the deity himself/herself is subject to the cycle of birth and death, thereby providing salvation to worshippers, who thereby become divinized. By bringing God down into the world of birth, death and rebirth, the worshipper hopes to escape the cycle, cross the barrier between the human and the divine, and achieve immortality.

Judaism renounced this hope. 'The dead do not praise You, nor those who have descended into silence.' Judaism divested the cycle of birth and death of divine significance and thereby released humans from the quest for divinity. They were released into humanity, accepting birth and death as their lot, but pursuing human aims as sanctified by the God of Heaven, who did not ask them to transcend humanity, but instead to worship Him as the sole transcendent Being. The chthonic gods became transformed into human beings. The birth-death cycle became a source of impurity, whenever entrance into the domain of the transcendent was required, but also a source of action and community planning, i.e. Torah and morality, outside the Temple. Impurity was not a sin (except in the actual presence of the Transcendent). It was the human condition, which had the approval of God when working out its own implications outside the Temple.

Yet the chthonic gods could not be entirely banished. The processes of generation, in particular, retained some of the divine aura and mysticism that they had in pagan religion. The fact that impurity was the Israelite substitute for a previous sanctity was revealed at times even in the Israelite ceremonies of purification. Though menstrual blood was one of the chief sources of impurity, its status as a magical generating substance had to find acknowledgment in the ritual of the Red Cow, the Mother/Virgin whose symbolically red body was distilled into the essence of menstrual blood, *mei niddah*. The ceremonies surrounding this survival of the chthonic Goddess are equivocal in their admixture of the clean and the unclean, hinting at the secret that impurity can be a transformation of a rejected holiness.[6] Though the Temple keeps the processes of birth and death at bay, chthonic rites, outside the Temple, continue to be performed, paying formal respect to the Temple, but also remaining a focus of primitive energy within Israelite religion.

---

[6] Milgrom senses this when he writes, 'The possibility exists that holiness and impurity were once both polaric and interchangeable; for example, the bones of the dead defile, but those of Elisha resuscitate the dead' (1991, p. 316).

Appendix A: The 'haberim'

A problem in the assessment of the function of ritual purity in Judaism is the role of the ritual purity societies (*haburot*), the members of which were known as *haberim*. These people cultivated the practice of ritual purity as an end in itself, not as a means of avoiding defilement of the Temple. The *haburot* existed while the Temple was still standing, and continued to exist after its fall. According to Neusner, these societies have a defining role in the history of Pharisaism and the subsequent rabbinic movement. They were the leaders of a new kind of Judaism which sought to transfer the holiness of the Temple to the home. ' ... the Pharisees held that even outside the Temple, in one's own home, the laws of ritual purity were to be followed in the only circumstance in which they might apply, namely, at the table. Therefore, one must eat secular food (ordinary everyday meals) in a state of ritual purity *as if one were a Temple priest*' (Neusner, 1979, p. 83). Neusner, in fact, equates the Pharisees with the *haberim*. A superficial justification for this equation is the fact that purity-devotees are sometimes called in rabbinic literature *perushim* and this word is identical to the name of the Pharisees. But the word *perushim* means several other things apart from 'Pharisees' (in some contexts, it can even mean 'heretics'). In ritual purity contexts, it means not 'Pharisees' but 'ascetics' (see Rivkin, 1969–70), and its abstract form *perishut* is used to mean the saintly virtue of asceticism (M. Sotah 9:15).

Against Neusner, it must be urged that the practice of the *haberim* was never equivalent to that of the priests. The grade of purity at which the *haberim* aimed was lower than the grade required of the priests. The basic aim of the *haberim* was to avoid imparting impurity to ordinary food (*hullin*) of the Land of Israel. While the priests had to avoid imparting impurity to the holy food (*terumah*) which was their perquisite, and which was susceptible to defilement even by a second degree of impurity (see Appendix B), the *haberim* were able to remain in a second degree of impurity without defiling ordinary food (which could be defiled only by a first degree of impurity). Thus the *haberim* were typically in a state of purity one degree lower than that of the priests.

Moreover, there is a vast difference between the position of the priests and that of the *haberim* in that a priest who defiled his holy food by eating it wittingly in a state of impurity was guilty of sacrilege, a Toranic offence (Lev. 22:3) carrying the severe penalty of 'cutting-off' (*karet*). A *haber*, on the other hand, who broke his vow or 'undertaking' by eating ordinary food in a state of impurity sufficient to defile it faced no greater penalty than to be ejected from the society of which he was a member.

It is thus incorrect to say that the *haberim* sought to behave in the home as if they were Temple priests. What then was the aim of the *haberim*?

Their aim was a voluntary one which was not prescribed in the Torah, and was therefore a supererogatory exercise of piety. That is why it was exercised in voluntary groups to which people sought to enter as members, in which they served a probationary period, and in which they made a declaration of intent, or 'undertaking'.

The debate that has taken place among scholars about the place of the *haburot* in Judaism has unfortunately paid little or no attention to the voluntary character of these groups. It is assumed by Neusner, for example, that these groups were offering a new kind of Judaism which they regarded as normative for all Jews. Even Sanders, who has opposed Neusner in this matter, citing evidence that the rules of the *haburah* were not generally observed or regarded as generally obligatory (Sanders, 1990, pp. 166–84) does not fully bring out the reason for this: that the *haberim* were volunteers whose self-dedication cast no blame or discredit on the majority who were not *haberim* but faithfully observed the laws of the Torah and the rabbis (note that the rules of the *haburah* did not have even rabbinical status as rules requiring general observance). Here the *haberim* must be sharply distinguished from the Dead Sea Scrolls sectarians, who regarded their special observances as obligatory for all Jews; that is why they expected the great majority of Jews to perish, as a punishment for their non-observance, in the coming eschatological war.

Hannah Harrington, on the other hand, in criticizing Sanders (Harrington, 1993, pp. 267–81), again seems to think that her task is to prove that the laws of the *haburah* were more widely observed than Sanders claims, allowing no weight to the fact that, when observed, they involved a voluntary 'undertaking' (*qabbalah*, see M. Demai 2:3), and were therefore not regarded as normative even by those who observed them (cf. the Rule of a monastic Order in Christianity, which is not regarded, even by members of the Order, as normative for ordinary Catholics).

Alon does address the fundamental issue directly (1977, p. 209): ' . . . we must determine whether, if it [eating ordinary food in purity] is a Halakha, it is confined to the community of the Associates, who 'undertook' to observe this practice, or is basically a specific custom of all Israelites, only the Associates took it upon themselves to keep the observance scrupulously'. His solution, on the whole, is that it is the latter. Yet his conclusion is so equivocal that it seems to undermine his own arguments: 'The Halakha . . . which calls for levitical purity when eating unconsecrated food was left undecided from the outset, for others ruled that that uncleanness applies only to the Sanctuary and to holy things . . . Hence the Halakha could not be firmly established and applied to all things, but remained for many a "precept of piety" [literally "abstinence"] and succeeded in being firmly applied in given cases only.' I suggest that the varied evidence presented by Alon is better interpreted by the view that non-priestly purity was always regarded with reverence, but never with insistence on its obligatory character (though in the case of communal leaders, it could be regarded as *de rigueur*).

The voluntary exercise of supererogatory ritual purity has a long history in Judaism. It begins with the Nazirite vow of the Torah (which continued to be practised in the Second Temple and rabbinic periods) and received further development in the *haburah* movement of the first and second centuries. This movement never aimed to turn the whole Jewish people into *haberim*, though it does seem at times to have sought to make membership of a *haburah* a requirement for communal leaders. The teacher who was chiefly active in promoting the *haburah* was Rabbi Meir, who rejoiced in his success in spreading membership.

The halakhic basis for the *haburah* rests on the question, 'To what extent does the ordinary food of the Land of Israel have sanctity?' All admitted that it did not have the same degree of sanctity as the priestly food, the *terumah*. All agreed, also, that it had *more* sanctity than the food of outside lands (that is why the Jews of Babylonia, despite their extraordinary degree of learning and piety, never formed *haburot*). A minority opinion was that it was actually 'forbidden to cause impurity to ordinary food of the Land of Israel' (b. Abodah Zarah 55b); if this view had prevailed, the *haburah* would have become the norm, though the prohibition would never have been regarded as equal in status to the prohibition against defiling priestly food. The view that did prevail was that while it was not forbidden to cause impurity to *hullin*, it was praiseworthy not to do so.

As Solomon Spiro has pointed out, there was also a practical reason for forming the *haburot*. This was that it was useful to have groups of people who preserved their ritual purity, so that the priestly dues could be separated from the crops at the proper times without danger of polluting them. Certain rabbinic passages show that at harvest times, it was the practice of the farmers to send a message to the local *haburah* to help in this process (Spiro, 1980).

Yet there was also a spiritual reason. If the Torah prescribed certain means of attaining purity before entering the Temple, there would always be those who saw the observance of these rules as a means of attaining spiritual progress. That is why we find that ritual purity was demanded of those who engaged in the mystical procedures of the *ma'aseh merkabah* and *ma'aseh bereshit*. If purity was required to enter the earthly Temple, it must surely be required to enter the heavenly Temple. This again was part of the voluntary character of the *haburah*, since noone was obliged to be a mystic.

The *haberim* practised purity outside the Temple; yet this was part of an old controversy or meditation centred on the question, 'What are the limits of the Temple?' Even within Leviticus we can discern two views about this, one of which sought to extend the boundary of the Temple to include the whole 'camp' (see p. 186). The Dead Sea Scrolls sect wished to include the whole of Jerusalem within the precincts of the Temple.

The *haberim* were thus not trying to transfer Temple practice to the outside world, but were playing a variation on the theme that the Land itself was holy, and its produce holy, even if not quite so holy as the Temple and its sacrifices and the priestly *terumah*. Even while the Temple was standing, the *haberim* were stressing that areas outside the Temple had their own sanctity which it was legitimate, though not obligatory, to honour. This honouring of the Land was, at the same time, an assertion of the old-established doctrine of the priesthood of the laity (Exodus 19:6).

After the destruction of the Temple, it was natural that, for a time at least, this doctrine should exercise a consolatory force. This accounts for the fact that voluntary ritual purity societies actually increased in popularity in the Land of Israel for a while, before eventually becoming quiescent and disappearing. The absence of the Temple eventually proved more potent a factor than the continuing presence of the Land.

Appendix B: The rabbinic system of grades of impurity

The highest degree of impurity is 'Father of fathers of impurity' ('abi abot ha-tum'ah). This is the corpse.

Whatever receives impurity from this is called 'Father of impurity' ('ab ha-tum'ah). Other 'Fathers of impurity' are not derived from the corpse: e.g. 'leper', zab, etc. A Father of impurity derived from a corpse is exceptional, however, in that persons or vessels receiving impurity from it become themselves Fathers of impurity, instead of moving one grade down.

Whatever receives impurity from a Father of impurity is a derivative impurity (vlad ha-tum'ah) and is called 'first-grade impurity' (rish'on le-tum'ah). This is also sometimes called tehilah ('first').

What receives impurity from a 'first-grade impurity' is a 'second-grade impurity' (sheni le-tum'ah).

A 'second-grade impurity' does not cause impurity to ordinary food (hullin), but only to priestly food (terumah) and sacrificial food (qodashim), which receive from it a 'third-grade impurity' (shelishi le-tum'ah).

A 'third-grade impurity' causes impurity only to sacrificial food, which receives a 'fourth-grade impurity' (rebiy'iy le-tum'ah).

A 'fourth-grade impurity' does not cause impurity to anything.

All impurities, from 'first-grade impurities' downwards are called 'derivative impurities' (vladot ha-tum'ah).

Derivative impurities differ from 'fathers of impurities' in that the latter cause impurity to persons and vessels, while the former cause impurity to food and drink, but not to persons or vessels.

214

The above summary (adapted from the *Entziqlopedia Talmudit*) is an outline of the system of transmission of impurity, but is much simplified. In general, the rabbinic system is a schematization of data derived from Scripture, but complications having only rabbinic authority were added.

References

Albeck, H. 1958, *Shishah Sidrei Mishnah*, 6 vols., Jerusalem/Tel Aviv.

Alon, G. 1984, *The Jews in their Land in the Talmudic Age*, 2 vols., Magnes Press, Jerusalem.

Alon, G. 1977, *Jews, Judaism and the Classical World*, Magnes Press, Jerusalem.

Baumgarten, Albert I. 1993, 'The paradox of the Red Heifer', *Vetus Testamentum*, XLIII, 4, pp. 442–51.

Baumgarten, J.M. 1980, 'The Pharisaic-Sadducean Controversies about Purity and Qumran Texts', *JJS* 31.2 (Autumn).

Berlin, M. and Zevin, S.J. 1947–, *The Talmudic Encyclopedia* (Hebrew), Talmudic Encyclopedia Institute, Jerusalem.

Blau, J. 1957–61, *Responsa of Maimonides* (Hebrew), Jerusalem.

Booth, Roger P. 1986, *Jesus and the Laws of Purity*, JSOT Press, Sheffield.

Boyce, Mary 1975, *A History of Zoroastrianism*, Brill, Leiden.

Breasted, J.H. 1959, *Development of Religion and Thought in Ancient Egypt*, Harper, New York (first publ. 1912).

Briffault, Robert 1927, *The Mothers*, 3 vols., Macmillan London and New York.

Büchler, A. 1928, *Studies in Sin and Atonement in the Rabbinic Literature of the First Century*, Oxford University Press, London.

Burkert, Walter 1983, *Homo Necans: The Anthropology of Ancient Greek Sacrificial Ritual and Myth*, University of California Press, Berkeley.

Burkert, Walter 1985, *Greek Religion*, Basil Blackwell & Harvard Univ. Press, U.S.A.

Caplice, R. 1974, 'The Akkadian Namburbi Texts: An Introduction', in *Sources for the Ancient Near East*, Undena, Los Angeles.

Culpepper, E. 1974, 'Zoroastrian Menstrual Taboos', in *Women and Religion*, ed. J. Plaskow, pp. 199–210, Scholars Press, Missoula.

216

Dahood, M. 1965, *Psalms 1–50*, Doubleday, U.S.A.

Danby, H. 1954, *The Code of Maimonides, Book* x: 'The Book of Cleanness.' Yale Judaica Series, Yale University Press, New Haven.

Daube, David 1956, *The New Testament and Rabbinic Judaism*, Athlone Press, London.

Dinari, Y. 1979–80, 'Customs relating to the impurity of the Menstruant: their origin and development.' *Tarbiz* 49:302–24.

Douglas, Mary 1966, *Purity and Danger*, Routledge and Kegan Paul, London.

Douglas, Mary 1994, 'Poetic Structure in Leviticus', in *Pomegranates and Golden Bells: Studies in Biblical, Jewish and Near Eastern Ritual, Law and Literature in Honour of Jacob Milgrom*, ed. D.P. Wright, D.N. Freedman and A. Hurvitz, Eisenbrauns, Winona Lake.

Douglas, Mary 1993, 'The forbidden animals in Leviticus', *Journal for the Study of the Old Testament* 59, pp. 3–23.

Douglas, Mary 1993–94, 'Atonement in Leviticus', *Jewish Studies Quarterly*, 1,2.

Dumont, Louis 1980, *Homo Hierarchicus: The Caste System and its Implications*, University of Chicago Press, Chicago/London.

Elijah ben Solomon (the Vilna Gaon), *Eliyahu Rabbah* (many editions).

Eilberg-Schwartz, Howard 1990, *The Savage in Judaism: An Anthropology of Israelite Religion and Ancient Judaism*, Bloomington.

Enziqlopedyah Talmudit (1947 ff.) (see Berlin and Zevin)

Eshkoli, A.Z., 'Halakha and Customs Among the Falasha Jews in the Light of Rabbinic and Karaite Halakha'. *Tarbiz*, 7: 121–25, 1936 (Hebrew).

Eves, Richard 1995, 'Shamanism, sorcery and cannibalism: the incorporation of power in the magical cult of Buai', in *Oceania*, March.

Feldman, Emanuel 1977, *Biblical and Post-Biblical Defilement and Mourning: Law as Theology*, Yeshiva University Press/Ktav, New York.

Frazer, Sir J.G. 1913, *The Golden Bough*. Part vi, *The Scapegoat*, Macmillan, London.

Gaster, T.H. 1969, *Myth, Legend and Customs in the Old Testament*, Harper, New York.

Girard, R. 1977, *Violence and the Sacred*, Johns Hopkins University Press, Baltimore.

Goldberg, Abraham 1955, *The Mishnah Tractate Ohaloth* (Hebrew), Jerusalem.

Green, A.R.W. 1975, *The Role of Human Sacrifice in the Ancient Near East*, Missoula.

Gurney, O.R. 1977, *Some Aspects of Hittite Religion*, Schweich Lectures, Oxford University Press, Oxford.

Haran, M. 1978, *Temples and Temple Service in Ancient Israel*, Clarendon, Oxford.

Harrington, Hannah K. 1993, *The Impurity Systems of Qumran and the Rabbis: Biblical Foundations*, Scholars Press, Atlanta, Georgia.

Harrison, Jane 1959, *Prolegomena to the Study of Greek Religion*, Cambridge University Press, Cambridge (reprint of 3rd edn, 1922).

Horowitz, C.M. 1890, *Baraita di-masseket Niddah. Tosfata 'Atiqata*, vol. v. Frankfurt am Main, n.p.

Howell, Signe 1996, 'Many contexts, many meanings? Gendered values among the Northern Lio of Flores, Indonesia', *Journal of the Royal Anthropological Institute*, June.

Hubert, H. and Mauss, M. 1964, *Sacrifice: Its Nature and Function*, University of Chicago Press (reprint of Paris 1898 edn).

Jacobs, Louis 1961, *Studies in Talmudic Logic and Methodology*, Valentine Mitchell, London.

Kapah, Y 1984–, ed. and comm., *Mishneh Torah*, Mekhon Mishnat ha-Rambam, Jerusalem.

Karo, Joseph, *Kesef Mishneh* (many editions).

Kaufmann, Y. 1937–56, *The History of Israelite Religion*, 4 vols., Dvir, Tel Aviv.

Klawans, Jonathan 1997, 'The impurity of immorality in ancient Judaism', *Journal of Jewish Studies*, 48,1, Spring.

Knight, Chris 1991, *Blood Relations: Menstruation and the Origins of Culture*, Yale University Press.

Krauss, S. 1902, *Das Leben Jesus nach juedischen Quellen*, Berlin.

Levine, Baruch A.(ed.) 1993, *Numbers 1–20*, Anchor Bible, Doubleday, New York.

Luzzato, S.D. (Shadal) 1965, *Commentary to the Pentateuch* (Hebrew), Dvir, Tel Aviv.

Levi-Bruhl, L. 1935, *Primitives and the Supernatural*, Dutton, New York.

Lévi-Strauss 1966, Claude, *The Savage Mind*, London.

Maccoby, Hyam 1984, 'Jacob Neusner's Mishnah', *Midstream* 30, 5.

Maccoby, Hyam 1988, *Early Rabbinic Writings*, Cambridge University Press, Cambridge.

Maccoby, Hyam 1990, 'Neusner and the Red Cow', *JSJ*, 31, 1, pp. 60–75.

Maccoby, Hyam 1996, *A Pariah People: The Anthropology of Antisemitism*, Constable, London.

Maccoby, Hyam 1994, 'Pharisee and Sadducee Interpretation of the

Menorah as Tamid', *Journal of Progressive Judaism*, 3, November, pp. 5–13.

Maccoby, Hyam 1986, *The Mythmaker: Paul and the Invention of Christianity*, Weidenfeld & Nicolson, London.

Maccoby, Hyam 1982, *The Sacred Executioner: Human Sacrifice and the Legacy of Guilt*, Thames & Hudson, London.

Maccoby, Hyam 1997, 'The law about liquids: a rejoinder', *Journal for the Study of the New Testament*, 67, pp. 115–22.

Magonet, Jonathan 1996, 'The riddle of Leviticus 12:5', in *Reading Leviticus: A Conversation with Mary Douglas*, ed. John F.A. Sawyer, Sheffield Academic Press, Sheffield.

Maimonides, (see Danby, H.)

Maimonides, *Mishneh Torah* (see Kapah, Y.)

Maimonides, *Responsa* (see Blau, J.)

Meigs, A. 1990, 'Multiple gender ideologies and statuses', in P. Sanday and R. Goodenough (ed.), *Beyond the Second Sex: New Directions in the Anthropology of Gender*, University of Pennsylvania Press, Philadelphia.

Melkman, Joseph 1971, 'Leper', in *Encyclopedia Judaica*, Jerusalem.

Milgrom, Jacob 1976, *Cult and Conscience: The Asham and the Priestly Doctrine of Repentance*, Brill, Leiden.

Milgrom, Jacob 1990, *JPS Torah Commentary: Numbers*, Jewish Publication Society, Philadelphia.

Milgrom, Jacob 1991, *Leviticus, 1–16: A New Translation and Commentary*, Anchor Bible, Doubleday, New York.

Milgrom, Jacob 1971, "EGLAH 'ARUFAH', in *Encyclopaedia Judaica*, vol. VI, p. 475, Jerusalem.

Mosko, Mark S. 1995, 'Rethinking Trobriand chieftainship', *Journal of the Royal Anthropological Institute*, pp. 763–85, December.

Neumann, Erich 1972, *The Great Mother: An Analysis of the Archetype*, Princeton University Press, Princeton.

Neusner, Jacob 1973, *The Idea of Purity in Ancient Judaism*, E.J. Brill, Leiden.

Neusner, Jacob 1976, 'First cleanse the inside', *New Testament Studies*, 22, pp. 486–95.

Neusner, Jacob 1979, *From Politics to Piety: the Emergence of Pharisaic Judaism*, Ktav, New York.

Neusner, Jacob 1975, *A History of the Mishnaic Law of Purities*, v, Ohalot, E.J. Brill, Leiden.

Neusner, Jacob 1977, *A History of the Mishnaic Law of Purities: the Mishnaic System of Uncleanness*, 22, Brill, Leiden.

Neusner, Jacob 1990, *Uniting the Dual Torah: Sifra and the Problem of the Mishnah*, Cambridge University Press, Cambridge.

Neusner, Jacob 1988, *A Religion of Pots and Pans? Modes of Philosophical and Theological Discourse in Ancient Judaism: Essays and a Program*, Scholars Press, Atlanta, Georgia.

Parker, R. 1983, *Miasma, Pollution and Purification in Early Greek Religion*, Clarendon, Oxford.

Philo, Loeb Classical Library, 10 vols., W. Heinemann, London, 1929–62.

Poirier, John C. 1996(a), 'Why did the Pharisees wash their hands?', *Journal of Jewish Studies*, 47, 2, 1996, pp. 217–33.

Poirier, John C. 1996(b) and Frankovic, Joseph, 'Celibacy and charism in 1 Cor 7:5–7: Paul and ritual purity', *Harvard Theological Review*, January.

Pritchard, James B. 1955, *Ancient Near Eastern Texts*, Princeton University Press, Princeton.

Qimron, E. and Strugnell, J. 1985, 'An Unpublished Halakhic Letter from Qumran', in *Biblical Archaeology Today*, ed. J. Amitas, pp. 400–407. Israel Exploration Society, Jerusalem.

Rivkin, Ellis 1969–70, 'Defining the Pharisees: the Tannaitic sources', *Hebrew Union College Annual*, 40, pp. 234 ff.

Sanders, E.P. 1990, *Jewish Law from Jesus to the Mishnah: Five Studies*, SCM Press, London.

Sanders, E.P. 1992, *Judaism: Practice and Belief, 63BCE-66CE*, SCM Press, London.

Sawyer, John F.A. 1996, ed., *Reading Leviticus: A Conversation with Mary Douglas*, Sheffield Academic Press, Sheffield.

Spiro, Solomon J. 1980, 'Who was the *haber*? A new approach to an ancient institution', *Journal for the Study of Judaism*, 2, pp. 186–216.

Thompson, R.C. 1908, *Semitic Magic*, Ktav, New York, reprint of London edn.

Vermes, Geza 1973, *Jesus the Jew*, Collins, London.

Wright, D.P. 1987, *The Disposal of Impurity*, Scholars Press, Atlanta.

Yadin, Y. 1983, *The Temple Scroll*, Eng. edn, 3 vols., Israel Exploration Society, Jerusalem.

Yerkes, R.K 1952, *Sacrifice in Greek and Roman Religions and Early Judaism*, Scribners, New York.

Zeitlin, Solomon 1914, 'Les Dix-huit Mesures', Revue des Études Juives, 67, pp. 22–35.

Index of quotations

221

Index of quotations

General index

Aaron   119, 143, 196
Abaye   57
Abel   86, 135
a fortiori   7, 50
air-animals
  do not convey impurity   69
Albeck, H.   36 n.
Alon, G   12, 211
altar
  immune to impurity   188
  inauguration of   179
animals, and purity Chapter 6, passim
anointing oil   133
'aperture'   14
Aqiba   35
Armstrong, Karen, n.   151
asceticism   206
'asham   131, 132
Assyrian sacrificial practice   84
Atonement, Day of   81, 86, 168
  does not atone for unrepented sins
    89
Attis   112, 164
Azazel   85, 86, 90, 182
  meaning of name   88

Baal   86, 135
Babylonian New Year   135
Babylonian religion   85
badad   110
Balder   86, 135, 138
baptism, Christian   112, 163
Baraita di-masseket Niddah   33
Baumgarten, A.   116 n.
Baumgarten, Joseph M.   96
  criticism of Neusner   100 n.
behemah   70

Berkovits, Eliezer   41
'bird in the gullet'   59 n.
blood
  from a wound   31
  shed by virgin   42
Booth, Roger   161, n.
boqe'a   22
Bouphonia   137, 139 n.
Brahmins   11, 197
Briffault, Robert   109 n.
Burkert, Walter   83, 111 n., 137
burnt-offerings   84

Cain   86, 135
'calf whose neck is broken'   91–93
Camp, definition of   185
Camp of God   4
Camp of Israel   4
Camp of the Levites   4
Canaanites   194, 199
'carrying'   8
castes, in Judaism   198
Catholic Church   194
'cattle'   70
Cave of Machpelah   2 n.
cedar   95, 135, 138
childbirth   47–50
Chthonia   112
chthonic religion, and immortality   207
Churching of Women   162
'comedy of innocence'   137
conversion to Judaism   9
corpse, does not convey *maddaf*
  impurity   52
Corpse impurity Ch. 1 *passim*
  as gas   21
  detailed survey of effects of   5

226

as punishment 120, 126
in fabrics and houses 127
result of infection 121
role of priest in 122
'shutting up' 122
total whiteness 124
Lévi-Strauss, Claude 204
Levites 133
live animals, as tents 24, n.
not source of impurity 67
locust 70
Loki 86, 135, 139
Luzzatto, Samuel David 31

ma'ahil 17, 18
Maccoby, Hyam 61, 98 n., 137, 154 n.
machaera 139 n.
Machaereus 139 n.
maddaf 50, 53
Magonet, Jonathan 50
Maimonides 5, 23, 34, 44
on rabbinic legislation 8
on Scapegoat 90, n.
makhshirin 77
mamzerim 198
Marduk 73 n.
Mary
visit of to the Temple 161
Meigs A. 111 n.
mei niddah 95
Meir 42, 212
Melkman, Joseph 144
menstrual blood, as healing agent 108
menstruant
awe of 36
prohibition against intercourse with
38–43
isolation of 33
not excluded from synagogue 2
menstruation
alleged dangerousness of 35
Chapter 3, passim
rabbinic system of 44–46
Meron 2 n.
metaher sheretz 74
metaphorical impurity 12
methodology 116
mezuzah 147
miasma 169
middot 60
Midian 11
Milgrom, Jacob 5, 7, 21, 30, 31, 36, 39,

44, 49, 55, 65, 69, 71, 72, 76, 80, 117,
137 n., 207
explains doubling of goats 135
on 'calf whose neck is broken' 92
on impurity and sacrifices 82
on Land-defilement 201
on leper's habitation 144
on leper's sacrifice 133
on sanctification by contagion 116
philological arguments 176–177
theory of biblical impurity 4, Ch. 14,
passim
theory of the Red Cow 105
view of graduated sin-offering 190
miqveh 38, 163
used by men 43
Miriam 119, 143
Mishnah 89
Mithras, Nativity of 151
miy'us 65
MMT 100 n., 102,
monastic orders 195
monotheism 128
morality, takes precedence over ritual
Ch. 16 passim
Moses 52, 120, 161 n., 179, 197
moshab 141
Mosko, Mark S. 109 n.
Mot 86, 135
mummification 112

Naaman 120
Nachmanides 31
Namburbi 134
naqi, neqiyut 66, 154
Nazarite 133, 166, 184, 212
nefesh, meaning 'neck', n. 59
Nehemiah 51
Neoptolemus 139 n.
Neumann, Erich 110
on menstrual blood 109 n.
Neusner, Jacob 14, 21, 22, 59, 76, 142,
195
contrasted with Milgrom 165
on haberim 96, 209
on impurity and sacrifices 82
on intentionality 79
on New Testament 152
on Philo 21 n.
on Red Cow 96, 100 n.
theory of discontinuity 97
New Moon 61

Made in the USA
Middletown, DE
05 September 2018